MW01232543

THE HANDLER
THE AGENCY SERIES

BY: MISTY BALLANTYNE

Copyright © 2015 by Misty Ballantyne

The Handler
The Agency Series
by Misty Ballantyne

Printed in the United States of America.

ISBN 9781498454186

All rights reserved solely by the author. The author guarantees all contents are original and do not infringe upon the legal rights of any other person or work. No part of this book may be reproduced in any form without the permission of the author. The views expressed in this book are not necessarily those of the publisher.

Scripture quotations taken from the King James Version (KJV) – public domain

www.xulonpress.com

DEDICATION

This book is dedicated to Angie whose friendship over the past 25 years I cherish and her enthusiastic encouragement to write this story was a nudge in the right direction. Thanks girl, I love ya. Here's to our "Handler", cheers!

ACKNOWLEDGEMENTS:

I want to thank my Lord and Savior for revealing these new characters to me and entrusting me with these stories to tell. To God be the glory!
To my husband, Earl who has set up my writing area with a new desk, new chair, and a Mack-daddy low profile back lit keyboard for those late nights when he is ready to sleep but I can't stop writing. Love you.
To my friends and readers who encourage me in all the little ways by sending texts, emails and Facebook messages spurring me onward. For those who lift me up every step of the way and pray me through the difficult times and celebrate all the little victories with me as though they were their own. I truly love you all so much.

Special Thanks to Lori Langston at Brownston Photography for the back cover headshot. Special thanks to Brandon Candee, Angie Groppe, Kelly Hain, Elizabeth Lowe, Paige Pittard, Victoria Pyles and Molly Towe, your input was invaluable. Seriously.

TABLE OF CONTENTS

Prologue xi

Chapter 1.   Radar 13
Chapter 2.   Practice makes perfect 23
Chapter 3.   Ready Set Go! 31
Chapter 4.   Winds of Change 35
Chapter 5.   Reports 47
Chapter 6.   And Baby Makes Three 53
Chapter 7.   Rear View Mirror 62
Chapter 8.   Safer 73
Chapter 9.   Comfort Food 79
Chapter 10.   Expectations 88
Chapter 11.   Down time 97
Chapter 12.   Moving 107
Chapter 13.   Back to Normal 123
Chapter 14.   Waves 132
Chapter 15.   Watching 139
Chapter 16.   Kisses 146
Chapter 17.   Uncertainty 154
Chapter 18.   Adventures 162
Chapter 19.   Upside down 172

Chapter 20. Spy games 183

Chapter 21. Miss-starts 194

Chapter 22. Sunrise 204

Chapter 23. Between you and me 212

Chapter 24. Bag of Cats. 218

Chapter 25. Court. 227

Chapter 26. Why Why Why?. 234

Chapter 27. Lull. 241

Chapter 28. Wedding Bells 247

Chapter 29. Reality Check. 250

Chapter 30. Make it go away. 260

Chapter 31. Comfort 268

Chapter 32. Spiral 275

Chapter 33. Answers 289

Chapter 34. Forever 298

PROLOGUE

T he only sound in the east wing hallway of the CIA headquarters in Langley, Virginia leading to the team conference room, was the clicking sound of the director's shoes as he made his way quickly down the corridor. He swiped his ID badge and let himself into the sterile looking room hosting thirteen chairs and a long conference table. Sitting alone in the room, at the far end of the table, facing the door was his number one agent Dean, who immediately stood upon seeing the director.

"At ease son." Director Johnson said with no discernable expression.

"Yes sir."

"Please sit, I have good news. An opportunity has presented itself and not only will it have a personal benefit for you, but we have been given the go ahead for your special project." The director stated searching Dean's face for a reaction. Dean's eyes remained fixed on the director's and only the slight turning of the corners of his mouth gave any indication to his state of mind.

"Sir, would I get to keep my current team?" Dean asked concerned.

"The only ones I can promise are the Driver, the Tech, the Interrogator and Ninja. We can build from there, but those are in stone."

"Thank you sir. I can work with that, I appreciate the opportunity. Will our mission be state side sir?" Dean asked respectfully.

"Potentially. Your permanent base will be, but of course depending on the scope of subsequent missions, travel outside the United States cannot be ruled out."

"Yes sir I understand. How long before we head out, so that I can give the team a heads up?" Dean asked.

"Four weeks. The new office front has already been acquired, I will split my time between Langley and the new site, and also unbeknownst to the Driver he has already been setting up his new facility from afar." The director said allowing a rare smile to form on his lips.

It was times like this that he reveled in being in a positon of power. His alpha team with Dean as his Handler, was one of the most sought after intelligence teams in the agency today. As a result they were inundated with missions and were fast approaching a level of burn out that the director was not willing to let happen. This move was basically unprecedented for a team of this caliber and he knew he had a lot riding on this move, but his gut told him this was the right thing to do. In a world landscape where there were so many blurred lines, this particular line seemed crystal clear.

"Sir are we…" Dean started.

"Pack your bags son, we are headed to the coast of South Carolina." The director announced with a huge grin spreading across his face.

CHAPTER 1

RADAR

A slight breeze would have been a nice touch, but since mother nature was sending near like gale winds there would be no outside dining today. Jesse Hardin, tried to rearrange the tables inside Reed's Café to maximize seating and clear a pathway for the take out patrons. Reed's was a popular breakfast and lunch eatery in the downtown office park that serviced the financial and shipping areas in the City of Ocean Side, South Carolina, Jesse was the hardworking, fast talking, head waitress and manager.

She had just finished moving the last two top tables to form a four top when an intense looking man in a black suit walked in and asked to speak to Mrs. Jesse Whitmore Hardin. Libby, another waitress who was filling the napkin holders at the bar, looked up when she heard his quiet, but commanding voice. She and the man locked eyes momentarily and she tilted her head in Jesse's direction.

"Yes? Hello, I'm Jesse Hardin." She replied, wiping her hands on her apron. It was quiet so far this morning only a few coffees and Danishes to go, so his presence startled her.

"May I have a moment of your time in private please? I have an urgent matter that I would like to discuss with you." He stated in a flat level tone, watching for her reaction.

She smiled pleasantly then asked Libby to go check on Johnny in the kitchen and get another pot of the French roast started. When Libby had gotten out of ear shot, she turned to the man in the suit and showed him to a table in the corner near a window where they were less likely to be over heard. He liked that she was discrete, that was a good sign.

"Of course, how may I help you, Mr......?" She replied trying to keep the nervousness in her stomach from rising and altering her voice.

"I am Mr. Johnson, and I am with the CIA." He stated showing her his credentials. "One of our agents in our field office here has observed you recently and has selected you for a program we are currently Beta testing. I would like to discuss this opportunity with you further at my office. It should go without saying that this is a matter that is not to be discussed in any way with anyone, not even your husband. I assure you, that at no time will you be in any danger or in harm's way." His gray eyes bored into her as he attempted to smile, a gesture meant to put her at ease, but it did not.

She shifted slightly and folded her arms across her chest then weighed what she would say next as her mind swirled with the realization that she had been under surveillance, and on the radar of the CIA... *What in the world???*

"Well, Mr. Johnson I am a little stunned and intrigued by your offer but I...." She began, but was interrupted by him handing her a business card with a time hand written on the back. He nodded his head then turned and walked out of the café.

Oh Lord! Am I in trouble?

Her thoughts were interrupted by a group of ladies scurrying in to get out of the wind, laughing and trying to get their hair back into place. Libby and now Hannah were on the floor taking care of the patrons, so Jesse excused herself to the back office for a few minutes. She eyed the generic looking business card, the embossed CIA insignia in the top left hand corner is the only thing that made it look official. She ran her thumb over it then flipped it over and stared at the time written on the back 5:42 p.m. *How odd that they specified THAT time. What is this all about?*

Jesse whipped out her cellphone to call her husband Jerry. She knew she wasn't supposed to discuss this, but wanted to let him know she might be home a little late tonight.

"Hello?" He answered impatiently.

"Hi honey, listen something has come up tonight, and I just wanted to let you know I might be a little late getting home." She said biting her nail and continuing to stare at the business card.

"Sure. Fine. I'm not going to be home until after nine anyway. If you are going to be later than that, just don't wake me when you get in." He stated as though he were distracted.

"Well I don't expect to be out *that* late, at least I don't think I will be. So are you eating dinner at the office again?"

"Yeah I'll pick up something. No need to cook. Hey Jess I've gotta go." With that, he ended the call.

Great. Thanks. Bye honey, love you too. Humph.
Unfortunately too many of their conversations were going this way and they rarely spent any time together anymore. He was working towards a partnership at the advertising firm, and long hours had become the norm lately. Thank goodness she had her dog, Casey for company on those long lonely nights at the condo.

She sat at her desk for a moment looking at the papers lying around and the corkboard that held a couple of pictures, business cards, and important to-do notes. Her eyes drifted back to a holiday picture of her crew at Reed's. Johnny in the back with his short brown hair, and lanky build, she loved his easy smile that matched his easy going personality. Then there was spunky Libby, her little spitfire with light auburn hair pulled back into a ponytail, she was a first year college student who had worked at Reeds since her sixteenth birthday. Then there was Hannah, with her big brown eyes, long dark curly hair and tentative smile. They all were very different personalities but all worked really well together, she was thankful for all their hard work and friendship.

The afternoon was pretty much a blur and she was grateful the time had passed quickly. It was "Let's have a Ruben" day Tuesday at the café and as usual they ran out. She finished up the deposit as Hannah and Libby finished loading the commercial dishwasher and mopping the floors. Jesse divided the money out of the tip jar and split it between the four of them. She knew the girls relied on those tips, and Johnny the cook, had a small family to feed. She on the other hand, usually put her portion in an account and used it to pay towards the Christmas party at the end of the year, or for cake when the staff had a birthday. Today was a very good day and they each walked away with approximately sixty one dollars in tips.

Jesse locked the front door, flipped the sign to 'Closed' and got ready to take the deposit to the bank across the street. Johnny finished unloading the truck for tomorrow's menu, and then closed the kitchen down turning off the lights as he went out the back door. She sat in the small office alone, listening to the hum of the refrigerator and dishwasher as they purred, pondering her upcoming appointment.

Standing, she began to untie her apron then hung it on the hook on the back of the door in an effort to get ready. She stood in front of the mirror and her big blue eyes stared back at her, she finger scrunched her short sassy blonde bob to encourage it back to its initial state of morning fluffiness. Then she reached for her purse to reapply some powder on her face to smooth out the effects of the busy work day. After applying a layer of lip gloss she put the deposit in her purse and made her way to the bank.

The address on the business card was an office building approximately half a block away. Jesse walked into the twenty five story building, her tennis shoes made very little noise on the tile floors as she made her way to the elevator. Most of the people were leaving so she was going against the flow of traffic. Once inside the elevator she pressed the number 2 button then looked around for cameras or anything high tech but only found mirrors on the ceiling and panels on the walls.

The doors opened slowly and she stepped into the lobby of the local CIA office, to the right there were two standard metal and dark brown pleather chairs with the obligatory faux Ficus tree in the corner, and battleship gray adorned the walls. A generic looking wooden desk sat in the middle of the back wall with a plain looking thirtysomething female with brown hair pulled back into a neat ponytail, manning the phones. She had on minimal make up but was not unattractive, nor was she attractive, she just seemed to blend. Her name tag identified her as Ms. Lane, she was also minimally courteous and Jesse wondered if everyone who worked for the CIA behaved like the receptionist and Mr. Johnson? If that was the case, she was definitely *not* going to fit in and considered turning back towards the elevator to leave.

The director's sudden appearance surprised her, "Mrs. Hardin, thank you for coming and for being on time. Please follow me." The director looked exactly like he did at 7:05 a.m. this morning, why she thought he might look differently this afternoon perplexed her. Jesse fell in line behind him and they walked in to what her active imagination determined to be an interrogation room with two way glass. She wondered who was behind there watching them and if they were taking notes. As the door shut behind her, she suddenly felt like she wanted to throw up.

"Please have a seat, may I get you anything? Water or a soda? Coffee?" He asked in a cordial manner.

"Thank you yes, I think I would. A Coke please, over crushed ice, in a Styrofoam cup with a straw." She smiled sweetly.

The man monitoring behind the two way glass let out a chuckle. *She knows what she wants and thinks we can't get her fingerprints or DNA from a glass if she uses Styrofoam. She is thinking on her feet. Smart girl.*

Upon hearing her order, the director gave a nod, approximately a minute or two later a knock on the door alerted them that her beverage had arrived as she requested. She thanked him, and then he sat down across from her to begin his spiel.

"Mrs. Hardin, I'll just be direct. This Beta program that we are testing is one where we enlist civilian people in our community to work with us in gathering intelligence. Intelligence that down the road could help cut down on crime in the local community, or God forbid a home grown terrorist attack launched within our shores. Now on your level there is absolutely no danger to you. You will go about your daily routine but will be equipped with special gear so that we can hear and see what you see. Any information you report back no matter how insignificant it may seem will be analyzed, and if it bears further investigation it will be given to an Alpha team who is highly trained to follow up." He paused to allow her to comment.

"Ok…When would this start and would I be trained or anything?"

"Those are good questions. When you start of course depends on you and your schedule. There will be training, but it's more like on the job training with your handler as to not disrupt your life. We ask for a six month commitment and should you want to terminate earlier that will be assessed on a case by case basis. Your handler will fill you in on the rest should you decide to accept our offer. Oh and you will receive monetary compensation, it's not a lot but may help with some bills."

"Who is my handler? Do I get to meet him or her at some point?" She asked fully intrigued.

"Yes and no."

She laughed nervously, then took a sip of her drink as she looked around the room then stood up to stretch. The man behind the two way glass was watching her and taking notes of how she moved, how many times she blinked when she smiled and estimated her breathing pattern. She stood directly in front of the glass and her big blue eyes intently stared into the two way mirror. For a moment he felt as though she could see straight through the glass at him and it gave him a cold chill. Jesse looked down at her well-worn tennis shoes, then lifted her head and turned back towards the chair and sat back down.

"I think I want to help you, I mean I love my country and feel strongly about our military men and women. I support them…we support them down at the Café when we can. I don't have any children right now, so if I was going to do something like this, now would be the best time. Ya know?"

"Yes. I think I understand your position. If you have time tonight I can introduce you to your handler and get you started. If not, then we can set up another appointment."

"I think I would like to go ahead and do it tonight." She said sounding more confidently than she felt. The director stood and asked her to follow him into another room. This room was dimly lit and she could feel her blood coursing through her veins as her heart felt like it was going to beat out of her chest.

"It's normal to be nervous Mrs. Hardin but, please try and relax. I am going to explain something to you and I need you to listen carefully. You are going to meet your handler now and his name is Dean. Just Dean. He will of course know what you look like so that he can protect you, but you cannot see what he looks like. That way if you cross paths in public, his identity will not be compromised and you will not have to worry about feeling awkward or explaining something we don't want explained. Do you understand?"

"Yes sir, I believe so." She said taking a cleansing breath.

"Ok, I am going to blind fold you now, so please hold onto my arm and I will escort you in, Dean is waiting and will explain the rest of the details to you." He stated pleasantly.

Jesse stood very still while he placed the blindfold on her then he gently placed her hand on his arm and they took a few steps into another dimly lit room. It was dark in there too she surmised since she could not sense any light filtering through the blindfold and then she felt someone take her hands. His hands were large, with long fingers that draped over her folded hands and they were warm, she immediately felt herself relax a bit.

"Hello Jesse. My name is Dean and I will be your handler for the next six months. I am here to explain what we are going to do together, and how this program works. Are you ok with that?" His voice was smooth as glass and had a calming effect on her nerves. She sensed he was very much in control, yet she truly felt like he was trying to put her at ease, which she appreciated.

"Yes Dean. Thank you."

"Ok, let's sit down, and I'll get started." He moved around to her side and took her by the elbow to help gently guide her into a chair. The ease in which she allowed him to do this showed him that he was already winning her trust. Trust was going to be crucial in this venture and he needed to know she could and would trust him.

"Are you comfortable?"

"Yes I am, thank you." She responded levelly.

He reached across and took hold of her hands again, partly to put her at ease, and partly to monitor her nonverbal responses.

"You are Charge 25. That is your technical name and during the operation that is how you will be referred to, this is for your protection. All we want you to do is live your life and as you observe things in your day to day work life or free time, report back on them. For example, you work at the Café and come into contact with no less than four hundred people in a week's time. Granted some of these people are repeaters, but you still talk to, touch and see hundreds of people in a week's time. We just want you to report anything that you feel is suspicious. Perhaps it's a vehicle that passes by six or seven times in a day, or a man who comes in for a coffee and sits alone for an hour or more."

"Ok, what if it's just a man sitting with no agenda? No harm, no foul?" she asked curiously.

"You will learn what behavior is concerning and what is not. There will be many days where there is nothing to report. Nothing extraordinary, nothing suspicious, and that is ok. Remember, anything you see, hear or over hear that is worth reporting will be reviewed by my team, and if deemed necessary will be escalated to an experienced team to investigate further. Your job is done. No one will know where the tips came from; your name will never be attached to any of the reports other than to say reported by Charge 25."

"OK, that seems simple enough but there has to be more, a catch of some kind?" She stated tilting her head a little to the right. His hands remained on top of hers and she made no attempt to move them under his, and she actually found this very soothing as they talked. She tried to focus on the sound of his voice and imagine what his facial expressions would be as he spoke.

"What are you thinking about Jesse?" He asked noticing her scrunch up her nose and mouth twist slightly.

"You. I'm trying to imagine what your facial expressions are as you are speaking. Your hands are soft, and your breath smells faintly of peppermint." He bent his head down smiling at her comments.

"That is a perfectly normal response. The situation you are in right now is *not* normal. You are doing great, and there is no catch. Now let me explain the equipment you will be receiving, it is extremely expensive so please do your very best to take care of it. There is a small ear piece you will wear that sits down low in your ear, with a transmitter and it acts as a two way radio so to speak. Once you have it in place you will be able to hear me perfectly and if you speak normally I will be able to hear you. I will even be able to hear you if you speak softly, we will test this very quickly tonight so that you can get a feel for how it works."

"Ok, that sounds good." She said letting out a small sigh and smiled.

"Jesse I am going to get up and come around to your right, and then I am going to touch your face, then your ear and insert the ear piece. Is that ok with you?"

"Um…yeah."

He patted her hands before fully removing his from hers. Then he stood, walked around the table, gently touching her arm, then her shoulder then he gently tucked her hair behind her ear, and then softly asked her to tilt her head to the left."

"I'm going to insert this ear bud. It may feel a little odd at first, but I promise you will hardly feel it once it's inside the canal and after a day or so will not even realize it is even there. It will just become a habit like brushing your teeth. Now this is an electronic device, it does not like water, please try to remember this if you take a shower, or go swimming. If for any reason while you are wearing this, if you cannot hear me or I cannot hear you that needs to be rectified immediately. Do you understand?" His warm minty breath floated across her neck as he spoke and she slowly nodded.

"You work in the Café correct? Then your equipment repair place is two doors down at the alteration shop. Walk in the alteration shop and say you need to pick up something for Dean. They will take you to a change out room, and you will be in and out in less than five minutes. I will contact you by cell phone or any phone I can tell that you are nearby if I can't reach you on the ear piece. Likewise there is a special number I will have programmed into your phone that will enable you to reach me 24 hours a day. The most important thing to me is your safety." He finished inserting the ear piece, and like he said it felt a little different but was not uncomfortable. He also untucked her hair, and then stood to walk to the far end of the room.

"Can you hear me?" He spoke softly then turned away from her to face the wall.

"Yes! I can." She said exuberantly.

"OK, lower your voice and speak in a normal tone." He said smiling to himself.

"Oh-my-gosh, I'm sorry Dean. That was probably loud, are you ok?" She said correcting to a normal tone, feeling like a failure already and it had only been two minutes. He laughed then assured her he was fine, that he was anticipating her response. She liked the way he laughed, it was natural and comfortable.

"Jesse, I want you to whisper something to me so I can do a sound check. Go."

"I am still very nervous." She whispered.

"Good job. I can hear you just fine, and don't be nervous. Now, let's discuss some of the lingo. I have mastered the art of multitasking and so I will be monitoring you daily from 7 A.M. until 6 P.M. and you will have Sunday's off. When you have something you need to tell me, you will need to say 'Report', that will get my attention and from there I will address you as Charge 25 and tell you to proceed. You will need to wait if you can until you are acknowledged first before you start your report. Do you understand?"

"Roger that." She said smiling.

He also smiled then grabbed a chair and brought it around next to hers, turning her chair towards him to where their knees were almost touching. Once again he took her hand into his, and she wondered if that was all part of the process or did he just like holding her hand?

"Jesse, I need for you to act as normal as possible. There is a go silent button that I will have the exit tech show you. Use this at times when you are in the restroom or places where personal privacy is required. Just be sure to turn it back on once you are finished, otherwise you will get a call or text from me, OK?"

"Yes sir, I understand."

"Good. Your husband cannot know about this, no one can. Can you do that?" He asked her calmly but firmly.

"Yes sir. I can." She formally replied.

"Please call me Dean." He said smiling.

"Yes Dean, I can, and how did you know I was married?" She asked.

"I can see the ring on your finger, not to mention all potential Charge recruits had background checks done on them before we approached you."

"Yes of course, that makes sense." She said quietly, almost to herself.

"Charge 25, I think we are going to be a great team. If you have any questions, just say 'Report', when I acknowledge you, then state you have a question. I will do my best to answer you. You will also be outfitted with a pin or broach that has a camera in it that will allow me to see all or part of what you are seeing. It's vital you wear it every day. That is one of the tools that will help me keep you safe, and help me navigate you in certain circumstances."

"So do you want me to start this tomorrow? Or wait until Monday? How does this work?" She asked earnestly.

"We will start tomorrow, unofficially so that you have a couple of days to get used to it, then Monday will be our official go live day. We will practice but not be as formal during the rehearsal time. How does that sound Jesse?"

"Ok, good, I like the idea of having a couple of days to practice. Thanks Dean. Oh do you have the time?"

"Yes it is now 6:55 p.m. is everything ok?" He asked concerned.

"Yes, I was just curious, my husband won't be home until after nine."

"Another late night, huh?" Dean remarked offhandedly.

"Yes, I suppose. How did you know that?" She asked curiously.

"By your tone, I surmised this was not the first time he has worked late. That is all." He said to cover his slip. However, that was not all. Once he had selected her as his potential Charge he started investigating her and her husband. However he was not at liberty to divulge any information he had uncovered since it was not pertinent to the immediate task at hand.

"Oh, well yes, he is working towards a promotion right now, and so unfortunately late nights are a part of that, but hopefully soon it will all stop. At least I hope so anyway." She stated melancholy etched her voice.

"I'm sure it will. Let's get you out to the exit tech and I will talk to you tomorrow. Ok?" He said encouragingly. He took her by the elbow and helped her stand, noting that the top of her head was level with his chest, and then he moved the chair out of the way so he could lead her into another area. The next thing she heard was the technician tell her that she could remove her blindfold.

She removed it then immediately turned to see if Dean was still there behind her, then she heard him through the ear piece say, "Goodnight Jesse", and she realized he was long gone.

"Goodnight Dean." She stated softly. The technician then showed her the proper way to take the ear bud out, showed her how to charge it, and then how to mute it or put it in silent mode. Then he assisted her with placing it back in position in her ear. He recommended she wear it home until time for bed, to assist in getting used to it. Then he gave her a spare ear bud so that one was charged at all times, then he fitted her with a camera pin and showed her where to pin it to get the best line of sight for Dean. He also took her cell phone then programmed Dean's contact information into along with a CIA passcode for when she called in so that she would be routed to the correct team. By 7:20 she was on her way.

CHAPTER 2

PRACTICE
MAKES PERFECT

J esse walked down the lit pathway that led her to the beat up Ford Escort she drove. She unlocked the sixteen year old car, buckled up the seat belt and prayed the car would start. She really needed to get a newer vehicle but Jerry said it could wait until he got his bonus. *A bonus that never seemed to come* she thought. Of course he drove a new car, a Honda Accord EXL, he rationalized that since he had to travel out of town occasionally it was warranted.

Please start, please start…. She said as she turned the key. The engine sputtered several times then started. *Thank you Jesus!*

Dean heard that whole exchange as he sat in the dark work room looking at the monitors and adjusting the sound to filter background noises. On his end he had the sound open all the time so that he could hear and monitor her, and would do this especially in the beginning to make sure she didn't divulge anything or run into any snags. He kept his mic muted and would speak to her only if warranted or when she had something to report.

He made a mental note to inquire about her vehicle, since he did not want his charge stranded on the side of the road anywhere. He listened in on her as she hummed along to the car radio and talked to herself as she drove home. He paid attention to what she said as she went through a local drive thru and ordered her dinner, and noted how polite she was to the staff who served her. She of course had no idea he was listening in so anything she did was not for show or to impress him, she was just being herself. Once he knew she was home safely he turned off the camera and ear piece then got ready to go home himself, tomorrow would come early and he wanted to be ready.

Jesse was up and dressed by 6:15 a.m. fully decked out in her ear piece and broach. The pin she wore allowed him to see into her small world and give him a glimpse into her lifestyle. He had gone out on a limb selecting her and desperately wanted to prove that an everyday citizen could be a tremendous help to the intelligence community. Police had their informants, this was a little different of course, since it was strictly on a voluntary basis, but same basic premise. He had observed her one day at lunch, he was sitting at a small table outside at Reed's on a busy Wednesday when a table of eight rowdy servicemen from a nearby base arrived for lunch. It was apparent she had waited on them before taking their ribbing and teasing in stride. She actually gave back as good as she got and they all had fun yet were respectful of her.

Calling them all by name, she was quick to ask after one of them who had been out for surgery recently, another whose child had a birthday, then chatted with one about his harem of women he was attempting to court. Her memory certainly impressed him as he listened to their conversations, but the men all remarked on what a great memory she had and thanked her for inquiring and following up with them. It's one thing to be friendly and attentive as a waitress but she took this to a whole new level and never missed a beat on their conversation, orders, refilling of drinks or their bill. Attention to detail was key.

Dean knew he had to have her, that she would make an amazing Charge, so he was beyond elated when he got word that she had actually shown up on time for the interview. Since Dean was the Project's team lead he had selected three of the five civilians that were interviewed and agreed to sign up. They were assigned to other handlers, also hand-picked by him, but he saved Jesse for himself.

He watched as she let her dog out, wiped down the kitchen counter, poured herself some juice then let the dog back inside and put her in her crate. Her movements were quick, controlled, but fluid and her living space appeared to be neat and tidy. Once again he listened as she encouraged her old jalopy of a vehicle to please start and get her to work one more day…then once again thanking the good Lord when the engine turned over.

The ride into work took her approximately eleven minutes and was uneventful. Even though he had been watching and listening since six o'clock he waited until seven before he came on line.

"Good Morning Charge 25, how was your ride into work?" He inquired innocently, as though he didn't already know.

"Hi Dean. Good, really good. I think I have everything on properly, is there anything you would like for me to adjust? Can you see stuff, is it up high enough?" She asked anxiously.

"Perfect, good job. Yes I can see, and hear you just fine. Now don't be nervous, just go about your daily routine. These next couple of days are just practice, so I don't want you to worry or be stressed out." He said his words smooth and encouraging.

"Thanks Dean, I am a little nervous, but excited. This could be really cool, ya know? A very good opportunity, well then again maybe not, since I probably couldn't put this on a resume." She stated laughing at herself. He chuckled too.

"Well this may not be a resume builder, but if you ever need a reference, I'll see what I can do. How's that?"

"Oh I'm just teasing about the resume, but that is so very kind of you to offer. Ok, well I just finished up this food order for tomorrow, and need to scoot outside on the floor and check on Libby since she was opening this morning. Talk to you later?"

"Of course. I'm always here." He said smiling to himself.

Dean went about his business at the office listening to her as she waited on people at the restaurant, dealt with staff and prepared lunches. She was definitely a hard worker and didn't ask anyone on her staff to do anything that she was not willing to jump in and do herself. He was impressed by that and was so far pleased with himself for selecting a responsible Charge.

It was about 3:20 when Jesse finally sat down to eat a bite of lunch. She sat at a two top near the window and gazed outside as she ate her vegetable soup and half of a turkey sandwich on wheat. It occurred to her that she had completely forgotten to ask about the compensation, and wondered if it might be enough over time to get her a newer vehicle.

"Report." She said cautiously.

"Charge 25, go ahead please."

"Question."

"Of course."

"Mr. Johnson mentioned there would be some compensation, and I completely forgot to ask about it, like how much and how often would I get paid?"

"Yes its two hundred dollars a week, before taxes. We will open a bank account in just your name and it will be direct deposited every Friday. I know that is not a lot, but hopefully it will help pay a bill or two. If you can swing back by the office today we can finish your paper work and get that set up so that next Friday you will get your first direct deposit."

"That sounds wonderful, perhaps I can use that money to get me a newer used car. I certainly need one." She stated emphatically.

"I think that would be a great thing for you to use the money for, something just for you." He stated earnestly.

"Who are you talking to Jess?" Hannah asked cautiously as she swept over near the window.

"What? Oh no one, myself. Just day dreaming really." She covered, then laughed at herself.

"Well you are right about the car thing, you need a new one bad girl. I am amazed you make it here and back home every day. Your husband is kind of a jerk for not letting you drive the new car if you ask me." She stated boldly which was unlike her.

"Hannah, please don't speak ill of Jerry. He does have to take clients out to dinner and travel out of town occasionally so he does need the newer car. Plus he is due for a bonus soon, and he promised we would look at getting me something newer when that comes in, so hopefully it won't be too much longer." She said making excuses for him as she cleaned up her lunch mess then went back into the kitchen.

Dean had to admit he agreed with Hannah, Jesse's husband was a jerk, but then again he knew things about him that Jesse didn't and hopefully never would know. If he was honest with himself he wanted Jerry to get what was coming to him, but not at her expense.

They finished cleaning the restaurant and Jesse decided to go and fill out her paperwork for the direct deposit and any other paperwork that Dean needed from her. She entered the lobby and signed in then gave the receptionist her passcode. Approximately two minutes later a gentleman in a suit came to take her back to an office so that she could complete the paperwork. As she passed different people in the hallway she wondered which one might be Dean and wondered if he knew she was there.

"Dean? Are you there?" She whispered.

"Jesse? Yes. I am here."

"Hi, I am at your office I just wanted you to know so that you wouldn't walk out and risk me seeing you." She said so seriously, still whispering. He could not help but grin, apparently she had forgotten he has seen her, but she had not seen him nor would she recognize him if she did see him in the hallway.

"Well thank you for letting me know. I thought I recognized that elevator when you stepped inside."

"Oh yeah…I forget you can see where I am." She replied sheepishly.

"Its fine, I'll let you get to your paperwork." He continued to look at the monitors and observe her as she filled out the paperwork. He knew he should keep his distance from her for a number of reasons, one of which she was a married woman, two she was working for him, and three it was for her safety. Yet there was something about her, strong and capable in many ways yet she was very innocent in others and he found something endearing about that.

The rest of the week went smoothly, he took notes while learning her schedule and patterns of travel behavior. It was important he have these mapped out in the unlikely event she ever went off the grid. They had worked on some basic observation techniques and exercises over the last few days and he was delighted at how well she did. With proper training she had the potential to be one heck of an agent, and again he was pleased with himself for having found her.

Sunday arrived and Jesse was looking forward to church this morning. They had a guest speaker in Sunday school with lunch in the fellowship hall after the main service. It was their church's annual homecoming, a time when old members and families gathered back together for a day of preaching and fellowship. Usually this was a pot luck affair, but the kitchen at church was undergoing renovations so the hostess committee decided to have it catered.

Jerry at the last minute decided not to go, which Jesse found to be a little embarrassing and frustrating. He had been fine all morning but then feigned a headache and stated he would not be going to church. She finished getting dressed and put in her ear piece to stay in the practice of wearing it. She pinned on her broach then looked into the mirror to spritz her hair in place.

"Is that what you are wearing?" Jerry asked sarcastically as he passed the master bathroom.

"Yes, why? What's wrong with this dress?" She asked turning looking side to side at it in the mirror.

"I don't know, have you gained weight or something?" He asked flippantly.

Quietly she stepped on the scale in the bathroom, fully dressed she weighed in at 123 lbs actually two pounds less than she weighed last Monday. She stepped off the scale and looked closely at herself in the mirror. Tears sprang to her eyes, and she tried desperately to blink them back so she didn't mess up her makeup.

Dean started monitoring her the minute she took the ear piece off the charger and it went live. Although Sunday was her day off, it was not necessarily his. The exchange he just heard between she and her husband, Jerry made his blood boil. Then seeing her look into the mirror with her big blue eyes filled with tears made him want to drive over there while she was at church and teach Jerry some manners.

However, that would not happen, at least not today. Dean knew he could not interfere in her life like that, regardless of how he felt about her sleaze of a husband. Their relationship had to remain above board and professional or he risked getting the plug pulled on this program, and he had worked far too hard to have that happen. So he would stow his feelings and regain control, he had to.

She sat on the front row in Sunday school soaking up every word the guest speaker had to say, he was speaking on relationships, and how your relationship with God was the most important one you would ever have in life. From there she sat on what looked like the third row on the left near the aisle, during the service she took notes on the Pastor's sermon and starred and underlined things that stood out or spoke to her heart. The sermon highlighted the fact that when unexpected things happen in our lives that God is not caught by surprise. He knows and even though we may not have all the pieces to the puzzle, we are to trust Him and His plan for our lives, and be obedient. Jesse immediately thought of the opportunity with the CIA and smiled. She didn't understand why the Lord had brought Dean into her life along with the Company, but she was going to do her best to be obedient.

Several people noticed that Jerry was not there and were sympathetic towards Jesse. A couple of older ladies invited her to sit with them during luncheon to which she graciously accepted their offer. She enjoyed spending time with them--their wit and wisdom was so refreshing. If only the younger generation would spend time with these women and learn from them. They are a fount of information and offer wisdom, which like the Bible is still applicable today. Jesse helped clean up after lunch and then went for a drive before going home. She stopped at a park near their complex and decided to swing on the swings, this always helped to clear her mind when she was upset or had decisions to make. Something very basic and therapeutic about just swinging back and forth.

It was just after two o'clock when she arrived home, and found that Jerry was not there. She called his cell phone and after the third ring he picked up.

"Hello?" He answered flatly.

"Hey, I'm home and you aren't here. Where are you?" She asked concerned.

"Did you expect me to wait on you all day? I got hungry so I went out for lunch. I'll be back later."

"So I take it you are feeling better then? No more headache?"

"Yeah something like that." He answered sarcastically.

"Drop the sarcasm Jerry. I'm tired of your attitude lately. I haven't done anything to deserve this treatment." With that she hung up on him. She was so angry, between his rude comment this morning, then him skipping church for no good reason, and now this. Unbelievable. She paced back and forth in the den for a few minutes then remembered poor Casey was still in the kennel crate.

"Oh precious. Momma is sorry! Let's go outside." Jesse bent down and unfastened the latch. Casey's tail wagged furiously. She reached for the leash and attached it to Casey's collar. Casey was a buff colored mixed bread, part miniature poodle, part schnauzer. Smart, well behaved and so loving. She proved herself daily to be Jesse's best friend and Jesse adored her. When all seemed dark and bleak in her world she could always come home to a happy Casey, tail wagging and sweet puppy kisses.

She walked Casey outside in the grassy area behind their condo until her business was finished, then they continued to walk around the complex so that Jesse could burn off some of the angry nervous energy. As she walked she kept muttering to herself and talking out loud to Casey, who would look up at her with a curious expression her big brown eyes expressing concern, then continue to trot next to her master. After two complete laps around the complex and down to the corner convenient store and back, Jesse finally decided she was ready to head back inside and think about starting dinner.

Dean had been listening to her as he putted around his apartment cleaning and tinkering with some of his computer and surveillance equipment. He continued to make mental notes of her schedule, daily routines, and continued with his dislike of her husband. When Jesse arrived at the house, Jerry's car was in the drive way and he met her at the door with Chinese takeout and a small bouquet of grocery store flowers.

"Hi honey, come on in, here let me take Casey for you." He said syrupy sweet.

"I'm fine, I've got her, thanks." She said as she bent down to unlatch her leash. Casey bolted off and scampered through the house finally settling on her small ornate doggie bed near the sofa.

"I took the liberty of getting us supper tonight, I got your favorite… Chinese food! I know how hard you work all week, and well I just thought it might be a nice treat." He stated attempting to make amends.

"Did you bring me flowers?" She asked incredulously, which caused Dean's radar to go off as he listened to their conversation. *What is that snake up to?* Dean thought to himself.

"You are right, I was in a terrible funk this morning and took it out on you today and that was unfair. I have been working so hard on the bonus for this month, it's supposed to be a big one, and well I am just not sure I'm going to make it. Even with all the overtime I have been logging, I'm just not sure it's

going to be enough. Plus I know you are needing work done on your car...."
He said with his eyes down cast, playing the sympathy card.

"Oh, it's ok. I'm sorry you have been under so much pressure. I wish you would just talk to me about it, I am a good listener." She said smiling giving him a light kiss on the cheek, unfortunately falling for it.

No Jesse, don't fall for his line of crap! Boy he is a piece of work. Dean said to himself now pacing in his bedroom agitated by the turn of events. *Wait. Dean come on man, you cannot get emotionally involved here. Stick to the plan, stay on track and keep this all business.* Dean sat on the edge of the bed and ran his hands through his short dark blonde hair. He listened as it sounded like Jerry was serving her dinner.

Jerry led her over to the kitchen bar and proceeded to take the plates out of the cabinet and set one in front of her as she sat down.

"I got us some fried dumplings, fried rice, Moo Shu Pork, and your favorite Chicken Chow Mein." He stated with a smile.

She didn't say anything but smiled slightly and nodded her head as he rambled on setting down the plates and serving up dinner, then Dean heard her mutter to herself softly 'I hate Chicken Chow Mein, and I prefer white rice.' *Oh well, it was nice that he was trying to make up for this afternoon.* She thought.

They ate in kind of an awkward silence, her trying to get the Chow Mein down, piling on the crunchy noodles, picking at the fried rice, and him shoveling it in like his life depended on it. She attempted to tell him about her day at church explaining how the sermon the pastor gave really inspired her to want to mediate and dive into the word more. He half mumbled an "uh huh" every now and then when she paused.

Jesse started cleaning the kitchen thanking him once again for the flowers and dinner, off handedly mentioning that next time she would love to try the Triple Delight with white rice, which was actually her favorite not Chicken Chow Mein. He patted her on the shoulder, then distractedly said, "Ok, yeah, sure." On his way to the couch to settle in and watch the history channel.

So much for the make-up session....apparently Jerry was done, and it was back to business as usual.

She let out a sigh and finished up in the kitchen and then poured Casey some fresh water. Then she wiped her hands on a dish towel and then draped it over the oven handle. Then she walked through the den over to the laundry area and got the basket of clothes that needed to be folded. She hummed to herself as she folded the clothes then put them away, Dean sat back in his recliner listening to her quietly humming and singing to herself. He found it to be soothing, so he closed his eyes as he leaned back in his chair and listened.

CHAPTER 3

READY SET GO!

Monday morning came early and Jesse had a hard time waking up. She was restless and didn't sleep well at all, tossing and turning most of the night. She scrunched her hair and applied minimal makeup, almost forgot her earpiece and then rushed to her vehicle. The car refused to start and her anxiety level shot off the charts. She pulled out her phone then called Hannah to tell her that she might be late and remember to pull the scones out of the refrigerator.

"Charge 25? Is everything alright?" Dean asked.

"No, not alright." She stated exasperated, almost in tears.

"Can you state the nature of your issue?" He asked calmly.

"I overslept, and today is our first day, now my stupid car won't start. I have special scones that need to be displayed, and well, I'm nervous and frustrated." She said with her lip quivering.

"Jesse please listen to me. We start whenever you get to work and are ready. There is no rush on my end, so please relax. We are good, OK? Now as far as this vehicle goes, I think you need a new starter and or a new battery. I know a guy who works on cars, so I will send him over to look at yours and let's see if we can't get you moving forward. So just take a breath for me and I will send Timothy over to your location."

"Thank you so much Dean. I'm so embarrassed."

"Please don't be, its fine. Let me know when he arrives." He stated reassuringly.

Within minutes a tow truck pulled up and a tall lanky guy with dark wavy hair in a blue jump suit with the name tag 'Timothy' stepped over to her window. Jesse slowly rolled down the car window and with an impish toothy grin he handed her Dean's business card to reassure her, then she stepped out of the car so that he could check everything out.

He looked under the hood and surmised at the very least she definitely needed a new battery, and possibly a tune up. He took the liberty of bringing a battery that would fit her car, and replaced it on the spot. Timothy said he would follow her to the café and then drive her vehicle over to his shop so that he could tune it up for her. She was so grateful, and relieved it was nothing more. It was an amazing feeling to turn the key and have it start up immediately. She relayed to Dean what had taken place, and that Timothy was very kind and helpful.

She arrived at the café and found everyone in their places with everything running smoothly, and let out a sigh of relief. Libby brought her up to speed on what had happened in the last hour, and proceeded to handle the morning crowd while Jesse got settled in the back office. She put a call into Jerry to let him know that she had to purchase a new battery for the car, but had to leave a voice mail message. She put her apron on, reapplied her lip gloss and hit the floor to start her day.

Jesse wrote out the sign for the street front to announce that today's specialty sandwich was the infamous grilled cheese and meat of your choice on sourdough bread. Another fan favorite at Reed's ranking right up there with the Ruben. She anticipated that they would serve no less than a hundred and twenty five of the sandwiches today. The take-out orders usually started ringing in around 10:45 a.m. all the way through until around 2:30 p.m. so they had their work cut out for them today.

Right at the end of the rush, Timothy walked into Reed's with her car keys. He promised Dean he would have her vehicle ready before she got off from work so that she would not be stranded. He explained that he did do an oil change, tune up and replaced her starter that was beginning to fail. Jesse held her breath as he pulled out the receipt for the work. She knew that starters could run upwards of a hundred dollars, as well and the other work that was done, it was going to be expensive.

"Here you go ma'am. If you have any trouble with any of the work that was done, please call me immediately and I will take care of it." His brown eyes crinkling as he smiled with wisps of his dark hair falling over his forehead.

She glanced down and saw that the bill was stamped paid in full. She reached over and touched his shirt sleeve hem, "Um, excuse me. How can this be paid in full?" Her big blue eyes searching his.

"Dean is a buddy of mine, and a friend of Dean's is a friend of mine. Plus, I'm a sucker for a damsel in distress. That car is super old, and the thought of you riding around in the dark in that car makes me shudder. If I had not fixed it for you, I would not be able to sleep at night." He winked then laughed.

"Well then the very least I can do is feed you. Please let me make you something to take with you, *anything* you like, just pick." She offered enthusiastically.

"I hear this grilled cheese thing is the bomb, I'll take one with turkey and bacon." He said still grinning.

"You are on, give me five minutes, and thank you so much for fixing my car. Really I can't believe your generosity. Thank you." She said sincerely.

As she walked back to the kitchen to place his order, he tapped into his direct line with Dean. "You there? Man she is so nice, and wow you could get lost in those big baby blue eyes. She is fixing me a sandwich for dinner, want me to get you one too?" He asked smugly.

"No, I am fine, and mind your manners Timmy. She's married." Dean said laughing. He and Tim went way back, they were at the Air Force academy together, and then were recruited into the CIA roughly at the same time. Although Tim was a couple of years older than Dean they got along great, almost like brothers. They were in the same department but different divisions, Dean was his supervisor and team lead on agency projects.

"Here you go, one special grilled cheese turkey with bacon. I put a bag of chips in there too, and what would you like to drink? Soda? Sweet Tea?"

"Oh the sandwich is fine, really, I have a drink back at the office. I really appreciate it." He said flashing a broad smile.

"No it is I, who is indebted to you. Thank you again Tim, you have given me peace of mind, and that my friend is priceless." She stated smiling.

"Like I said, my number is on there, call me day or night. I run the shop, so it's not a problem. Talk to you soon." He said waving as he walked out with his sandwich.

She folded up the paperwork and slid it in her apron pocket. Libby asked about the visitor and Jesse explained that she had called him this morning when her car would not start and he came immediately to assist her. She nodded, and then went about wiping down the rest of the tables and restocking table supplies. Jesse was happy she didn't press for further details.

Once again, they finished cleaning up, and then Jesse prepared the deposit to take to the bank. She went into the back office to tally up the receipts and separate the tips out. Today she was disappointed in the tip contribution, since the total only yielded $42.50. Hannah lightly tapped on the door, and peeked around the corner to ask, "So what is our tip situation?" her dark curls tumbling over her shoulder.

"Were there any problems today that I need to know about?" Jesse asked concerned.

"I don't know? Maybe a few. That accountant guy was in again, and of course hated everything. I'm beginning to *hate* him, he is such a pain, and he never tips." She said with a frustrated huff.

"Next time he comes in I will wait on him. I have an idea that just might work. I didn't hear him yell or cause a scene today, when did he come in? I can't believe I missed him."

"Oh well today he wasn't loud like he was last time, but he all but threw his sandwich at me because his lettuce wasn't placed right. Really? Can't we ban him or something?" Hannah said exasperated.

Then they heard Libby chime in from the counter, 'Yeah let's ban him!'

"Guys, I know he is difficult, but again, I think I have an idea that will turn this around. Next time he comes in, if I am busy come find me and I will handle him." Jesse soothed.

"No problem he is *alllllll* yours." Hannah relented laughing, then went back to her chores.

Jesse finished closing up, gave the staff their tips, and then headed over to the bank. While walking she was taking extra care to notice people and her surroundings more. She saw a couple of business men, a few young guns and one or two women out power walking around the square. Nothing special really, or out of the ordinary for that time of day.

"Report" She said softly.

"Charge 25 go ahead."

"Nothing of significance to report today, headed into the bank to drop off the deposit, then heading home."

"Thank you Charge 25, have a good night."

"Dean?"

"Yes..."

"How late do you work? I mean if I saw something in the evening, can I just talk to you or would I need to call?"

"Some nights I work late so I monitor, so just try Reporting in, but if I don't answer immediately please call the number on your phone."

"Ok, thank you. I was just wondering. Good night Dean."

"Goodnight Jesse. Be safe."

CHAPTER 4

WINDS OF CHANGE

After several weeks of working together, Jesse and Dean were developing quite a rapport with one another with their long philosophical discussions while they were doing training exercises. One afternoon Jesse stumbled across a man and his associates having a luncheon outside an upscale Chinese bistro across the office park from Reed's. She saw them as she was delivering a small office box lunch order at an attorney's office located on the third floor of the twelve story building.

There was just something about their demeanor and the way the two main business men sat surrounded by what looked like body guards that caused her new found radar to go off.

"Report." She stated levelly.

"Go ahead Charge 25."

"Wu's Original Chinese bistro. Seven people, 2 primary, 5 guards. Looks intense. Happening right now."

"Roger, can you get me a visual?"

She retrieved her cellphone from her pocket and pretended to be talking to her sister Susie as she walked in front of the restaurant, so that she could get good video line of sight for Dean. "Hey girlfriend. Yeah, I'm on break, oh no I'm over here at …let me see Wu's Bistro. Oh yeah… I love their spring rolls." She said lining up in front of the business men, fluffing her hair with her free hand as she held her phone in her right hand.

"You're doing great Jesse, I am getting it all now. Move a little to the right I need to see blue blazer's face better." He stated in a calm reassuring voice.

"Oh Sue did I tell you, that there are *three* stores I found that are right up your alley? Yeah three, and one of the big gun department stores that I am sure you would go for."

"Confirm. Are you seeing three major players, and one of them has a gun?" he said his voice slightly elevated.

"No silly, three carrots and six sparkly diamonds all around it in a silver, no dark gray setting." She said laughing and walking back and forth positioning herself in front of the man in the dark gray suit.

"Got it, three principals, surrounded by six guards, one in the dark gray suit has a gun."

"Perfect. Oh hey, listen I need to start back to work I guess, can I call you later? I have some more things I want to share with you." She asked.

"Roger that, call and check in when you can. Thank you Charge 25."

"Ok, bye! Love ya." And with that she ended the call not realizing what she had said and then turned to walk in the direction of the café.

Ok bye...love ya? Her last words floated through his head for the next two hours as he worked reviewing the footage of what he got off her camera today. She may actually have something here and he was encouraged with this report, the guy in the dark gray suit was someone he recognized but didn't know his name. He started running the facial recognition program on the stills he had collected from her video feed and should have some names soon.

Jesse checked in right after the lunch crowd vacated the restaurant, she moved back to the tiny office while the girls cleaned up the front, and Hannah worked on the deposit for a change. She had reorganized the small space so that the desktop was now visible and there was a stacking tray that held papers in a specific order, like bills, food orders, payroll and miscellaneous paperwork.

"Charge 25?"

"Here, Dean." She replied, anxious to see if her discovery yielded anything he could use.

"Great work today Jesse. We have some firm leads and the video was invaluable. It has been escalated to an alpha team. I'm impressed, good call."

"I am so excited. What an adrenaline rush. Did I make sense when I was pretending to call my sister?"

"Took me a minute but yes, it was great. Whatever works for you so that you blend while we are trying to gather Intel? You say whatever you need and we can decode it later as long as you remember what you heard." He said with a chuckle. He was so proud of her, and the small training exercises they had been doing after work and while she walked Casey in the evenings were well worth the time spent.

Jesse went on to relay that she thought she overheard one of the men say that the deal was set for Tuesday. She didn't really know what that meant but thought he should know. He took down those notes and again thanked her for the lead. She asked if there was anything else she needed to do, and Dean assured her that the Alpha team would take it from there.

She stayed at the office another hour, doing some prep work for tomorrow's specialty sandwich which was chicken salad. So she went to the refrigerator and pulled out the celery, red onion and fresh parsley. Jesse reached for her favorite knife and cutting board, starting with the celery first and dicing into small cubes then transferring them to a large glass bowl covering them with saran wrap. Then she took on the red onions, dicing them in record time. Again she put those in a glass bowl wrapping the bowl and placing it back in the refrigerator next to the celery. Last she chopped the parsley in fine bits then placed them in a zip lock baggie. Chopping veggies had a uniquely calming effect on her today and she looked around to see if there was anything else that needed dicing. She washed off the cutting board and knife and put them back in their place.

Jesse wrote out the check list for tomorrow so that everyone would be on the same page. Although the homemade chicken salad would be the feature sandwich, there were still dozens of sandwiches on the menu. They needed to be prepared for any and all of them, Johnny was terrific at keeping on top of everything back in the kitchen, but when Reed's was busy, it was hopping and all hands were needed on deck.

Reed's was owned by Reed McMillan and his wife Ann. Reed ran the restaurant for years until Ann was diagnosed with cancer. She survived her cancer scare, but Reed never recovered, it shook him to his core to think that his beloved Ann could have become a victim to this disease and leave him and his girls alone. He decided to pass the torch to his right hand gal, Jesse and retire early so that he could spend more time with his family. Ann is a professional photographer, who still works freelance for various national magazines. However, now when she has to travel for an assignment, the whole family can go.

Jesse was twenty two years old when she took over the reins and started managing the store. Reed checks in a couple of times a month now, but overall leaves the business to Jesse, who is this year an eight year veteran at Reed's and one he trusts implicitly. She made one last pass through the diner, checked the front door lock, and then made her way to the car. Casey was getting low on dog food, so she swung by the grocery store to get a few items.

Dean continued to monitor as she meandered through the grocery store aisles selecting a few vegetables for dinner, shrimp from the meat/fish department, and flour tortillas. It looked like she was planning on shrimp fajitas for dinner he deduced based on the groceries selected so far. She picked up a bag of dog food for Casey along with some doggie dental treats. Jesse used the self-checkout then proceeded to her vehicle, just as she began to load her bags into the trunk her phone began ringing.

"Hello?" She said breathing a little hard.

"Uh hey Jesse, listen I'm sorry for the last minute change but we have clients in from Cincinnati so management wants me and Mark to entertain them for supper tonight. I think we are going to take them to Antonio's for Italian." Jerry stated, almost sounding apologetic.

"Oh, ok. Well I haven't started supper yet, so I guess that's good. Do you know how late you will be?" She asked as she loaded the last of her groceries.

"No not really we are still here at the office and probably will be until around 7:30 or so, then we will head out and try and get a table. I'd say maybe by 11:00 p.m. or so."

"Ok then, I guess I'll see you later or in the morning." She said sounding somewhat dejected. She pressed end on her call then placed the phone in her front pants pocket.

She started the vehicle and pressed the button for the Christian radio station. A prerecorded sermon was on that she had already listened to, so she turned the radio down. Then she started talking to herself as she drove home.

"Ok girl, once again it's just you and Casey. Dinner for one. *Why* did I get married? Please explain that to me again? Do I just want to get some take out? But… nothing sounds good at the moment. I really had my mouth set for the shrimp fajitas." She said out loud as she drove home. Dean listened to her as he continued to write up the reports for the facial recognition data on the men she identified at the Chinese restaurant for the pass off to the Alpha team. This was the least glamorous part of his job, but one of the most vital parts, information disseminated and passed along to the Alpha team had to be accurate or lives would be in jeopardy. That was not liability he wanted hung around his neck, so he always double and triple checked his data before passing it along.

His heart hurt for Jesse as he sensed her frustration over being alone once again. This was something he was all too familiar with since he lost his fiancé several years ago. They also met at the Air Force academy his junior year, she was a senior and on track to be a fighter pilot. He was immediately enamored with her drive and intelligence, she was captivated his magnetism in return. They were inseparable, until her first assignment after graduation which took her abroad. They remained devoted to each other, skyping and spending weekends together whenever they could. Claire's job was to be a short term training assignment for six months then she would be stateside again. By then he would be close to graduating so they had planned to get married. However, her assignment got extended and she was to be overseas through his graduation, which made it hard on the young couple.

He received the news the day after his graduation that she had died during a training accident. They were doing integrated combined exercises with the Eastern European unit they were assisting with training. He was absolutely devastated, she was everything he had longed for in a mate and he grieved for years after her death, throwing himself into the Agency and his work. It was only in the last year or so that he had even begun to casually date, but always careful to not ever let it get too far. His work and family seemed to be enough, until just recently when he began to feel himself yearning for more.

Dean completely empathized with her going home to a dark empty house again and eating alone, the only difference between him and Jesse at this point was that she had Casey. Maybe he needed to get a pet? He rationalized that wouldn't really be fair since his job was unpredictable and pets needed a sense of normalcy and routine.

Jesse arrived at home, unloaded the groceries then took Casey out for a walk. While walking through her complex she decided to reach out to see if Dean was around. "Report." she said tentatively.

"Charge 25 go ahead." He replied.

"I'm sorry nothing is wrong, nothing to report." She stated now embarrassed.

"What's on your mind Charge?" Hearing the melancholy in her voice.

"Never mind Dean. I'm so sorry." She stated sounding forlorn.

"Jesse, wait!" He said trying to keep her on the line.

"I just wanted to hear a friendly voice is all, I know you're busy." She said her voice trailing off.

"You sound really down, are you ok? Where are you?" He asked concerned.

"Walking Casey around the complex, I'm fine really, just feeling sorry for myself. Ugg I hate feeling like this, I should just call my sister and complain and not call you, this is completely inappropriate. Can we just scratch this conversation? It won't happen again, I promise." She pleaded.

"Jesse, you are under a lot of new pressure with this assignment, it adds another layer to your life. There is nothing to forgive or worry about, ok? It's all good. As long as you are ok?"

"Yes Dean, I am fine." She stated wearily.

"Why don't you head on home and get something to eat. We will talk tomorrow." He encouraged.

"OK, thanks. Goodnight."

"Goodnight Jesse." He said softly.

I have lost my mind! What was I thinking? Oh Lord forgive me for reaching out to another man, I need to get home and call my sister and vent... and maybe eat some food. I'm hungry all of a sudden.

"Come on Casey let's get home girl. I've got some fajitas to fix." She said walking in a more determined manor toward the condo.

She arrived back at the condo and made a bee line for the kitchen, she pulled out the small onion, and peppers then began chopping and slicing for the fajitas. She pulled out her trusty skillet and drizzled some olive oil in the pan, then threw her veggies in to start sweating. Then she rinsed her already peeled and deveined shrimp under cold water. Once the veggies had started to sweat becoming tender she threw the shrimp in until they turned pink, then she turned them onto the other side, then gently stirred the seasonings in with a half a cup of chicken broth. The kitchen smelled fantastic, and Dean had a front row seat to this cooking show episode and was quite impressed. He just wished he was there to taste it.

She plated up her tortilla then placed a healthy scoop of shrimp and veggies in the middle, folded it and took a big bite. *Oh wow that is good, even if I do say so myself.* Jesse finished eating, then plopped on the couch next to Casey. Reaching for the remote, she turned on the television, then flipped through the channels until she found the Romance movie channel. She settled in watching a movie for about thirty minutes then when a commercial came on she hopped up to put the left overs away and placed the dishes in the sink.

Her phone started ringing so she bolted from the kitchen to find her phone. It was her older sister Susie.

"Hey Sue."

"Hi Jess, what are you up to?"

"Just finished eating supper, and I'm watching a little television with my hot date Casey. Probably going to bed soon, it's been a long day." She confided.

"Oh I'm sorry honey, you sound really tired. Is everything going ok? What are you doing this weekend? Maybe I can get Matt to watch the baby and we can go shopping or something, what do you think?"

"Oh yeah, that sounds nice Sue, thanks. I would love to go shopping, or maybe hit a few yard sales?"

"Ok great, I will talk to Matt and give you a call tomorrow. Hey maybe we can even cruise a few used car lots? Sis you really need a new car, is that bonus ever going to come through? I'm seriously beginning to doubt it, I mean really does he even really work for an advertising firm? Or is he just blowing smoke?" She said snickering.

"Ok, ok…I know. I have days when I wonder the same thing, but it's coming, I just know it. Call me tomorrow. Love you." She said smiling.

"Love you too Jess."

The next couple of days went along without a hitch, there was nothing of significance to report, and so one day just seamlessly flowed into the next. Finally it was Friday morning and Jesse was really ready for the weekend. Today's sandwich special was the sourdough BLT, and the whole diner smelled like bacon. Jesse was busy wiping down the tables outside, sweeping the side walk, and watering the baskets that hung in front of the plate glass windows in the front of the store.

Jesse entered into the café again to wash her hands and review the already growing list of takeout orders. One name caught her eye, Justine Willis. Her husband Dr. Ned Willis was in the hospital with heart issues and was mentioned in the prayer time during the Wednesday night service at church. She had been meaning to reach out to Mrs. Willis to see if there was anything she could do for them, knowing she was stopping by today set Jesse's mind into motion. She asked Johnny to create two special box lunches for Mrs. Willis with all the condiments on the side, so that she could take them up to the hospital and not worry about having to leave him or endure hospital food. *Perfect!*

The morning was ramping up nicely and so far things were running smoothly. Jesse was at the register when she spied her table of eight minus two of the regulars, it was the rowdy bunch of Navy men that she secretly adored. They were fun, loyal, and good tippers. Libby took over at the register while she went to take them their drink orders.

"Where are Joe-Bob and Tiny?" She asked as she set the drinks down in front of them.

"Joe-Bob is on assignment, and Tiny is sick." Yoshi piped up to explain.

"Assignment? Is it a top secret one?" She teased as she passed out the menus. "And poor Tiny, I hate that he feels bad, can I get you a to-go order for him?" She asked sincerely.

"Well we- could- tell you… but then we'd have to *kill* you." Yoshi said flashing his fantastic grin, then laughing at himself.

"Tiny is having stomach issues, so I doubt he'll eat anything, but that is really nice of you to offer." Doc said.

"You guys take a look at the menu, and Mack, step outside the box today and try something new!" She encouraged smiling at him. "I'll be back in just a minute."

They were really a great bunch of guys, Doc was actually a doctor on the base, Mack was a mechanic built like a Mack truck, and Yoshi was the self-proclaimed ladies' man of the group. He had jet black hair cut short and tight, and a megawatt smile and dimples that would melt any woman's heart. He was really more of a cut up than a ladies man, but Jesse didn't doubt for a moment that the women threw themselves at him. Yoshi, Tiny, Leo and Jack were all pilots. Joe-Bob worked in the tower, and the Duke was a mystery. He was the strong silent type that actually looked like John Wayne when the Duke was in his twenties. Uncanny really.

She ran back inside to check on the crowd and to get a new order pad. Most of the tables inside were starting to fill up and two of the five seats at the counter were already taken. She smiled at the two ladies at the two top near the inside corner and grabbed the water pitcher off the counter and refilled their glasses as she passed by.

Dean was in full tilt watching her work her magic, Yoshi's comments had gotten his attention until he realized who she was waiting on. He was taking his lunch break and decided to eat in the war room and monitor his Charge.

"Ok fellas...what will it be?" She asked.

She smiled as they rattled off theirs orders, then winked as she snatched up the menus and made haste to the kitchen to get their orders started. Jesse had just filled Johnny in on the air crew when Hannah walked back into the prep area almost in tears.

"He's here. I told you he'd come back." Hannah said completely frustrated.

"Who?" Jesse asked as she helped pack a few takeout orders.

"Mr. Patton! That horrible accountant who terrorizes us every week."

"Hannah take these sandwiches out to my table of six outside when it's up. I'll handle Mr. Patton. Johnny please get my materials we discussed ready. I've got this one." She said with a determined tone.

Dean sat up and took notice as she marched right out to greet her patron who sat on his stool looking like he was ready for a fight. *This is gonna be interesting.*

"Hello Mr. Patton, I'm Jesse the manager here at Reed's. It's been brought to my attention that we have not been able to satisfactorily present you with a sandwich for lunch that has been up to your standards. Today I intend to rectify all of that, since I will be waiting on you and I plan to get to the bottom of this mystery. You see we are a sandwich shop, and we do this all day, every day and it pains me to think that you have left here so many times with your expectations not being met. I would like to think that we pride ourselves on customer service and we want all of our patrons happy." She said with a smile plastered to her face and a lilt in her voice.

"I just want to eat a decent lunch in peace, but apparently here that is *too* much to ask." He said snarling back at her. Undaunted she continued in her rapid fire style.

"Certainly it's not too much to ask, and that is why I have asked Johnny to prepare something special for you today. Will you be having your standard smoked turkey on fresh whole wheat, with mustard, lettuce and mayo? With a half and half sweet tea?" She asked.

"Yes that is what I would like, if you can *manage* it and a bag of plain chips." He stated tersely. She called for Johnny who brought out a cutting board with all the ingredients needed for his sandwich neatly laid out, a clear glass and a small bowl of ice cubes sat to the side. Mr. Patton sat there incredulous as she put on a pair of sanitary gloves and waved her hand over the tray of food as if she were a game show host.

"Here is what we are going to do today Mr. Patton, may I call you Carl? Carl, I am going to have *you* make your sandwich today and I am going to take notes. Step by step notes so that I can recreate your exact moves the next time you come in for your lunch. You see, this is a five dollar sandwich, not a lobster meal at Chez Diane's. Therefore the angst and anger that you thrust at my staff on a regular basis is proportionally skewed. We take pride in our repeat customers, in that they take the time to come back and choose us to spend their lunch hour with, when there are so many other options in the office park." She said still smiling pleasantly. Dean was grinning from ear to ear listening to this exchange. Inside the restaurant, she now had the attention of everyone eating lunch, and you could have heard a pin drop.

"This is ridiculous. If I had wanted to make my sandwich, I could have done that at home." He blustered.

"Indeed Carl. That is my point. You always order a basic sandwich, one I am sure we are capable of making, but you always seem to find fault. So today, once and for all, we are going to resolve this ongoing issue. Life is too short to waste your lunch hour getting completely worked up over a five dollar sandwich. So please, these ingredients are entirely fresh, the bread was baked this morning and the meat was not sliced until you came in, so if you will please? I am now ready to start taking notes." She lifted up her note pad and pen and was poised on the ready.

He hesitated when he picked up the knife, and now with all eyes in the diner on the two of them, the show began. Jesse expressed keen exaggerated interest in the amount and technique in which he spread the mayo on the first piece of bread, and then the manner in which he applied the mustard. She then noted the way in which he layered the meat and the number of slices to get the bread to meat ratio correct. Then she made special notes on how he placed the lettuce leaf on the meat stack before placing the top piece of bread on the sandwich. Then he took the knife once more to cut it in half and *not* on the diagonal, which was duly noted. The lady sitting next to him at the bar seemingly had held her breath the entire time while he made his sandwich, then audibly exhaled relieved once it was cut in half.

Jesse then prompted him to pour his half and half tea into the glass. Again noting the exact amount of ice he placed in the glass first, and the ratio of sweet tea to unsweet tea that he poured out of perfectly marked tea pitchers. Once that was finished she slapped a plain bag of chips down next to his plate, then proceeded to clean up the personalized sandwich work station that she had brought out. Even the table of eight with minus two were riveted by the powerful displayed of 'putting a person in their place' that went on at the counter. Their respect for Jesse just exceeded level ten, as did Dean's.

"Please Carl, enjoy your lunch. I'll be back to check on you in a moment or two." She said sweetly. Jesse noticed Mrs. Willis at the edge of the counter and darted back into the kitchen to get her food. She came out with a medium sized brown bag with woven straw handles.

"Hello Mrs. Willis, I have your order right here."

"Hello dear, thank you so much." She said smiling through the tired expression on her face.

"Please take this, and it's on the house. I know Dr. Willis is still in the hospital and hopefully this will feed you for a couple of meals, and save you from the ghastly hospital canteen food." Jesse said with a smile.

"Oh no, dear, please let me pay you for this…" the older woman protested.

"Absolutely not. Please it's the least I can do, you both do so much for our community, and it is my privilege."

Jesse walked her to the door then bent to give her a hug. "Please give him our best and tell him that we are praying for a speedy recovery." The woman nodded and smiled as she walked back to her car. Jesse stopped to check in on the accountant, who was quietly eating his sandwich, trying not to make eye contact with anyone in the restaurant. He indicated that he was fine, and so she moved back to her table of eight minus two, who by now had finished eating their lunch, but hung around to say good bye to their favorite waitress.

"Girl that display of power and awesomeness in there was *sick.*" Mack said enthusiastically. Seconded by Jack and Yoshi.

"Sick is good, right?" She asked innocently and they all burst out laughing. Doc spoke up and clarified for her that 'sick' in this context was equivalent to awesome.

"Cool." She said smiling back at them. "I'm sorry I was diverted, but as you can see I had a serving emergency that had to be handled. I'll make it up to you next time. Can I get you guys a refill?" She said flashing a grin at them.

"Heck… lunch and a show? Who can top that?" Yoshi said grinning from ear to ear. "Nah we are good, but we gotta head back or they will send out the dogs to search for us."

They all either hugged or high fived her as they left, then she picked up the last of their plates and brought them inside and handed them off to Libby. Once again she was standing in front of Carl as he took the last bite of his sandwich.

"Was everything to your specification today?" She asked smiling tilting her head slightly to the right.

As much as it visibly pained him, he took his paper napkin then wiped his mouth and admitted that his lunch was 'fine'.

"Really? Fine?" She asked again with her arms folded.

"Ok, you have made your point Jesse. It was good. Can we please end this spectacle?" He said quite contrite.

"Carl, yes this whole thing was done to make a point. We do want and appreciate your business, truly. However, you taking your anger out on my staff repeatedly week after week is not ok. We would love to have your future business, but if you don't feel like we can handle your orders, then perhaps you need to consider bringing your lunch to work, or trying a different restaurant in the park. I sincerely hope we see you back again, and soon. Here's your ticket, Hannah will check you out." She said handing him the bill. "Oh and don't forget to tip….." Then with that said, she disappeared into the kitchen to wash her hands.

Johnny although busy, stopped to make her a fresh soda and clapped when she turned around to face him. She grinned and then did a small curtsy. She took a long sip of the soda and let out an exhale.

The next thing she heard was Dean in her ear say, "That was amazing Jesse. *You* are amazing. I spent my entire lunch watching you handle that disgruntled customer. Nice job, and never once did you lose your temper. I just wanted to say I am so proud of you Charge 25."

"Why thank you." She said to Dean, but was still looking at Johnny.

Dean let out a chuckle and then said he would check in with her later. She smiled and then walked back out front to see if the crowd was thinning out. Hannah was cashing another client out and waved as they walked out the door. Tim the mechanic was the next in line, Hannah walked around Jesse to get the table at the window a to-go box leaving Jesse to cash him out.

"Timothy, what a pleasant surprise. Are you here on business?" She said smiling pleasantly at him.

"I had to come back for one of your signature sandwiches, I must say ya'll have it going on here at Reed's. Well that, and I wanted to check to make sure your vehicle was still running ok for you. It's pretty old." He said with a sheepish grin.

"Oh, thank you. That is so sweet of you. It's been cranking each morning, so I can't complain. It's a burden off my mind."

He handed her his ticket, and she rang him up. She thanked him again for stopping by to check on her and had Libby bring him a sweet tea to go. He smiled and waved as he left.

"Jesse is fine Dean. She completely handled the angry patron, you were worried for nothing. But hey, it's ok, I had a great view of the smack down and a very tasty lunch." He said ribbing his old friend.

"Shut up Tim and come on back in. Dean out." He said as he tossed his pen across the room. Tim busted out laughing, then Dean started shaking his head, laughing at himself.

CHAPTER 5

REPORTS

Susie arrived to pick Jesse up Saturday morning at 8:00 a.m. to treat her to breakfast and a whirlwind day of shopping. They selected a mom and pop restaurant near the edge of town that was known for its breakfast bar. They were seated by a window and the waitress explained the buffet bar, and the specials on the menu. Jesse decided on the Pancake explosion breakfast off the menu, and Sue decided on the breakfast bar.

Jesse was appreciative to have this time alone with her sister, which was rare anymore. Sue always had the baby with her, whom Jesse loved dearly, but she missed having one on one time with her sister. They were usually very close, and generally spoke several times a week, but somehow life just got in the way and lately they rarely got to chat for any length of time. They sat talking getting caught up with details they usually had to thrust to the side for the sake of expediency due to time restraints or interruptions.

While Dean was monitoring her this morning he held his breath a few times thinking she was going to divulge their secret, but she never did. She was confiding so much in Sue, that part of him felt guilty for listening in, especially when she mentioned that maybe she and Jerry should have a baby soon. Jerry had really been pushing her to have kids early in their relationship and she was the one who was holding off, but she really wasn't sure why. Maybe if she said she wanted to have a baby he would want to stay home more with her and spend quality time together?

Sue never encouraged her one way or another, but listened and explained that things appeared to be tense between them and adding a child into the mix would only amplify things that were wrong, not make things right. Dean wanted to march right into that diner and hug Sue, but instead decided to go to the gym and burn off some of this raw energy he was feeling.

They finished eating then drove to the mall. A cousin of theirs was getting married in July and they both needed dresses for the event. They were not part of the bridal party, but were close with this cousin and his fiancé. Peter was Susie's age, they had all grown up in the same neighborhood until he went away to college. He would come home on breaks bragging of his college exploits trying to impress his cousins, but they knew deep down he was a nerd and came nowhere near being as cool as he bragged he was being at college. He landed a great opportunity after graduation and threw himself into learning his new job. Peter was now a successful business analyst for a firm across town and that is where he met his sweet fiancé Emily. She was a temporary secretary there but now taught second grade at an elementary school on the west side of town.

Jesse located the Indigo dresses first and waved Susie over. They were the perfect shade, and came in several different styles. Sue preferred the boat neck with the dropped waist, and Jessie tried on the round neck, A-line cut dress which looked like it was made for her. *Sold!* They both exclaimed as they walked out of the dressing rooms to stand in front of the large display three way mirror. Their find was made even sweeter when they went to the counter to check out and the clerk told them the dresses were thirty percent off. *Cha-ching!*

Next, they went on a quest to find shoes to match. Four shoe stores later, Susie found a three inch wedge heel in the matching indigo trim, and Jesse leaned toward the nude colored strappy sandals with a low one inch heel. To look at the two sisters they could not be more different, Susie was tall and willowy with shoulder length strawberry blonde naturally curly wavy hair and big expressive blue eyes. She was sassy and witty, but fiercely loyal and so much fun to be around. Jesse adored her and her bold personality. Jesse was petite at 5'3 and average build with big blue eyes that twinkled when she smiled. Jesse had a sweet temperament but could be firm when she had to be, and she and her sister did share the same sense of humor. Their cousin Peter was the brother they always longed for but never had, Sue had snapped pictures of the dresses and texted them to Pete, who texted back that he wholeheartedly approved.

After three hours of cruising the mall shopping, the two women stopped for a giant salted pretzel and a soda to replenish their spent energy reserves. They sat at one of the tables in the food court to enjoy their snack and people watched. Jesse checked her phone and saw that she had missed a text from Jerry. He was going into the office to meet with the art director on the latest campaign, and wouldn't be home until after four and feel free to continue shopping with Susie. She texted back that it was fine and that she and Sue would be out for a bit longer and might even eat dinner while they were out shopping.

Jesse decided to run all the packages out to the car and sit down for a minute since Susie had run into an old high school friend, and they were chatting away near the food court. While she was on the way to the car she wondered what Dean was up to and tried to imagine what his Saturdays were like, did he have a house or an apartment, and was he married?

She loaded the packages into the back of Susie's car and sat in the back seat for a moment to stretch her legs. While sitting there she observed two women, with their arms loaded down with loose clothing, shoes and necklaces stop at a vehicle parked right in front of Sue's car. They opened the panel van's back door and started tossing the stuff in back, looking wildly about as if to make sure no one was seeing them.

"Report? Dean are you there?" She stated anxiously.

"Charge 25?" He responded perplexed. "Go ahead."

"I think I'm witnessing a robbery in progress or at the very least some serious shoplifting. Which of course you know is stealing which is robbery, I think? Well maybe if they had a weapon which I don't currently see." She stated in a hushed tone almost breathlessly. He tried not to laugh since she was being so serious about it all.

"Proceed." He encouraged.

"Ok I am at the Coastal Mall, parking lot "B" on the Macy's side. There are two, suspects at this time with a White and dark green panel van. Ford. License plate South Carolina B5X-112. White female with dark brown black hair might be partially Hispanic, tattoo on shoulder that runs partially down her arm, looks like a floral pattern. She is wearing jeans and a tank top. The other woman is a very tall African American woman, maybe 5'10, smooth shoulder length hair, she is wearing plaid Bermuda shorts and running shoes. Hold up, there is a white male, a little late to the party who is also carrying an arm load of clothes that looks like it's from the Old Navy store. I know this because I saw a sundress there I wanted, but decided not to get it at this time, and he's carrying one in his pile. He is average height, maybe 5'10 or 11 and weighs about twenty pounds more than he should all in the gut area, he is also wearing jeans, black t-shirt, tennis shoes and he has a snake or worm looking tattoo on his left forearm." She rattled off, and he smiled as he filtered her details onto the report. *Who gets a worm tattoo? She is a hoot!*

"Jess where are you? Can they see you?" He asked concerned.

"No. I am in the back seat of my sister's car resting and I'm seeing this unfolding right before me. Dean I think they are getting ready to leave. What do I do?" She asked hurriedly.

"*Nothing!* Please do not exit the vehicle. I am calling Coastal P.D. right now, and yes you are correct Jesse, I am hearing all kinds of chatter from the mall security channel. I am also contacting the Highway Patrol, are you certain of the license plate?"

"Positive, it's only like 15 feet in front of me. I have actually been taking a video of them while we were talking. I just hope it turns out." She said feeling proud of her quick thinking.

"That is awesome, I will of course need you to send that to me. What lucky timing that you were there and could give the locals a real lead to catch these criminals. I am..." She interrupted him with another update.

"Dean! They just pulled away, headed towards the traffic light and are going....... Right, they are going right as if to head out toward the interstate." Jesse exclaimed in her excitement.

"Great job Jesse. Really, I am so proud of you. These kind of solid tips are what is going to make this program a success. Get me that video as soon as you can, ok?"

"Sure. Wow that was kind of exhilarating. I mean, my heart is beating 90 miles an hour. Woooo, is this what your life is like all the time?" She asked.

"Sometimes, I can't lie. I am a bit of an adrenaline junkie. That is why I have done so well in this field, but even with that being said, I remain very calm on the outside which I guess that's just training. You have really done great Jesse. I have been tallying up some stats since you've gotten started and so far you have had 9 valid reports and 6 have led to Alpha escalations. That is amazing for someone who is not formally trained for this kind of detail." He said trying to encourage her.

"I have a really great coach." She said smiling. "Oh, here comes Sue, I have to scoot. Talk to you later ok? Love ya." She said out of habit. *What??? Oh no, I hope he didn't catch that.*

"Ok...I'll talk to you soon." He responded cautiously, smiling again at her obvious slip.

"Oh, I'm so sorry. I mean, I didn't mean to say *love ya,* it's just a habit. I'm so sorry. This is weird. I feel weird now." She stammered. Which once again caused him to grin from ear to ear listening to her try and explain.

"It's ok, I totally understand. That is usually how you sign off when you are talking to people you are close to, I have heard enough of your conversations to know that. It's fine. Really, no harm no foul." He said chuckling.

"Ok...well um bye, ok? Talk to you in a bit. Bye." She stuttered sheepishly as she ended the call.

She tried to compose herself as Sue approached the car, and acted like she had dozed off. They decided they were not really hungry and were winding down from their marathon shopping excursion, plus Sue had gotten a phone call from her husband, Matt something about needing diapers and frozen peas. So the sisters headed back to Jesse's condo.

Headed home now, are you there yet? ~Jesse

No in the middle of something, sorry gonna be late. –Jerry

Think I may let Casey out, then go to a movie. It's early so I can hit the matinee, is that ok? ~Jesse

Might as well eat dinner while you are out too since I won't be home, and there is no need for you to cook just for one. Treat yourself. –Jerry

I just might, thanks honey. See you later tonight. ~ Jesse

They arrived at the condo. Sue leaned in to give Jesse a hug, and then Jesse removed her bags from the back seat, thanked her sister and blew her a kiss as she drove off. She laid her packages near the couch and let her sweet Casey outside to go potty. Jesse stood at the door watching her scampering around the mini-side yard they had that was fenced in, and thought about how much she loved that little silly ball of fur who was always happy and ready to see her. Then she reflected on how lonely she would be if something ever happened to her. She was truly the bright spot in any given day for Jesse.

After Casey finished her business she trotted in past Jesse and then circled around her pillow before plopping down and looking up at her master with her big brown eyes. Jesse did not have the heart to put her back in the crate so she left her out to rest on her fluffy pillow. She would be fine for a couple of hours until Jesse or Jerry returned home. Jesse took her packages into the bedroom and laid them inside the closet. Then she grabbed her phone and uploaded the video she took to Dean, and texted him that he might want to filter out their conversation. She also checked the local movie times and if she hurried could make the next show, which was still at matinee rates.

Grabbing her keys she headed out the door, as she approached her car, Dean checked in. "Charge 25, are you there?"

"Yes of course, did you get the video and can you use it?" She asked as she entered her vehicle.

"Yes, once again, great work. Wanted to let you know that the Highway Patrol caught them and they are headed to jail. Apparently they have been hitting malls and outdoor shopping outlets up the coast line pretty heavy as of late, and well, they were happy to finally catch them. Lots of charges being pressed at the moment, they are even thinking they hit the jewelry store in Wavecrest last week." He reported.

"Wasn't that an armed robbery?" Jesse asked incredulously.

"Yes, the Hispanic-looking woman and the man were involved in that incident based on the descriptions the store clerks gave the police. That is another reason they were thrilled with the reliable tip. Hey are you headed back out again?" He asked.

"Oh just going to see the latest Shane Hartselle action movie, I hear it's a good one. Going to the matinee, and if I hurry I can make the 4:15 show. Do you ever get to go see any movies?" She asked genuinely interested.

"Occasionally, but not like I would like to, work just doesn't really permit it, but I do really enjoy going to the movies and I am a complete sucker for the 18.00 dollar container of popcorn. Ridiculous I know." He stated sarcastically.

"No I totally get it, I *love* the popcorn. Jerry never wants to pay for it though so I usually don't get any…but since I am going alone and he said to treat myself to dinner, I think I am going to get a barrel of the hot buttery stuff and a big drink and call that supper!" She said as she drove down the boulevard to the theater.

"Good for you Jesse, wish I could share it with you, think of me as you dive into that bucket of buttery popcorn love." He stated laughing truly wishing he could go sit with her in the dark, sharing the popcorn and drink. However, this would be yet another work night for him spent alone, and this made his chest feel tight.

CHAPTER 6

AND BABY MAKES THREE

T he theater was not very crowded and Jesse found a seat on the aisle about twelve rows back from the front. There were approximately twenty five people at this showing so the sound was a little loud throughout the auditorium since this room usually held up to a hundred and twenty five people. Dean had no trouble hearing the entire movie and could see the majority of it since Jesse's broach placement today was more near the top of her shoulder than below her clavicle. Yes, technically that was cheating, but he would take it for now, since it allowed him to feel like he was actually with her.

She appeared to enjoy her popcorn, eating nearly the entire bucket, which made him smile in spite of himself. She exited the theater, looked around the parking lot and stretched before getting back into her car. Jesse turned the key in the late model Ford and it jumped to life. *Thank you again Tim and Dean.* She muttered as she put the car into gear. She noticed that the time on the clock was 6:37 p.m. so she headed back towards the condo. As she pulled up to her parking spot, she observed that Jerry's car was in its spot and so apparently he had gotten home sooner than he expected.

Jesse unlocked the door and the house was eerily quiet, the television was not turned on and oddly Casey was back in her crate whimpering. This caused Jesse's curiosity to peak and she quietly laid her keys down, and walked towards the bedroom. *Perhaps he is taking a nap?* She turned the door handle and opened the door, what she saw next caused her to shriek out loud nearly deafening Dean and scaring the fool out of her spouse.

Standing there in the doorway with her hand covering her mouth in an attempt to stifle the screams that were still trying to escape.

"What are you doing here? Get out!" Jerry screamed back at her.

"Get out? *Get-out*? This is *my* house Jerry! What are you doing here naked with that bimbo?" She screamed back at him causing Casey to bark furiously in her crate, scratching trying to get out.

"You are pathetic Jesse, I *hate* you. Don't you dare call her a bimbo! I love this woman, she is the mother of the child I am having, so I want a divorce and I want you out of my house *Right NOW!*" He rapidly spat at her.

"How long have you been cheating Jerry? And how dare you bring this into our home?" She stated still in shock, waving her arms wildly about.

"What does it matter? I love her. I don't think I *ever* loved you or that miserable mutt in the other room. As a matter of fact, I'm about ready to *kill* that barking flea bag." He taunted her.

Jesse picked up the nearest thing she could get her hands on which was a picture frame that sat on her dresser and flung it at Jerry's head. Unfortunately it narrowly missed, causing Jerry to stand up in his naked state and come after her, screaming something about killing her as well as the dog, but thankfully his mistress jumped up, grabbed his arm and pleaded with him not to hurt Jesse. *At least she looked remorseful. What lies has he told you mistress?*

Dean finally got his bearings after nearly being deafened and began talking Jesse down, he had to get her out of there safely and get her to him A.S.A.P.

"Jesse, sweetheart, it's Dean. He just threatened your life, do *not* antagonize him any further. I want you to start slowly walking backwards out the door, get your pocketbook and keys and get out of that house *right* now. Grunt or say something to let me know you understand what I am saying. I need for you to trust me right now Jesse. Can you do that for me?" He stated calmly listening for a sign from her.

"I want to get my Casey, then I will leave." She bargained with Dean and Jerry.

"You are not getting that stupid dog until I can account for all of my stuff. If I don't find everything I am looking for, I will kill that rotten bag of fur and dump her on the side of the road." Jerry hissed back at her.

Dean heard her gasp so he started once again. "Jesse, please trust me, he's not going to harm Casey. I swear it. He's only trying to hurt you more emotionally. Don't react. Just please walk out of that apartment right now, and meet me at Reeds. I'll be waiting at the back door. Jesse, start walking... *now!*" He implored her.

Slowly she began walking out of the bedroom they used to share, she spotted her keys on the end table and grabbed them. Jesse looked back one last time at Casey, and then ran to her car leaving her beloved friend behind barking frantically. She entered the vehicle then burst into tears, crying so hard she didn't know if she would be able to drive or not.

"Please stop crying sweetheart, I know you are very upset at the moment and rightfully so but I have a plan. Please come, I am waiting for you, I have on a dark blue baseball cap and a dark navy windbreaker. This will all be ok, I promise. Jesse, please meet me at Reed's." Encouraging her in the calmest voice he could muster.

She turned her car in the direction of the restaurant as tears streamed down her face. Dean let out a heavy sigh of relief knowing she was on the way. He knew it would take her about fifteen minutes to get to Reeds, so in the meantime he rang Jerry's cell phone. When Jerry didn't answer Dean rang the house phone, his mistress's phone and his simultaneously. He loved that he had access to such toys, and was keenly adept at using them.

"Hello?" Jerry answered gruffly somewhat disoriented with all the different phones ringing at the same time with the same number.

"Jerry, you don't know me, and trust me, you don't want to know me. But I know you, and oh too well. First of all, don't you *ever* threaten Jesse's life again if you wish to keep yours? Second, you will not harm that dog in any way, shape, or form. Do you understand me? Because if I find out that you have, I will find you and the beat down you will receive will make you wish you had never been born. Third, you are going to give Jesse the divorce, provide for Jesse financially, and buy her a new car of her choice. Brand new and paid in full, you have jerked her around long enough."

"Who are you? How dare you threaten me? You know nothing about me!" Jerry bellowed in protest.

"I know you have been dating Cindy for seventeen months, and that she is four months pregnant. I also know that you have $69,365.27 sitting in a savings account in just your name that you have hidden from your sweet wife. All the while poor mouthing to her after promising that you would buy her a newer car, one that you had no intention of ever providing. You have exactly one hour to get your crap out of that house and vacate the premises. Again if I find out, and I will, that any harm has come to Casey or that any of Jesse's things are missing or destroyed you will answer to me." Dean stated in a low menacing voice.

"What, are you spying on me? How do you know this stuff? Tell me, I demand to know!"

"You are not in a position to demand anything. You have one hour." Dean stated then hung up.

Next Dean called another agent, nicknamed Ninja on his way to Reed's. He briefed her on what had just taken place with his charge and that he needed her on standby for an evac. She of course agreed and stood ready to assist him with anything he needed.

He stood in the shadows and watched Jesse pull into the parking lot, thankfully the light at the back door was dim and with his hat pulled down low, and with her crying it's doubtful she would see his face. She came around the corner with her head down, tears still freely flowing, so he softly talked her into his arms. He leaned against the back door and she flung herself into his mid-section with her head turned to the side, then he wrapped his arms snuggly around her petite frame.

He spoke very gently, very softly to her and she clung to him as though her life depended on it. He knew he was risking so very much to be here with her, but in this moment, there was absolutely no other place he was willing to be but right there consoling her. Regardless of the consequences he might potentially face, she was worth it.

She never attempted to look up at him but kept her head to the side with her cheek resting on his chest. She vacillated between anger, fear, rejection, grief, sadness, disbelief and back to anger again. He tried to empathize with her wave of emotions as they rolled through her small body. In retrospect his range of emotions when being confronted with something such as this would be anger, possibly hurt then it would all be shut down. Banished from his mind then he would compartmentalize and move on. He envied the fact that she was able to express her raw emotions with him, and he unashamedly treasured that it was his shirt that was stained with her tears. For the first time in many years he longed to have a woman of substance in his arms, and for him Jesse was that woman.

"Jesse, I know this has knocked the wind out of you, but I have a plan. First of all no harm will come to Casey. I have seen to that, I promise. I have someone, a friend of mine that is going to go with you back to your house tonight and you are going to get your essentials out of there for now. I am putting you up in a safe house that is being renovated and I want you there for at least two or three days, or as long as it takes. Reed can come in and run the restaurant for a few days. You never call in sick, and now you need some "me" time and you are going to get it. Second, you have to find a new place to live, so I have a couple of ideas and if you can afford at least $700.00 a month in rent then I know the perfect place. I would love to see you in there, so I will call and check availability. It's close to your work place, very safe and dog friendly. Third, I know it doesn't feel like it right now, but you are going to be ok. You are going to be better than ok, and I need for you to trust me. Do you trust me Jesse?" He asked, holding his breath until she answered.

"Yes Dean. I trust you." She whispered.

He leaned down and gently kissed the top of her head, and then slowly rubbed her back making no attempt to release her, and she made no attempt to move.

"Sweetheart, I can't physically be with you, but I am here, know that I am always close and you can talk to me anytime. My friend, Ninja will be escorting you back to your condo tonight to get Casey and your things. She drives a big S.U.V so load it up, the safe house you are going to is at the beach. It's very private and very *very* safe. Please do not disclose the location of where you are, if Susie asks, just say you are staying at a client's house for a few days. I have a hunch that Jerry will start divorce proceedings right away, so prepare your heart and mind for that, ok? Also, he will be buying you that new car, so don't you worry about having reliable transportation. He is going to provide it." He stated with authority.

"Dean, how can you do all this? I don't want you to get into trouble because of me. I appreciate everything you are trying to do for me, and I will admit I am a bit lost and devastated at the moment. Honestly, I don't even know where to begin. How in the world did you get Jerry to agree to a new car? This is all so overwhelming." She said letting out a long sigh.

"I know you are overwhelmed. Please let me help you Jesse. There is no need to worry about me, I will land on my feet regardless of what happens-- if anything. I will be fine, seriously. Do not worry about me, let's just focus on you. Jerry will be all too willing to accommodate you with a vehicle you were promised, believe me, with what I have on him, he is going to comply. Again, do not worry about the method, just know I am in your corner and will do what I can to help you. I care about you Jesse, probably more than I should." He said earnestly.

She squeezed him even tighter and still clung to his taut muscular chest. Then it hit her what he said about Jerry... how did he know all of that?

"Dean, so you knew about this affair all along, and you never told me?" She said starting to pull away. He immediately held her tight with one arm and gently pressed her head back to his chest with his other hand and held her there.

"Jesse...please understand it's my job. I am/was forbidden to tell you any of the information I discovered during the back ground check on Jerry. I could be *fired*. So I had to keep it a secret from you as badly as I felt about it. So since I couldn't tell you, I promised myself I would be available to help you pick up the pieces when this all hit the fan, and I knew one day it would. I am so sorry, I would have told you if I could have. I hated to have to lie to you. There are many things about my job that are top secret, and cannot be divulged for ethical and safety reasons. I hope you can understand and forgive me."

"It's just all so much to take in right now. My head is pounding..." She said in a whisper, again letting out a heavy sigh.

He just stood there holding her, she was exhausted and made no real attempt to leave even though she knew she should go. So many things were running through her head but most of all she was worried about Casey.

"I need to go get Casey, I'm worried about her."

"Yeah I know I need to let you go so that you can meet Ninja and get your stuff. First, I want you to head to your local ATM and transfer all but $50.00 out of your joint account into your private account where we pay you. You are going to need some relocation cash and he just got paid. I'll be around tonight so if you run into a snag or need anything at all, I'm a call away." He leaned into her drinking in her scent then lightly kissed the top of her head again.

"What about Jerry and our bills? How will he pay them? That will leave him no money until next pay period."

"Believe me, he will be fine. He's been hiding money from you Jesse. Do like I say, it's your right, that is a joint account and you are entitled to the money in it. The bills are in his name, he is responsible for them, let him be for once." He stated flatly.

"Wow, he truly is a cheat at his core. Cheating on me and then cheating me out of money too. Perfect." She said sniffing.

"I am truly sorry Jesse, about everything. I really am." He stated sincerely.

"I know Dean, and it's not your fault. Any of it. I really do appreciate all you are doing for me, I really don't know what I would do without you right now." She took her hand and tried to wipe away her tears that were still intermittently rolling down her cheeks, it was as though she had no control over them. He gave her a few last minute instructions and then sent her on her way to meet her escort. His heart was heavy as he watched her slowly walk away from him with her head bent down. There was work to do so once he was sure she was on her way, he hustled back to the office to finish planning her escape from the oppressively cruel Jerry.

Tentatively she pulled into the parking lot of her condo and Jerry's car was gone, in its place was a large dark blue Suburban S.U.V. Jesse parked and exited her car, once she was on the side walk a very petite woman with long black hair tied back in a tight neat ponytail walked up and introduced herself as Ninja. That of course was a nick name, and Jesse wondered what her specialty in the CIA was since she was three inches shorter than Jesse and weighed all of 95 lbs. soaking wet in full gear she suspected. She seemed very pleasant and Jesse was thankful for the company.

They entered the apartment and Jesse made a bee line for Casey who was still in her crate, perfectly fine. Dean must have made one heck of a threat for Jerry not to have touched her. However, it did look like he had kicked the crate as some of the frame was dented on the side. She could not wait to get her out of here and put her someplace safe where no one would ever yell at her or kick at her cage again. They loaded up several baskets of clothes, shoes, a couple towels and her toiletries. Ninja grabbed her laptop and small printer along with all the cords and accessories that went with it. Jesse went over to her small table top jewelry box to get her engagement ring and a small ruby and diamond necklace that she had gotten for Christmas one year. The rest of the items in there were few, a couple pairs of costume jewelry ear rings and her high school class ring. When she opened the lid she was furious to see that her diamond ring was missing.

"What? Are you kidding me?" She exclaimed. Ninja came around the corner to see what was wrong.

"Jesse, what is it?" Ninja asked levelly. She noticed that once again tears started rolling down Jesse's cheeks, but this time she was angry.

"That snake took my diamond engagement ring!"

"Don't worry, we will get it back. Is there anything else missing?" Ninja asked.

"No ma'am, I don't think so. What should I do about plates and pots and pans stuff like that?"

"Does any of it really mean anything to you? Like family heirloom stuff?" Ninja replied as she carried Casey's dog food and the fluffy pillow out to the S.U.V.

"No not really, just my knives. I have an awesome set of cutlery. Professional grade." She stated as she started rummaging through her drawers to find the paring knife that always seemed to get missed placed. She found it in the Silverware drainer in the sink so she wiped it off then put it in the block with the other knives and found the carrying case for them on top of the refrigerator.

"Ok, let's make one more pass, are there any dog toys, special pillows, movies, music/CD's... anything else that needs to be moved at this time?" Ninja asked surveying the premises.

"Honestly I can't think of anything else right now, I really don't have a lot of *things* so to speak. Most of the books are his, the television is ours and the furniture. But of course knowing what I know now, and after seeing what I saw today, I don't want any part of anything he ever sat on or anything else he might have done on a piece of furniture. He can have it." She said turning on her heels and walking out of the apartment.

Ninja watched her walk out and truly felt for her in that moment, so she took that as her cue to lock up the condo and move on to the safe house. She tapped into Dean to quickly report that the dog was unharmed but the diamond engagement ring was missing. Dean made a note of it and told her to check back in once they arrived at the safe house. It was only a couple of miles away and right on the tip of a secluded cove on the shore. They were to leave her car there at the condo for now. If she needed transportation there was a car at the safe house.

The ride over was quiet, as Jesse leaned her head back against the headrest and closed her now swollen eyes. Once they arrived at the safe house, Ninja unloaded most of the items and then set her computer equipment up on the small desk in the den. Jesse put Casey on a leash then walked her outside in a small grassy area so that she could go to the bathroom. For a moment she was completely mesmerized by the sound of the ocean in the dark, lapping at the shore. Amazed that the water obeyed God's command and went no further than it should as it chased small sea creatures into the sand then retreated back to the security of its volume. *Thank you Lord for the comforting sound of the waves and the steady rhythm they provide. Truly nature's lullaby.*

She walked up the stairway that led to the front door of the house, and found Ninja had unloaded just about everything for her. She felt a little guilty and rushed in to see what she could do to help.

"I'm sorry Ninja, I got distracted. What else can I help you do?" She asked self-consciously.

"No problem girl, you've been through a lot tonight, and this place is meant to be a distraction for you. Since you are here now, let me show you a few things. Here is the alarm, must be set while you are in here and if you leave for any reason, even to take the dog out. Ok?" Ninja stated firmly.

Jesse nodded that she understood as she accepted her alarm code that Ninja handed her.

"Here are a few features, and I have Dean already programmed in as the emergency contact. If you hear or see anything remotely suspicious you are to call in, we will immediately determine the threat level if any. Groceries are delivered daily as necessary. Here is a list, you call the specified number and place your order, if you have a special need or medication, please tell Paco who answers, and he will get you what you need within a three hour window. There are staples that are kept here in the house and inventoried weekly for freshness and edibility. Make sense?"

Ninja made them a drink and they both sat outside for a few minutes. She made Jesse a virgin frozen strawberry daiquiri and made herself a real one. They sat outside on the deck and just chatted casually. Jesse began to finally feel at ease and was enjoying the girl company, she shared with Ninja about her shopping excursion that turned into a Report for Dean. Ninja told her a few funny stories and they both laughed and sipped at their drinks. Once the agent felt like her guest was sufficiently settled and not motivated to jump off the roof in a fit of angst or grief she explained that she needed to shove off for the night, but that Dean was most assuredly on standby for her if she needed anything at all.

Jesse thanked her profusely and invited her to come back over tomorrow if she didn't have anything else to do, which Ninja found endearing. No wonder Dean was enamored. She was really a nice sincere person, but was she the right person for Dean? Ninja had her reservations, but then again it was hard for her to trust people. Dean and Tim were two of the few people in her inner circle.

"Boss, it's me." Ninja said.

"How is she? Is she settled? It pisses me off that he took her ring, but I am not surprised. We'll get it back. Then if she wants to pawn it or sell it, she can do what she wants with it." He said aggravated.

"She is really a nice gal Dean. However, I am not sure she is the right girl for you, it's too early for me to tell. You know I love you with all kinds of platonic love, right? So what I am saying is out of concern for you. I just know how hard you have worked to establish your career and I don't want to see you jeopardize all that for a woman. But if you say she is the one, then you know I will have your back 100%. You know that's how we roll." She stated.

"Thanks buddy. I know what you mean and I am happy you have my back. She is the one. It's hard to describe, but I felt it the first time I saw her, I knew. I just knew. Thank you so much for helping me tonight, I owe ya one."

"Well, you owe me like twenty, but whose keeping score? Oh yeah… that would be *me!*" She said laughing.

She continued to fill him in on what they moved and that she stayed per protocol to make sure that the Charge was comfortable and settled in, and not feeling overly anxious or suicidal. She also offered some observations and made a few suggestions for him regarding housing and explained her furniture needs among other things. After about twenty minutes they finished their conversation and he locked up his office and got ready to head to his place to unwind.

He texted Jesse to remind her to call or text Reed to let him know she would not be in Monday, and that more than likely she would not be Tuesday either, but would check in to let him know what her plans were. She assured him that she would.

CHAPTER 7

REAR VIEW MIRROR

D ean walked into his dark apartment and headed straight for the fridge, he wasn't even sure he had eaten lunch today. Nothing in there looked appealing so he just mixed himself a protein drink and then walked into his bedroom and flung himself down on his bed with his arm laid across his forehead. He laid there making a mental list of what he needed to do tomorrow and re-prioritized his list one more time. He kicked off his shoes and adjusted his pillow when he heard a very faint *"Dean are you awake?"* Immediately he shot straight up in bed and answered her.

"I'm here Jesse, are you ok?" He asked calmly, his insides churning.

"Oh sure, I'm just sitting here in the middle of the floor looking at this magnificent place. This whole day has been surreal. Did I wake you up, because if I did, I can let you go?" She said, melancholy weaved through her hoarse sounding voice.

"No I am home now, I'm fine. I've just been concerned about you. Ninja called to give me her update, so I know about the ring."

"She's really nice, so very helpful and smart. You work with some great people Dean. Her and then of course your friend Tim. I'm lucky to know you and your people."

"Yeah, I know some pretty amazingly talented folks that is for sure. I'm just so happy she was available to help."

"I miss my sister Dean. I can't go to her with this right now, but I will have to tell her. Jerry was never her favorite anyway, so she will be *thrilled*. Do you have any brothers or sisters? Or can you tell me that kind of information?"

"Yeah, I have a big family. Twins run in our family, I have two brothers and two sisters. Mom and dad are both still living, but that's really all I can tell you. We are all very close and one of my brothers works with me." He stated thinking about his large crazy family and how lucky he was to have them.

"Wow twins that's cool. There's just me and my sister Susie. As older sisters go she is like the best. She was always *that* sister, you know that had your back when things were rough at school? She could be a real junk yard dog. I really enjoyed our time together today, I miss her. My day was going really well ya know? Then BAM! It all changes. I guess life is like that, one minute you are fine, and then the next minute chaos." She stated absent mindedly, lost in her thoughts.

"Never a truer statement was made my sweet lady. My dear kind mother is living proof of that, you see my first set of sibling twins are five years older than me and my twin brother. My mom had us all at the park and the two older ones were playing, running around and I was just starting to walk. She was watching me while my brother, Camden lay sleeping in the stroller not more than a foot away. The older ones were playing hide and seek with friends at the park, so about six children came running past us and one of them knocked me off balance causing me to fall. I of course started crying and my mother immediately scooped me up and was checking my injuries which were mainly a few minor scrapes and hurt feelings. She was soothing me when she looked back over at the stroller and saw that my brother was gone. Missing. She started screaming for help and within minutes the other parents had formed a task force searching the small park for him or anyone who might have taken him.

My father who was in the military was called in from the base, and the local police, F.B.I and Military police were dispatched. However he was nowhere to be found. So one minute my family was happy and intact, the next minute chaos."

"Oh my sweet Jesus. No! Dean I am so sorry, how did your mother survive that kind of loss?" She asked as once again tears filled her eyes.

"Prayer and lots of time. She is still not over it, but she deals. We lived in another state when it happened and have moved many times since. He and I were identical twins. I think that is one reason why I went the route I did in my career, hoping that one day I would find him somewhere out there in this big world of ours and bring him back home to her." He stated his voice trailing off at the end.

"I will be in prayer over this Dean. Sincerely I will be, no family should ever have to go through this kind of tragedy. This just makes my heart hurt for you and for you sweet mother. I am so sorry Dean for your loss and your family's." She said trying not to let on that her tears were once again freely flowing at the grief this family must have endured.

"I didn't tell you this to make you sad, but to let you know that you are stronger than you know. That what you are going through right now, although it has rocked your world, you too will eventually be ok, and be able to love again. At least that is my hope for you Jesse." He explained.

"Dean what happened to me today surprised me but it was not a surprise to God, he knew. Just like you knew eventually one day this would come to light, and so you were also not caught by surprise. I just have to be open to his plan for my life and try to follow and be obedient even though right now my path is so unclear to me. Thank you for being my friend, and for helping to guide me through this maze of emotions and uncertainty. I am so grateful for you." She said earnestly. "Oh my, I am so tired, my eyes are dry and burning from crying so much. Plus I need to let you go so you can get some rest…"

"Hey don't you worry about me, I am fine. I'll stay up and talk as long as you need me too. Why don't you go get settled in the master bedroom and get ready for bed? That mattress is the best money can buy and I guarantee you will be sound asleep within minutes of lying down. Sleep in and enjoy your time at the beach. I'll be around all day tomorrow if you need anything, you just let me know."

"Thanks Dean. I don't know what I would do without you right now. Be sure and get some rest yourself."

"I will, goodnight Jess. Sleep well." He stated, his heart yearning to be with her again.

After several minutes of silence he heard her say very softly "Dean it felt so good to have your arms wrapped around me tonight. No one has ever held me quite like that before. I really needed that…I just thought I would let you know. Night." She stated drowsily.

He was right, within minutes she was asleep.

Jesse woke with a start Sunday morning forgetting where she was for a moment. The sunlight streamed into the bedroom through plantation blinds thinly veiled in sea foam colored sheers. The hardwoods under her feet felt smooth and cool. Casey was perfectly content to lay at the foot of the bed and merely allowed her big brown eyes to follow her master as she stood and stretched.

She walked into the living room area and pulled the heavy curtains back so that she could see the glorious view in front of her. It was strange, she grew up on the coast and as a child they always went to the beach on the weekends and for various events since they were only twenty minutes away or so, but as they became adults who worked for a living, making it down to the beach was rare anymore. Being here right now in this moment during this difficult time in her life is just what her soul needed. She reached for the handle then remembered the alarm, so she disarmed it.

It was 7:20 a.m. and the cove where the house was located was quiet except for the subtle sound of the waves lapping at the shore. In the distance she could hear the sea gulls and noted that it was slightly overcast today. Still not even rain could dampen her hopeful outlook. Last night was indeed a shock, but in retrospect, if she were completely honest Jerry was never really checked in as a spouse to her, loving and kind like he promised in church on their wedding day.

She set about to pray but took Casey down to the grassy area first. Once that was taken care of, she went to the furthest point on the deck and knelt on a welcome mat she found at the back door, then began to pray. There was so much to be thankful for even amidst the confusion and hurt she was experiencing.

Dean was up until the wee hours of the morning, and actually was still asleep when the sweet sound of her voice saying her prayers woke him up. He was so tired he had forgotten to take his ear piece out, so when she started quietly praying on the deck, he had a front row seat to her version of church this morning. He was careful to be quiet as to not distract her, the fact that he could hear her meant she had her ear piece in too. He closed his eyes and listened to her as she praised God for providing help in the middle of her storm and for the provision he had provided through Dean. She went on to pray for everyone she could think of, including Dean and his family and beseeched God on behalf of the lost brother.

Lying there quietly in his bed, Dean was almost moved to tears listening to the honest emotional prayers of Jesse, especially the ones on behalf of his family. *She is truly a kind woman with such a gentle spirit.* Dean's faith was underneath that hard exterior somewhere, his job really did not permit regular church visits and therefore he was woefully out of practice. Not to mention his job gave him a certain sense of independence that gave him a false sense of security as though he really didn't need God's help. Not that he had ever outwardly or verbally expressed that notion, but he lived his life as though it were true. *Self-reliant.*

She remained in prayer talking to God for a good thirty minutes or more. Casey's barking at something in the distance distracted her and so she finished up and then looked to see what Miss Priss was barking about. Way in the distance she could see what looked like a man walking a larger dog. Not sure if the dog was on a leash or not, but since Casey thought she was the size of a Great Dane, Jesse went ahead and ushered her back into the safety of the house.

She walked over to the refrigerator and opened it up to see what was inside, there was juice, milk that was fresh, and some freshly cut fruit plus a couple containers of yogurt. Dean must have been paying attention or either that was their standard fare for "guests" who stayed here? Either way she was pleased with the selection and selected the cantaloupe and the mango-orange juice. She located a bowl and the glasses and then took her light breakfast out on the back deck to sit at the table and chairs there. The breeze was perfect, as was the temperature. She leisurely ate her breakfast and then pondered what she was supposed to do for the rest of the day. Normally she would be going to church, but decided that she just wasn't up to seeing all those people today, not to mention her eyes felt like they were swollen from all the crying. She hadn't even bothered to look yet this morning but they felt scratchy and tight, a sure sign.

Her phone buzzed with a text from Reed who was concerned, but agreed to work for her for the entire week if she needed it. He also insisted this would be paid time off since she literally never took a day off. The only time he could remember was when she left early on the Friday before she got married to attend the rehearsal dinner, and then she took Monday off for the brief honeymoon that they took. Other than those two days he could not remember her taking a sick day or a vacation day off in eight years.

Jesse held her phone in hand and stared at Dean's name in her directory. *Should I reach to him this early or not? I'm not sure what I'm supposed to be doing. Maybe I'll just text him…*

Hi Dean…Good morning. Just checking in, I'm not sure if I'm supposed to be doing anything right now or not. Just let me know if there is something you want me to do. Ok? I hope you slept well. I slept like a dead person for being in a new place for the first time. Ha. ~Jess

Hey you! I am happy you slept well, I told you that bed was the best. This day is yours to do what you want. Sleep, go to the beach, watch movies, anything you want to do you can. Just stay close. If you want to start looking at cars, please do that and I will send you a link to the apartment I was telling you about last night? I'm going to hop into the shower and I will call you in a bit. -Dean

Sure, great thank you so much Dean. And thank you for breakfast, it was perfect. ~Jess

Y.W. :--) Dean

He finally pulled himself from the comfort of his bed, and headed for the shower. The pulsating shower head was just what he needed this morning to jolt his sore muscles from their rebellious state. His workout yesterday was a little more intense than he intended. He stood there for a long while allowing the water to just course over his body before ever reaching for the soap to wash up. Finally he finished his shower, brushed his teeth and then decided to fix himself some breakfast, since dinner last night was a protein shake.

He splurged on a Jimmy Dean sausage muffin and a glass of juice. Ahhh the life of a bachelor. Then he went over the paperwork for the apartment he wanted her to be in, it would of course be her choice he just hoped she would like it and agree to move in there. It truly was perfect for her he thought. He fired up his laptop and proceeded to send her the link. Several single people from the Agency lived there, it was close to the office, affordable and close to the amenities. It was an older complex that had been completely renovated and now was the best kept secret in town.

Tim actually lived in the complex but in a different building towards the back of the complex, the one that currently had a vacancy was the first unit in the complex. There were four units in a building, the two bedroom units were on the first floor and the one bedroom units were upstairs. All the apartments had new hardwood flooring, new vanities in the bathrooms, new kitchen cupboards, sinks and counter tops, and of course were repainted after each tenant vacated. You walked in through a main door and the bottom units were on either side of a large wide staircase. The entrance was nicely done and the mailboxes were on the outer wall of the first floor. The lower units had nice patio areas and the upper units had small but nice balconies.

Jesse made the bed, took a shower and tried her best to put on makeup that concealed the kind of night she had had last night. Once she was finished she looked better but you could see the after effects of all that crying. Then she fired up her laptop to check her emails. She was happy to receive the email from Dean. She opened the email and then clicked on the link that took her to the apartment site. It looked really nice and she thought for the price it looked fantastic, the kitchen was amazing for an apartment unit. Although she was very nervous, she was also starting to get a little excited too. Daring to dream of a different life than the one she had, the one she thought she was content with until all of this came crumbling down around her.

She also had an email from Jerry. Quite nasty, he was demanding she call off whatever dogs or private eye's she had on him, and that hell would freeze before he bought her a new car. That the money he had saved was for his new life, his new wife and family...not for her. She immediately forwarded this onto Dean, along with his demand that she return the money to the joint checking account, or he would have her arrested for stealing. She recognized that his last remarks were a blustering intimidation tactic that for once in her life was not going to work on her...*not this time*! Two minutes after she had pressed "Forward" on that email she heard Dean come on-line in her ear.

"Hey you? Are you ok?" He sounded concerned and a little irritated. She knew it was not directed at her, but at Jerry's email.

"Hi Dean. Yes I am fine, was a little caught off guard to have gotten an email from him, but you would be pleased, I did not let him upset me with his strong arm tactics."

"Good Girl. You leave him to me, he'll be begging to buy you a new car by the time I am finished with him. Punk. It galls the crap out of me to see how he speaks to you. Hey did you get the email I sent? What do you think about the apartment complex?" He stated then held his breath.

"Oh yes, I saw it. Has that place been renovated? It looks new. I mean if they have an opening and if I can afford it, I think it would be perfect. The first and last month's rent might be kind of tough. Maybe Susie can help me out with that, since I will also have to put up money for utilities, since currently they are all in Jerry's name not mine. I don't have credit that way, if you know what I mean?" She stated in a worried tone.

"Jess, we've got this, I promise you it will all fall into place. If you decide after seeing it that you like it, we will make it happen. Tim offered to show you around his place so that you could get a feel for it, if you want to that is? No pressure. Were there any other places that you wanted to look at while we are lining things up?"

"Uh no, not really. I'd love to see this place, based off the address I think I pass it on the way into the restaurant, but like I said I can't really place it."

"Yeah it's a bit hidden off the road that is one of the things I like about it. It's in the middle of everything but with the park like setting that it sits in, you feel like you are out in the country. Its pet friendly and from what everyone says the people who do live there are really nice. Mostly young professionals and a few older couples, not many kids that I have seen, but then I am not there much."

"I like the fact that there are only six units in this complex, and that it doesn't have two thousand people living there all trying to use the same small swimming pool. I think I would enjoy the smaller community. I would totally love to see it, just whenever. I guess I need to call and make an appointment?"

"Tim has a key and can take you around. I think the property manager has a huge crush on him and since he said he wanted a place for his little sister, she was all about helping him out. I'll give him a call and see if he can swing by and pick you up. I'll contact you again once I have firm plans from him, does that work?" Dean explained, then finally shared with her that Tim was more than just his best friend, but one of his agents too.

"Yes, I have already had my shower so I am good. Just let me know when. Yikes."

"Yikes? What's wrong?"

"Nothing, it's just that I'm kind of excited. That's all." She said grinning.

"Perfect! I'm happy to hear that you are entertaining the possibilities of the new life ahead of you. I'll talk to you in a bit." He stated, a huge smile now plastered across his in need of a shave face.

Jesse took Casey for a quick walk down to the beach to stick her toes in the water for a few minutes. It was so beautiful today, and looking out over the ocean definitely took her mind off her woes and put things into perspective. There were so many things to be thankful for, she was alive, at a beautiful place, she was safe and surrounded by people who cared about her. God is good. About an hour later her phone started ringing and it was Dean.

"Hey Jesse, everything ok? I think your ear piece died. Can you please swap it out?" He stated, his tone a little gruff.

"Oh I'm so sorry I didn't realize it. I'll go do that right now. Please don't be upset with me?" She pleaded, his tone distressing her.

"No honey, why would you say that? I'm not angry I was just worried." He was trying to explain as his phone went dim. The call had ended. *What just happened? Jesse?*

She took off for the house to change out her ear piece and saw that he had hung up. Jesse was confused and upset that he was so short with her. This was the first time her battery had ever gone dead and it was just because she had lost sight of changing it out with everything else that was going on. As she approached the steps, something caught Casey's eye and she bolted away from Jesse causing her to drop her phone on the deck as the leash flew out of her hand. She took off in a full sprint to catch her beloved dog who raced down the beach toward who knows what?

Dean in the meantime was trying to raise Jesse again on the house phone, and her cell phone and got nothing but voicemail. *Jesse! Where are you? What is going on?* Trying not to panic he called Tim who was already in route.

"It's Tim."

"Get to the safe house now, something upset Jesse, now I can't get her back on the phone. Her headset is dead." Dean said trying to remain calm, but Tim knew that voice.

"Dean I'm sure it's innocent and she is fine. I'm about two minutes out and I will call as soon as I get there. Hang on." Tim said in his reassuring best friend voice.

"Where are you now?" Dean asked impatiently.

"I'm on the lane now pulling up to the house. Let me see if I can find her and I'll call you right back."

"Hurry."

Tim parked his 1969 Ford Bronco in the driveway of the safe house and looked around the outer perimeter for Jesse, he slowly un-holstered his side arm as he walked up to the deck landing. There was no sign of her as he punched in his agent code to enter the premises. He slowly walked through the house and once he had cleared it he called out her name. No Response. He opened the French doors that led outside and immediately he saw that her phone was laying precariously on the deck. Now his gut was starting to churn. He looked around the deck then walked down toward the shore, and there was not a person in sight. The waves methodically lapped at the shore and aside from the air conditioning unit humming and the sounds of the ocean, it was quiet.

Once again Dean was beeping into his ear. *Crap.* "Hey man, I'm here... looking for her" Tim started.

"What do you mean looking for her, where is she? Tim, what is going on buddy, speak to me please." Dean commanded.

Just as Tim was getting ready to talk Dean off the ledge, he thought he heard Jesse. He all but hung up on Dean telling him he would call right back. Dean started pacing back and forth talking to himself trying to get a grip on his emotions. Maybe this having feelings thing was way over rated if it makes you feel like this on any kind of a regular basis. He started checking his email and monitor set up so that he could work more from home as a diversion while he waited for Tim to call back.

"Jesse?" Tim called out.

"Here!" She shouted back. "Coming, sorry my dog lost her mind and just ran a beach mile on me." She stated coming around the hedge of tall sea grasses out of breath and carrying a proud wet looking Casey. Tim met her half way and took the pooch from her to give her a break. He couldn't help but smile at the whole scene.

"Well, you have given our *friend* quite a scare missy." He stated mock scolding her.

"Great..." She stated tears filling her lovely blue eyes.

"Whoa, hey girl, what's wrong? I'm teasing. I mean he is very worried about you, but he's fine. Please don't cry Jesse." He said setting Casey down securing her with the leash and a deck chair. Tim walked over to her and leaned his lanky 6'3 frame over to give her a big bear hug.

"I'm sorry, I don't know what's wrong with me? I was fine a few minutes ago." She stated muffled into his shirt as once again tears spilled down her cheeks.

Dean was tapped into the short circuit on the safe house, witnessing this whole display wondering what was being said. He tapped back into

Tim's earpiece. Tim gave Jesse a squeeze then sat her down in a chair in front of him.

"Talk to me Jess. What happened earlier to start all of this?" Tim asked, his big expressive brown eyes searching her tear filled blue eyes. Dean with his birds eye view sat there monitoring all of this intensely watching her body language. *She had been fine, almost sounded happy...what turned all that around?*

"I was just standing at the water's edge thinking about everything that is going on and thinking how grateful I am to have all of you guys helping me. Then Dean called me, and he was angry that I had let my headset go dead and he couldn't reach me. So I was headed back inside to change it out when Casey caught wind of, I still don't know what, and nearly jerked my hand off tearing down the beach like she was on fire. I guess I dropped my phone in the process and then it took me several minutes to catch up to her. She scared me to death, I don't know what I would do if I lost her too. Not right now, it would just be too much, ya know?" She said snubbing slightly.

"I wasn't angry with her Tim, please tell her that!" Dean yelled in his ear. Tim shook his head as though to shake Dean out of his mind, then regrouped his thoughts.

"Oh honey, Dean wasn't angry with you. He was just worried that he couldn't raise you. Then when you two lost cell connection too, then he really got worried. He knows you have been through a lot, so he's being super over protective right now. I understand you getting emotional that is normal, especially thinking that someone you count on is upset with you and then almost losing your best furry friend is distressing." Tim reassured.

Just then her phone started ringing, and it was Dean. Tim handed her phone back to her and took Casey inside to get her some water, wipe her down, and secure her in her crate while Jesse spoke to Dean.

"Jess, honey?" Dean stated calmly and softly.

"Hey..." She said trying her best not to cry again.

"I am so so very sorry that I was short with you and caused you to think that I was angry with you. I am not and I was not. I was distracted by some equipment I was setting up that was not going the way I wanted, then I realized I couldn't raise you on the ear piece and I guess my equipment angst transferred over to you. That is no excuse and it won't happen again. Please forgive me, you have had enough of men speaking harshly to you and I will not be a part of that." Dean offered.

"It's ok, I guess I'm still just..." Her words trailed off.

"Fragile. Duly noted and I will behave accordingly. Are we ok Jesse?"

"Of course. You have been so great to me, and honestly I just can't stand the thought of disappointing you. That's all."

"You don't disappoint me Jesse, I doubt you ever could. Jess, I am not going anywhere, and it takes a lot to make me angry. I cannot imagine you ever getting me to that point. Sweetie go get ready and you and Tim get out for a bit and take a look at that apartment. That is if you are up to it?"

"Yeah, I am, I just need to get cleaned up... again." She stated exasperated.

"Ok, you get cleaned up and give me a call later if you like. Don't forget your ear piece, OK?" He said trying to make his voice smile. Secretly crushed that he was the cause of her latest tear filled episode.

"Ok, thanks. Bye." She sat there for a minute looking at her phone as it flashed *Call ended*. Dean sat there watching her on the deck wishing he could envelope her in his embrace.

Tim was sitting on the couch programming channels for her on the large screen television when she walked into the living area. She set her phone down and grabbed a napkin off the counter to blow her nose. He sympathetically looked over at her as Dean chatted away in his ear.

"Tim, I think we have that misunderstanding cleared up but she is still pretty emotional, see if you can divert or cheer her up, OK?"

"I've got this man, don't worry." Tim responded quietly.

"Just don't be too charming so that she falls hopelessly in love *with* you." Dean teasing cautioned.

"I would never do that to you man, you have to know that? Seriously. Not that I sweat you necessarily, but Ninja scares the crap out of me, and I know she would take your side on this one." He said grinning.

"And I would use her too if it went that way Buddy." Dean said stifling a laugh.

"She's getting freshened up now, so we will be leaving shortly. I may take her for lunch and then go see the apartment. Just so you know." Tim stated matter of fact.

"Ok, thanks again for taking time out of your day to do this for me. I owe you one man." Dean said.

"Yeah, well you owe me like twenty." Tim said laughing, then signing off.

CHAPTER 8

SAFER

J esse emerged from the bedroom, redressed and refreshed. She had gotten back into the shower to quickly rinse all the sand and sea salt off and put on a pair of capris pants, a patterned tee-shirt and her sandals. Tim stood up as she entered the room, he smiled at her and then started locking up the safe house.

"Soooo?" He inquired.

"I feel better, thank you." She replied sheepishly. "I have my ear piece in fully charged, my phone is with me and I am ready to see the apartment. Could we maybe swing through a drive thru on the way back home? I'm starving." She stated with a grin.

"You got it. I am here to serve." He said unleashing his full set of pearly whites on her, his shaggy dark brown hair framing his tan dimpled face.

"You my friend are a mess!" She stated laughing at him. Dean rolled his eyes at Tim, the goofball, but smiled upon hearing her laugh again.

They finished locking up, then Tim escorted her down to his ride. She literally swooned at the sight of his candy apple red and white fully restored 1969 Ford Bronco. Tim not only was a fine mechanic fully versed in just about any car ever created, but he also had a photographic memory when it came to all things automotive. Restoring vehicles was his hobby and something he did on his down time, and this was one of his pride and joys.

"Wow! This is amazing Tim." She exclaimed. "Is it yours?"

"This little lady is all mine. I've had her for a while and finished her about eighteen months ago. Hop on in my friend." He stated proudly.

"I absolutely love it. You are very talented." She stated earnestly.

"Thanks, I enjoy it. I usually drive it on the weekends, and drive the company car or work truck through the week. The agency has been great for me, I'm not just the motor pool coordinator; I have actually gotten to do some serious driving and undercover work. Getting to be a grease monkey too is just a perk." He said once again flashing her a dazzling grin.

They drove for approximately twenty minutes and soon came to a very familiar part of town near their offices. As they approached the hidden drive that led to the apartment complex, he pointed out the small cheesy sign that identified the complex: Seafoam Estates Apartments or SEA for short. Tim navigated the turn and drove approximately an eighth of a mile to the first Building. He pulled up in the empty parking spot next to a black Mustang Cobra then came around to open the door for her.

"Wow it does feel secluded here, like there is nothing around you but trees. The outside is really cute and I like the side patio areas on the lower units, they are big and really nice." She said.

"The complex is owned by a private owner, ex-military man not a conglomerate which makes all the difference. He is very particular about who he rents too, and he tries to maintain a certain atmosphere for the tenants. He is very strict but it benefits everyone who lives here and calls this home. The upstairs unit to the left is the one that is available. I used to know the guy who lived here, he is in the military and got transferred to Alaska." He led her into the foyer area of the building, and to the right was unit 4A a lovely wreath adorned the door and the welcome mat stated *The Smiths*. To their left was 3A and the mat in front of that door merely said *Welcome*. The eight foot wide stairway in the center had large wooden double plank steps that led to the second floor landing. There was a large iron chandelier that hung above the alcove to illuminate the entry way.

While they were standing there admiring the interior, the tenant from 3A stepped out from within his apartment to put some mail in the outgoing box. His tall fit physic, short sandy blonde hair and piercing blue eyes got her attention. He was barefoot, wearing a pair of Levi's and a snug blue tee-shirt that had an Air Force insignia above the pocket.

"Hi there. Are you guys looking at the unit upstairs? It's really a nice unit." He said smiling showing off his dimples.

"Well I already live here, building six on the back side, but we are looking at this unit for her. Do you know your neighbors in this building, are they nice?" Tim asked the stranger.

"Yeah, the Smiths are a great older couple, she works part time at the library and Mr. Smith works downtown in the Sutton Building. She loves to bake, I owe my last five pounds to her." He said smiling. "I'm Carter James by the way."

"I'm Tim and this is a good friend of mine, Jesse." Tim offered.

"The guy upstairs is a programing spook. He works mainly from home, and generally keeps to himself. He's a nice guy, never cooks and regularly eats take out that delivers, but he's cool." Carter explained.

"So what do you do Carter?" Tim inquired.

"I'm in Information Technology. I work at a firm downtown, but have the ability to work from home too. I have a pretty decent network set up here in my second room. So some days I'm here, and other days in the office. Just depends on what's going on. So ah, Jesse? Where do you work?" He asked smiling at her as he leaned up against his door jamb.

"I manage a restaurant downtown in the office park called Reed's." She stated, feeling herself flush under the powerful gaze he had fixed upon her.

"Oh I know that place, I have eaten there. Great Rubens." He said relaxing his gaze and smiling at her.

"Yes! That's us." She said smiling back at him.

"Well I'll let you guys get to your business. If you have any questions feel free to come back down and ask me. If I can help you I will. I have lived here for about two years now." He said shaking Tim's hand.

"Thanks, we will. Nice to meet you Carter." Tim said smiling.

"Yes, very nice to meet you, and thank you for the information. Next time you are at Reed's please say hi." She stated smiling at the would-be neighbor. He nodded and grinned stating that he would.

She and Tim walked upstairs as Carter went back into his apartment. Tim unlocked the door and had her wait on the landing while he cleared the apartment. He came back with a smile on his face and invited her inside. She walked into the living area, and to the immediate right was the kitchen with a long bar with seating for four. Through the living room was the bedroom and on suite bathroom. There was a small hallway behind the kitchen that held a large storage/linen closet, washer and dryer and a small half bath for guests. Off the living room was the balcony large enough to hold a small grill and a small table with two or four chairs. It overlooked the patio area where Carter lived, which she was thinking might be a perk.

It was almost as if Tim could read her mind, and spoke up breaking her concentration. "So, the balcony is pretty sweet, right? I bet the view on any given day would be pretty sweet too." He said teasing her.

"Tim..." She started realizing she didn't know his last name, so then she began again. "Timothy. Please." She said in her pretend stern maternal voice.

"So you are telling me you didn't notice Mr. Ripped Carter James downstairs?" He said giving her the eye.

"Ok, yes I did notice him, and yes he was mighty *fine* looking, but we don't even know him. He could be some kind of I.T. serial killer or nerd crazy person playing Call of Duty all night with Mr. I-don't- leave- my- house- ever, next door." She replied back with her hands on her hips.

Dean was listening in on this exchange and couldn't help but smile at her feistiness. He was torn, because in all reality due to his position and career, a life with Jesse would never be possible. As much as he was growing to care for her, he had to really evaluate his situation and hers. Was he being selfish thinking that they could actually be together one day?

"Good point. I'm a pretty good judge of character and I think he is probably on the up and up, but I would of course run a full back ground check on him and everyone else in this building before letting you move in here. Actually I am pretty sure Dean has already done that for you." He said chuckling to himself, knowing his friend as well as he did, he could probably bet his next pay check on it.

"What is wrong with me? Technically I am still a married woman. Married to a creep who lied, said cruel things and cheated on me, but still I can't be looking at other men right now. Even if they resemble a Greek god like Carter James. Tan, blonde, so very fit and those intense blue eyes, that crinkled when he smiled." She caught herself getting lost in the moment, then tried to recover.

Tim stood there laughing at her shaking his head. "Come on you, have you seen enough or do you have some questions for Captain America downstairs?" He quickly jumped out of the way as she swatted at him for his sassy remarks.

"I'm good I think. Well on second thought I do have a question if you don't mind stopping by there on the way out." She said with a serious expression on her face. Just then Dean came online in her ear peice.

"So what do you think of the apartment? Do you like it? Could you see yourself there?" Dean asked.

"I think I could actually. It's really pretty back here and so private. I just have a few questions because I am worried about my budget since I will no longer have any of Jerry's money to rely on. Your buddy Tim here is giving me a hard time about a neighbor we met." She said making a face at Tim who stood there laughing at her.

"Oh, which neighbor?" Dean asked slyly as if he didn't already know since he had been tapped into Tim's ear piece.

"Oh the one downstairs, below where I would be living." She said not giving up any of the details. Dean continued to prod her.

"Yeah, so what's he like? Is he nice?" Dean asked.

"I suppose, I mean he's very handsome, and he seemed fine. I would have to get to know him better of course before I could really say one way or the other." She stated trying to sound logical and reasonable.

"Dean don't believe a word she is saying! Her eyes are dilated and she is swooning over Captain America downstairs." Tim interjected laughing and staying out of the reach of her swat once again.

"I seriously don't see how you work with him day in and day out Dean. He is a total goof ball." She said exasperated. Dean started laughing at both of them and said he would certainly have to check this guy out. Then he told Tim to take it easy on Jesse, since she was not used to his constant ribbing like the rest of them were.

"Well you guys keep me posted and I'll talk to you in a bit." Dean stated signaling that he was signing off.

Jesse made one more pass through the apartment trying to imagine herself in each and every room, and then tried to imagine the place with furniture. Furniture that she currently didn't have, but needed to get. *Oh Lordy, more expenses. I will need at least a bed, a couch and an end table. The rest I will have to get as I go.* Tim watched as her brow furrowed and he wondered what she was thinking about. The afternoon had started off a little edgy but was turning out to be a pretty fun day.

They locked up the apartment and walked back downstairs in the direction of Apartment 3A when Tim noticed someone looking at the Bronco. So they headed outside first, and it was Carter.

"This is a sweet ride man, is it yours?" He asked as he walked around the back side of the vehicle. "Mines the Cobra."

"It's nice. Yeah among other things, I restore cars in my spare time. This is one of my favorites for sure, I worked on her for about two years before I got her just like I wanted her." He said beaming with pride.

"So Miss Jesse, what do you think of the apartment upstairs? I think it has nice lighting in the bedroom and the balcony gets morning sun, so it's perfect for the afternoons." Carter asked glancing up at her from around the vehicle.

"I liked it a lot. I do have a couple of questions that you may or may not be able to answer for me. Do you know what the utilities run for that size unit here? And well, I have a dog, so I was wondering where I might take her to do her business? The only real grassy area I see nearby is really close to your patio space, and I wouldn't want to do that to you." She said grinning.

"And I appreciate your consideration." He said unleashing a knee weakening grin. "But there is a place behind the apartment that is designated more for that kind of activity. Basically if you look out your bedroom window, it would be in that space back there, near the tree line. As far as the utilities go, I would not think they would be very much, since these places are insulated like crazy. Nothing like today's cheap construction. I run an insane amount of electronic equipment here, plus the air conditioner and mine averages about a hundred bucks a month and remember mine is a two bedroom unit. If that helps you decide?" He said now checking the tires out on the Bronco.

"It does, thank you." She stated sweetly.

"Well we are going to grab a bit to eat I think. Again, nice to meet you Carter." Tim said shaking his hand.

"Sure thing, and Jesse, I hope to see you around here soon." He said tipping his head in her direction and giving her a wink. She blushed and smiled then said "Me too."

CHAPTER 9

COMFORT FOOD

She and Tim got into the Bronco and he drove her around to show her where his building was located. Then they headed in the direction of the main city strip that had the majority of the restaurants and shopping. Tim slowly came to a stop at a traffic light then looked over at Jesse, she caught him out of the corner of her eye, and once again he busted out laughing at her.

"What you Cheshire Cat?" She asked him as she folded her arms across her chest continuing to look directly in front of her.

"Ok, ok...I'll quit teasing you. What's on your mind? What do you think about the place? Seriously?" He stated in a more serious tone.

"I don't know I have so much floating in my head right now. I do like that place, but Tim I do not have a single stick of furniture. I have no bed, no dresser, no sofa, and no table. I have nothing. I'm not saying I have to have it all immediately or anything, I am fine with getting a piece at a time, but I at least need a bed and they are expensive. Then with utility deposits, etcetera...It's just overwhelming, and I'm angry. Angry that Jerry has put me in this position with no consideration for me at all. I mean what did I ever do to him? I finished putting him through school, I kept a clean house, cooked and his clothes were always ironed. I was frugal with money. What did I get in return? A big fat nothing and heartache." She stated tearing up again.

"Jesse..." Tim started.

"I guess most people would say I was stupid to put up with him, or I deserve what I am getting, but is that fair, just because I believed him when he said he would love me forever? Take care of me and honor our vows? I just feel like screaming really loud and then punching something. Then I see a nice looking guy who is polite to me and I feel a fluttering in my stomach? I must be completely mental. What is wrong with me?" She stated as a single tear rolled down her cheek.

"Jesse there is no doubt you are getting a raw deal. This guy definitely tops my list of people I'd like to punch right now, and I don't even know him. I know all this seems overwhelming, but I promise you, Dean and I will not let you live in a cardboard box. Now I could be wrong, but I think you have existed in a marriage where you received very little real attention. Attention like you deserve anyway, and the fact that you felt a stirring when a nice looking man smiled at you and was kind, is *not* crazy. It's normal. I mean heck if I was a girl, I'd do him." He stated grinning from ear to ear.

She was feeling consoled until his last statement, and then she burst out laughing. That Tim was something else she thought.

"You are incorrigible! What am I going to do with you Timothy?" She scolded still laughing.

"I'm just saying that you are being too hard on yourself. I mean you were not the one out sleeping with someone other than your spouse. It was not you out there lying your butt off so that you could selfishly pursue your own agenda. And now that he is going to have a kid? I pity that child having that man for a father. Listen this is all going to shake out, you don't have to figure it all out today. You have options." He said sincerely.

"Thank you for being so sweet Tim, really. I seriously think you drew the short straw today getting stuck with me, who has had all of her emotions hijacked by Sybil." Jesse said with a slight grin.

"Listen, I have seen and handled much worse, believe me. Heck I am the lucky one, at least I get to be in the same room with you. Poor Dean is relegated to only his ear piece."

They ended up driving out of town and she had no idea where they were headed. Tim seemed focused and for a quick moment she was feeling anxious. "Where are we going?" She asked nervously.

"Oh, I'm sorry I had an idea and wanted to drive out to see if this place I like is open yet, he's seasonal. It's the best kept seafood secret you will ever eat. This guy has been a sea captain forever and has this great little hole in the wall beach shack restaurant. Is that ok? Did you need to be somewhere?" Tim asked.

"Oh that's fine. I love seafood. I hope he's open, I'm starved." She said, her stomach now rumbling.

"Me too, but if he's not, I have a backup seafood place that is open year round. No worries." He said smiling. They continued driving down the coastal highway, for another thirty minutes or so, she leaned back in her seat and just watched the scenery go by as he drove. Intermittently she could clearly see the ocean and she found that to be comforting. He started slowing as they entered a small coastal community called Ocean Creek, Tim pointed a few places of interest like the second hand shop that sold antiques, called Dolly's, and a small local pharmacy that still sold homemade ice cream at the soda counter.

After a couple of turns he was nearing the marina, and the place where Wex had his boat and diner if you could call it that. Wex was a weathered looking seaman, who was a retired Navy veteran who fought in the Viet Nam war, and was one heck of a great guy. His real name was Mortimer Wexler, hence the nickname Wex. No one wanted the name Mortimer, that's for sure, Tim explained. They pulled up and a huge chocolate Labrador came bounding up to Tim as he exited the vehicle.

"Hey Godiva!" He said bending down to pet her head. If she was here that was a good sign. He heard Wex whistle for his pet, turning the corner he then realized he had company.

"Well I'll be a son of a gun, Timothy my boy. Get over here." He exclaimed happy to see his young friend. Tim walked over and shook the older man's hand then hugged him. Wex was wearing a white tee shirt and overalls with work boots on. He was tan and unshaven, and although he had to be in his late sixties, he looked like he was maybe in his fifties she observed. Tim waved her to get on out of the car then he turned to explain to Wex who his other guest was.

Godiva came running up to Jesse, but never jumped up on her, she leaned down to pet the top of her head and Diva's tail thumped Jesse's leg in excitement as she squirmed around enjoying the additional attention.

"Well hello there Miss, I'm Wex." He introduced himself. "Timothy told me you are not his date, and I said that was a shame. He said you are working for Dean." He said with a smile.

"Yes sir, well sort of. We are friends...sort of." She stated flustered not knowing how to really answer him.

"Well if you have a sister, please introduce her to Tim here, he needs a good woman to keep him straight." He said laughing at his own joke patting Tim on the shoulder.

Tim just smiled, shook his head at the old seaman and winked at Jesse. You could tell there was a real bond there, and she wondered what the back story was on those two. It was a grandfatherly/grandson type relationship at first glance. He walked them around to this building that looked like a storage facility, but in reality was the restaurant.

"Ya'll take a load off and I'll fix you something to eat, your timing could not be any better. Tim are you spying on me again son?" He laughed.

"No sir. Not since 2008." Tim replied flashing him a toothy grin.

"What will you have today? I've got Red Snapper, shrimp, and clams and I have one enormous tuna that snuck in." He called out to them from the kitchen.

Tim explained quickly that the shrimp scampi was to die for, best he had ever eaten, but that the crab stuffed Red Snapper was also five star, and if you liked clams he made some of the best fried clams with a horseradish ranch sauce to dip in. She was wide eyed in amazement at the selection and sat frozen not sure what to pick out.

"Never mind, too late, I'm doing a buffet. Since your lady friend, who is *not* your date, is here we might as well put on the dog for her." Wex called back out again from the kitchen.

Tim let out an ear splitting whistle expressing his excitement over the dinner selections tonight, causing the dog to go berserk and for Wex to burst out laughing. She sat down at one of the tables that had a plastic checkered table cloth and Tim followed right behind her.

"So what is the story here? Is he your long lost grandfather or something?" She asked him placing her chin in her hand.

"Well, of sorts I guess you could say. I am an only child and my parents are very formal, and I was raised to be living amongst proper people in proper society. Needless to say my parents are miserably disappointed in their only child. They only see the outside since they really don't know what I do for a living, but I will say their formal training has come in very handy on certain missions. Wex was someone they used to get their fresh seafood from when they had parties or entertained. That is part of his business, selling fresh seafood. Well one day I had come home filthy from school, I had gotten into a fight, after some kids had ganged up on me. My shirt was torn and my pants ripped at the knee, anyway my mother was terribly upset, and I of course never told her I was being bullied. She just thought we were a bunch of boys roughhousing and that I just was not taking proper care of my things." He said making a face, then he continued.

"So my parents decided I needed to understand what it would be like to have to really *work* for a living, and not live the life of privilege they were providing since I didn't seem to appreciate it. So they sent me to work with Wex for a month. Every Friday night he would pick me up and we would take the boat out, he taught me how to sail, navigate waters, tie ropes, mend nets, clean fish and cook. I would stay with him until Sunday morning when I would then return to my parents to attend church with them. What they didn't count on was that I would love it and the punishment they intended was more like a vacation for me." He smiled. "So what started as a month long punishment, turned out to be one of my greatest joys."

"Oh Tim, that is extraordinary. Did Wex understand what they were doing to you? And why?" She asked fully engrossed in the story.

"Oh sure, not much gets past Wex. You see he and his wife had a young son who tragically died when he was two years old. His wife never recovered and became an alcoholic, Wex did everything he knew to do to try and help her, console her, but nothing worked. One night she was at a local bar, got drunk, walked out into traffic and was hit by a pick-up truck. Wex was out to sea on the boat picking up his nets when it happened. He has seen a lot of tragedy in his life time. So by the time I met him, he had been alone for many years. We just clicked and he seemed to understand me whereas my parents did not. I seriously think I was adopted, because I do not seem to share one single gene of similarity with either one of them." He said then got up to fix them a soda from the soda fountain.

"Need any help Wex?" Tim hollered into the kitchen.

"Nope, you just keep courting that girl you are not on a date with, I've got this." He stated with a mock gruffness. Tim just laughed shaking his head. He brought her back a soda, a pack of crackers and a silverware packet along with his drink. She thanked him and took a long sip of her drink and opened the crackers.

"Yeah, well Wex picked up right away that I was being bullied at school. He showed me how to handle it so that next time an incident came up, I would not only not have to be afraid, but I could handle it by myself. He also taught me how to fight, and to fight dirty, since life is messy and people don't always follow rules. Again, things that have time and again have actually saved my life, I will be forever indebted to him. He also showed me how to have fun too, how to work hard, and how to work smart. We would sit on that boat while it rocked for hours with no television or books or toys to play with, just nets to mend and stars to watch. He would tell me stories and we would talk about life. I would not trade my time with him for any amount of money, fame or treasure. He is family as far as I am concerned. Just like Dean is my brother, not just my best friend." Tim stated emphatically.

"Tim what a great story. He seems like an amazing man, I mean just think about how God saw your need, and saw Wex's need and put the two of you together. What a blessing, I know you have probably blessed his life in many ways too." She stated earnestly.

"Blessed me? Why heck no, he eats me out of house and home every time I see him, and I've lost more nets in that ocean than Carter has pills, due to that fly boy. But I reckon I'll keep him, since I'm all he has...well that and

I can't seem to find him a decent wife." Wex said walking up on the end of the conversation setting a huge platter of broiled stuffed Snapper in front of them along with the shrimp scampi and garlic toast on barbeque bread. Next he brought out a corning ware dish that had scalloped potatoes in a creamy cheese sauce in it, along with a bowl of green beans.

"Ya'll get started on this while I drop the clams, they should be up shortly." He said with a sly grin.

"Please wait and say the blessing for us first before you go Wex." Tim asked.

Jesse was blown away by the humble prayer offered up by this sweet gruff of a man that Tim called family. He was eloquent yet so very sincere and she felt like God's presence was there in that beach shack in that brief moment. When he finished his prayer, he leaned down and kissed the top of Tim's head, then walked back into the kitchen. This gesture of love caused Jesse to tear up, realizing she was witnessing real love between two grown manly men. Neither ashamed of the affection they had for one another. A son in search of a father who would love him for what he is, and a father's whose loss of a son left a 6'3 size hole in his heart that only Tim could fill. A Jesus filled moment for sure.

Tim helped her plate up and then he served himself. Godiva found her place right at Tim's feet, knowing for sure that something would be dropped, he was no stranger to her. Wex brought in the last plate of fried clams then sat down with his guests and began to fix his plate. Tim immediately jumped up to fix Wex a drink and get him a set of silverware.

They talked and ate until Jesse was sure if she tasted one more thing then she would explode. Her stomach was really taking a hit today, between the fantastic food, and all the laughter listening to those two tell stories, she was sure at one point they were going to have to call 911 for her, since she was laughing so hard she could barely catch her breath.

Jesse offered to clean up and let the two of them visit, since she needed to move around and work off that fabulous dinner he had cooked. He scuffed and fussed not wanting her to clean since she was company, but he had met his match in her and it was her way or the highway tonight. Finally he relented and sat back down allowing her to win the argument. She could see the relief on his face as he sat back down after catering to them all night. He needed to rest.

Dean sat back in his recliner listening to them and his heart was heavy. He wanted to be the one there with her, not Tim. But he also understood why his best friend went to Wex's house. That was Tim's happy place, his go to retreat when the world or life got too hard for him. He loved that old man more than he loved anything or anyone, even his parents Dean suspected.

Tim knew Jesse was upset and depressed so of course in his mind, Wex can fix anything, Dean should have realized he would take her there.

Dean's insecurity was starting to kick in, Tim was a good looking guy, funny, and oh so charming. Jesse was vulnerable and desperately in need of positive male attention to boost her self-esteem that was crushed by her snake of a husband. Tim was great at that, he was a fantastic wing man, and often didn't realize he had stolen the girls' right out from other men. His fun, approachable, self-deprecating sense of humor resonated well with the ladies. Dean selfishly prayed his magic would not work on Jesse.

As Wex walked them back towards the Bronco, Godiva trotted right behind him. This was the most excitement she had seen in weeks and her tail was wagging low and slow as they got ready to leave, also sad that their visit had to come to a close. Tim gave Wex a long solid hug and whispered that he'd see him soon. Wex stood there smiling but his eyes were filled with sadness as he watched his boy leave again, not knowing when he would pop back in to visit.

Jesse walked over and gave Wex a hug then kissed his cheek. She thanked him profusely for dinner and his hospitality on zero notice. He told her that she was welcome to come back to visit him anytime, since she passed the dog test, not to mention he was taking a shine to her too. He said she could come with or without the tall lanky boy, that she was welcome either way. She assured him she would be back and looked forward to seeing him again. They hugged one last time then Tim helped her get back into the truck.

He fired up the Bronco, took one last look at Wex then pulled away, waving as he drove off. Once they were back on the highway, he pushed a CD into the player and turned the music up. It was Foreigner's greatest hits and Dirty White Boy was playing. Irony. They drove for several miles before he spoke again.

"So what do you think of my restaurant shack?" He said studying her.

"I am honored you took me there. He is *great* and well the food is unparalleled. He loves you so much Tim, you can tell, but he's getting older and that has to worry you some. Yes?" She replied.

"Yes. I really cannot bare to think about him not being around. I try to see him at least once or twice a month. If I take vacation, often I'll just go down there and hang out with him. I always split my Christmas holiday time with him and the family. He gave me this old Bronco when I turned eighteen that is why I cherish it so." He said softly.

Reaching over she placed her hand over his and he let her. It was done as a gesture of comfort, not one of romantic intentions and they both seemed to instinctively understand that, so there was no weirdness between them. They drove with the music as the backdrop, and the passing of oncoming head-lights had a mesmerizing effect on her. He proved to be an excellent driver and she expected no less from him as a professional driver since that was a huge portion of his job. Jesse felt very safe with him.

Finally they reached the safe house and he made a point to check the perimeter first then he entered the house and cleared it. Once that was done, he put Casey on the leash for her and let Jesse come inside. He stayed while she walked the dog, once they were back inside he said his goodbye's and then left for the night. She locked up behind him and then spent some time with Casey who was going crazy sniffing her pants having picked up the scent of another dog.

Tim called Dean on his cell phone and informed him that he had dropped her off and she appeared to be fine, all locked up for the night. He was not in the mood to chat so Dean thanked him again and let him go. Dean under-stood leaving Wex was hard and getting harder each time Tim went, but he should be fine by in the morning. Or so he hoped.

Jesse crawled into bed and turned the television on. This had been a full day and she was exhausted, but she needed to check in with Dean.

"Report." She stated softly.

"Hey girl, how was your day, you guys are getting in kind of late aren't you?"

"Yeah I suppose. I missed you today. I feel like we got off to a rocky start then I just didn't have much interaction with you, and well it's left me feeling kind of sad. Is that weird? Or are my emotions still whacked out? It's hard to tell right now." She stated solemnly.

"Look you have been through a lot in the last twenty four hours. Give yourself a break ok?"

"Are we O.K. Dean? I need to know that we are, Ok I mean." She stated with a sigh.

"Yeah honey we are fine. No issues here. Are you still upset with me? I would understand if you are, what happened this morning was totally my fault."

"No, I'm not angry or upset with you at all. We are good."

"So you liked the apartment at S.E.A? Do you think you could live there and feel safe?" He asked.

"I do, I'm just worried about the logistics and all. It's like I shared with Tim tonight, I have no furniture Dean. None. Zero. I don't even have a micro-wave. I would need to at least start with a bed and that is one of the most expensive items. It's just depressing." She said wearily.

"I'm working on a few things, please give me a day or two ok? I want you to really rest up tomorrow and make a list of everything you will need. This is going to work out, I know it will. So you get some rest and we will hit it hard tomorrow."

He could tell she was not ready to sign off and truthfully he was not ready to let her go, he had missed her terribly today, and hearing her with Tim all day was sheer torture, even though nothing happened between them. They stayed up talking about everything and nothing for another two hours. It was after midnight before they both signed off.

CHAPTER 10

EXPECTATIONS

I t was another day in paradise, as the sun once again gently filtered into the master bedroom of the safe house. She was dangerously close to getting spoiled and never wanting to leave this new sanctuary he had invited her into. She rolled over looking for her phone to find the time, it was 8:30 a.m. Casey lazily stretched but made no real attempt to get up either.

"What a bunch of lazy bones we are Case. If we don't get moving our whole day will be spent." She stated in her puppy love voice. Casey yawned, then reluctantly stood up and shook as though she was shaking the previous night's slumber off. Jesse watched her and wished that humans had that *shake thing* going on, but since they didn't she stood and stretched instead.

She unarmed the alarm, fastened the leash and took her to the side yard for some doggie business. Casey was on top of her game this morning and they were back inside in no time. Jesse decided to eat the rest of the cut up fruit in the refrigerator and a yogurt. She was amazed that she was even hungry after all she ate last night. Frankly after spending that much time with Tim yesterday and getting to know him she was kind of stunned that he did not have a serious girlfriend. He would be quite the catch, he was very good looking, boyishly charming, funny and so kind hearted. What's not to love?

She had not checked her phone since she woke up, so after eating she went and retrieved it off the night stand and saw that she had eight missed texts. Mostly from the staff wondering where she was, and wishes for a speedy recovery, and one from Reed wondering where the paperwork was for the bread delivery truck. She texted Reed back the location of the papers and explained where he could find the menu for the week and the daily food draws.

After she felt like the staff was squared away, she fired up her laptop to check her email. She did so with one eye closed half expecting another nasty gram from Jerry. There was another email from Jerry which made the hairs on the back of her neck stand up considering how foul he had been just thirty six hours earlier. It was amazingly civil and cordial, he informed her that he had filed for legal separation, that he has admitted his adulterous affair and is seeking the most expedient method to dissolve this union. He also informed her that he would be giving her three thousand dollars for relocation fees, and would be willing to buy her a car up to twenty five thousand dollars. He also stated that he had inadvertently taken her engagement ring and would be dropping it off at Reed's today at lunch time.

Wow. Did Dean get to him? Or is he having a crisis of conscience?

"Report. Dean are you there?" She asked. But there was no reply. That is strange, so she tried again, and again nothing. Something is wrong she thought, so she texted him and still got no reply. Now she was panicking. Just as she was getting ready to call the office with her pass code, she received a text from an unknown number. It was Tim, stating that Dean was in a "meeting" and would not be available until 11:00 a.m.

Thanks Tim for letting me know, everything is fine. Just received an email from Jerry and was going to inform him. I can wait. Hope your morning is going well. Thanks again for yesterday, I had a great time. ~Jess

Me too, I will relay the message when I see him. -Tim

Since he was going to be tied up, she started cruising the internet making her list and looking at options for furniture now that she was going to be receiving some relocation money. She was usually pretty frugal, so the money he was offering should take her pretty far. She looked through the wants ads and classifieds to see if there were any bedroom suites for sale. She found one that looked nice in the picture on the local Coastal Swap site. It was a mere $200.00 for the headboard, and chest of drawers. That would be enough to get her started anyway, then all she would have to get would be a mattress and box springs.

Another furniture store was having a spring blow out and had a full bedroom set, with a platform bed which only required a mattress. That was also very reasonable and so she listed it as an option. From there she searched for Sofa's and saw a beautiful cottage style overstuffed sofa with a light blue floral print accented in pale yellow. Now that one she just might have to have, and cringed as she searched for the price. It was normally $899.00 but was on sale for $525.00 and if you applied for their in store credit card option you could get an additional twenty percent off if approved. That would reduce the price to $420.00 plus tax, and she could swing that price. Now she was starting to get excited.

Time passed quickly and it was 11:00 o'clock before she knew it. Dean came on line sounding tired.

"You are in trouble because of me aren't you?" She asked him directly.

"Yes and no, it's my fault. I pulled some resources without authorization, so I had to explain to the director what was going on. Its fine now, and I was able to justify it since Jerry threatened your life, so there is no reprimand or damage done. I just have to be careful. Thankfully the director likes me and I am doing a good job, but still, there are rules and I must obey. How are you this morning? Is everything ok?" He asked getting his mental ducks in a row.

"Yes I forwarded the latest email from Jerry. I am quite stunned at his cordial tone. Can I assume that is your doing?" She inquired.

"Yes, I explained to him the consequences of him being unkind to you in detail and that he had a choice to make, so I see he is attempting to make the correct one. How is your list coming along? Finding any of the items that you are looking for?"

"Actually yes, I am. It's kind of exhilarating. Especially now since I know I will be receiving some relocation money. I have book marked a couple of things." She said with a lilt in her voice bordering on excitement.

"Fantastic. Ok here is the deal on the apartment. I called the owner and stated that we had a hardworking recently single gal with excellent references that desperately needed a place to live. He seemed sympathetic to your plight and agreed to waive the first and last month's deposits, and is only requiring the $200.00 Pet deposit. He said you could pick up the keys at any time and start moving in whenever you are ready." He stated then waited for her response. He had actually paid her first and last month's rent for her, but did not want her to know that for fear that she would refuse it.

"What? You mean I am in? Really? Oh- my-gosh, I have my own place to live?" She squealed, which made him smile.

They discussed some of the items she was looking at on line, and she sent him the links to the things she had found so far. He also told her he had gotten her utilities set up without a deposit by providing an excellent reference for her and setting up her accounts to be directly drafted. So that took another burden off her plate. He was also able to secure her a cable package at a premium rate by using agency privilege perks, now all she needed was a television.

He had another meeting to go into so he needed to close for now, but said he would pick back up with her later in the day around 2:30 and they would develop a plan. She went back to cruising the internet looking for other deals when her phone started buzzing with more texts. Reed texted her that word had gotten out that she was out sick, and already two bouquets of flowers had arrived for her and two cards. Several patrons sent their well wishes and prayers for her. She was touched by their out pouring of love for her and thanked Reed for letting her know. Hannah offered to bring them to her, but she stated she wasn't at home but was recuperating at a friend's house.

Tim happened by the Café for lunch and saw the lovely display of flowers on the counter. He mentioned to Libby that he was working on Jesse's car again and would be happy to run those items out to her. Libby texted Jesse to confirm and she said that was fine if he wanted to bring those items when he brought her car back to her. So he carried his load back to the work truck and made plans to run those out to her later in the afternoon.

Jesse spent the remainder of the afternoon walking along the beach and then she took a nap. She didn't realize how tired she was until she laid down after her walk. Dean was not able to get her via the ear piece and she didn't answer her phone so as a last resort he tapped into the houses video system. He could see that she was lying down and did not appear to be in distress. He decided to let her rest and would just speak with her later.

The ringing of the doorbell is what finally woke her up and as she made her way to the living room she could see Tim loaded down with flowers at the back door. She rushed over to unlock the door to let him in.

"Hi, I'm so sorry I laid down and fell asleep. I must have really slept hard, since I missed several calls I see. Thank you so much for running these out here, you really didn't have to do that, I know it's out of your way." She said sincerely.

"It was no problem, plus I feel like I was kind of moody when I left last night and I wanted to apologize. So here I brought you flowers!" He said with a goofy grin.

"You were fine, I could tell you were sad about leaving Wex. It's understandable. There is nothing wrong with him is there? I mean he is not sick or anything is he?" She asked concerned.

"No not that I know of, he promised he would tell me if ever anything came up, but he is terrible about going to the doctor. So more than likely he would be dead before I would ever know and could worry."

"Men." She said with a humph. To which he just grinned, and handed her several cards that had stacked up for her. It was sweet that she was missed that much, there was even a card there from Carl, the accountant. She had to sit down for that one. It was very simple but very sweet and expressed his wishes for a speedy recovery because he wasn't going to eat there until she came back, signed with a smiley face. She shared that one with Tim since he was there the day she had him make his own sandwich.

The largest bouquet of flowers was from the table of eight. Her Airmen, the bouquet was as diverse in its arrangement as they were in personality. She felt almost guilty about telling them that she was sick, but Tim said it was for the best until she was settled. "They would understand, and if they didn't it was ok." He stated.

"Um, Tim. I know I really don't have a right to ask, but I have a favor? I mean I know you are busy and you have a life, right? But I am sure Dean wouldn't mind you helping his Charge, and since I am so pitiful and in need of assistance…." She said sticking her lip out trying to look as hopeless and pitiful as she could possibly look to sway him.

"Ok, ok, ok…your emotional blackmail is working. What do you want girl?" He said in mock exasperation with his hands on his hips.

"I saw a car that I would like to check out, but of course I have never bought a car before, and I don't know how to negotiate, and even though I might like the way it looks I need to know it's in good shape and healthy. Ya know? I thought maybe you and I could go see it." She said sitting on the couch. He walked over and sat next to her on the couch,

"Have you mentioned this to Dean?" He stated flatly, not wanting to over step any boundaries with his best friend.

"No. Oh no, I've messed up again haven't I? Never mind then. I will figure it out, thanks anyway." She said now embarrassed, looking away from him.

"No, its fine, I just didn't know if you had talked to him about it yet? That's all." He said, now wishing he hadn't opened his big mouth.

She stood and picked up her phone and texted Dean.

Dean, I found a car and asked Tim if he would check it out to see if it's a good car since it is used. But apparently I should have run all this past you first and I am sorry I didn't. He brought me some things from the Café and I just spontaneously asked him. I'm sorry if I crossed a line. ~Jesse

Jess, I have no problem with Tim looking at a car for you, he is my go to guy for those things anyway, but I appreciate your candor and honesty. Tell Timmy to give me a call. -Dean

"He wants to talk to you." She asked looking ashamed.

"Sure."

"I'm fixing dinner, do you want some. Since you came all the way out here, let me make this up to you."

"Let me see…I'll be back in a minute." Stating as he stepped out onto the deck.

Tim called Dean and explained what happened. He too thought that she had just gotten excited and wanted his opinion since he was the 'car' guy. Tim was just trying to make sure that she wasn't relying too much on him, and cutting Dean out of the picture which Dean picked up on and appreciated. Dean understood Jesse's heart and motivation, so he felt secure with Tim being his right hand on this one since he could not physically go with her to see it. Dean left it up to Tim and his comfort level as to whether he wanted to go with her or not.

Tim came back inside and watched her as she prepped away in the kitchen. He sat at the bar watching her cook, knowing she was feeling guilty, and it was his fault.

"Hey girl, so tell me about this hot rod you found. Where is it?" He asked trying to get her to open up.

"I can send you the link if you guys want to look at it. Then you can let me know what you think, if it's not a good car, then I can keep looking." She said evenly, as she continued to chop the onions and peppers for the shrimp fajitas, not able to look at him for the moment.

"Jess, I don't mind looking at it for you, I really don't. I'm so sorry I said anything..." He said sounding contrite.

He got cut off by the abrupt sizzle and steam cloud as she dumped all the veggies she had just cut up into the sauté pan. She let the veggies sweat a bit then threw the shrimp in and poured a splash of chicken broth to help everything cook and meld together. Tim's phone started ringing and he excused himself to take the call.

"Jess I am so sorry, I have to go. Company business. Listen send me the info on the car and I will look at it tonight when I get in and call you tomorrow ok?" He said truly sorry he had to leave.

"Wait. Hang on a sec, I'll make you one to go."

He watched as she grabbed the flour tortilla and held it over the veggies and shrimp and steamed it slightly, then she laid it on a piece of tin foil then scooped the shrimp and veggies and rolled it up burrito style. Then took the foil and wrapped it so he could take it to go. He took it and kissed her on the cheek as he started for the door.

"Thanks for dinner Jesse, I'll call you later..." He said on his way out.

"Thanks Tim for bringing the flowers out to me. I appreciate it." She said locking the door behind him.

In that short period of time she had lost her appetite. She found a storage container so she put the meal in the Tupperware and put it in the refrigerator. Dean tried to raise her through the ear piece but she was feeling very out of sorts and didn't answer. She texted him instead and said she wasn't feeling well and asked if she could call him later? He of course agreed, but was worried about her. He tapped into the close circuit on the house to keep an eye on her and watched as she laid down on the couch and started crying. This was ripping his heart out. He knew she was confused, still so overwhelmed and all he wanted to do was hold her.

He watched as her tiny frame was racked with grief and confusion. Casey was pacing the floor, upset that her master was unhappy. He monitored for as long as he could and then he left his place and headed for the safe house. In the meantime, Jesse desperately tried to pull herself together. She felt like everything in her life was slipping away. She was the reason Dean was in trouble at work, and now there was going to be weirdness between Tim and Dean because of her. The one person she had come to rely on for advice, who she felt like was a true friend, and support, might be taken away because of her. It was all becoming too much to bare, the humiliation from Jerry that Dean had witnessed, the emotional roller coaster she was now on was threatening to fling her off with no one there to catch her. She was slowly unwittingly alienating all of them and she didn't know how to stop it. *Why can't I get it together? What is wrong with me? Please Lord help me, I am scared and I feel so alone.*

Dean pulled into the driveway of the safe house and cut his lights off. He knew he shouldn't be there, but he had to see her, and try to talk to her. He could see that she was melting down under the pressure of the last few days and he could not just sit by and idly watch it. It was too painful. As he exited the vehicle to get a better look inside, he heard the French doors fly open and she bolted out of the house running towards the ocean.

He immediately ran around to the corner of the deck to see if he could see where she was headed. From his position he could see that she ran into the water, and was just standing there ankle deep as the water crashed over the lower part of her legs. She stood there facing the expanse of the sea and then let out a blood curdling scream into the night that seemed to last forever, before dropping to her knees. By the time she hit the sand he was behind her.

"I'm here baby. I'm sorry... I just couldn't stay away, I knew you were upset and I just wanted to hold you. Can I please hold you once again?" He said over the crash of the waves.

Her body language gave him the permission he sought from her. She collapsed into his arms and he walked her back a bit out of the waves to the water's edge. He sat down in the sand, and set her in front of him as he placed his strong muscular arms around her and she leaned her head back against his chest.

"What is wrong with me Dean, I'm messing everything up. I don't mean to, I hate feeling like this, all this crying and confusion is not me." She said as hot tears continued to flow down her cheeks.

"Baby it's ok, you haven't messed up anything. I promise you haven't. I know you have all these emotions fighting for position in your head and heart, and I know you don't know what to do with some of them. I know I am not helping either. I promised to keep you safe, and to be your Handler. I have crossed so many lines with you and it's not fair to you. I was supposed to keep my distance, stay formal, only monitor you from 7am to 6 pm, but observing your husband like I had, and knowing the things I knew, I stayed on longer to protect you. My knight in shining armor syndrome kicked in and I over stepped my boundaries because I have come to have very strong feelings for you." He stated breathlessly.

"What?" She whispered.

"Feelings I am not supposed to have, but can no longer fight. Tim understands this development, and me better than anyone. He is crazy about you Jesse, he too has grown to love you but in a sisterly kind of way. He is so naturally charming that women normally just hurl themselves at him which usually causes him to run. He just didn't want to confuse you or the situation. He told me how great you were with Wex last night, and that sealed it for him, you are now in the inner circle and one he considers as a close friend. I know I am in danger of losing my position, and my project that I have worked so hard for, but I don't care. It's been a long time since I have had feelings for someone, and being with you right here right now is where I want to be." He said kissing her neck and holding onto her even tighter. Her breathing was less ragged now, and she just sat there her full weight against his chest and her arms wrapped around his left arm, with her head turned slightly to the left resting on his muscular bicep.

"Dean, I too have feelings for you that run so deep that I am not sure I can properly articulate them. I have also come to rely on you, maybe too much? All I know is the thought of losing you causes a panic in my soul that takes my breath away. But with that being said, I do not want to be the cause of your career going up in flames. We are a great team Dean, we have to get back to that, show the director what great rapport we have and show him what we can do together. Please don't let me be the one to take that away from you." She pleaded with him.

"You won't Jesse. I will figure something out. Just know that I care about you... so much, I want you safe and happy." He said softly in her ear.

"Right now, right here, I am happy." She whispered back to him.

They sat there quietly for hours. He thought at one point she had fallen asleep she had gotten so still. He was content to sit there in wet sand holding her while listening to the waves as they crashed on the shore and for the first time in a long time he began to earnestly pray.

"I need to lay down, and I need to let you get some sleep." She said softly not wanting this moment to end, but she was afraid if she didn't go now she would definitely be waking up on the beach.

The weariness she was experiencing made her bones feel heavy like they were weighted down. Dean stood, then effortlessly lifted her to her feet. Staying behind her he guided her through the darkness to the side of the house, past the tall sea grasses where the outdoor shower was located so he could help her rinse the sand and salt off of her and himself. She braced herself against the wooden privacy wall while he took the hose wand and gently washed her from the waist down. Even though it soaked through her clothes, he would eventually wrap her in a towel and send her inside. He finished rinsing off himself then patted himself dry and laid the towel on the deck.

He made sure the house was secure, and she was in bed, then he drove home to the comfort of his own bed. *Please Lord, let her get some sleep. Clear her mind, and give her peace.* He prayed before he also succumbed to sleep.

CHAPTER 11

DOWN TIME

J esse woke the next morning feeling like her head was in a vice. She wasn't sure if it was from not eating, all the crying, dehydration or all of the above. She made her way into the kitchen and grabbed a bottled water out of the refrigerator and proceeded to down the entire bottle. Apparently dehydration was playing a part in her body's current physical state. She threw the bottle into the recycle bin and then rummaged through her belongings to find some Advil.

Casey was now up and scampering around alerting Jesse that it was time for her regular morning outing. As Jesse walked around the side yard waiting for Casey to find that perfect blade of grass to do her business on, she thought back on last night and wondered if she had just imagined it all? She so badly wanted to see Dean and be held by him, and then have him tell her that everything in her upside down world would be fine. She knew she had to get a grip though, that he could not continue to risk everything and have his career ruined so that he could console her.

Jesse was amazed that someone like him would jeopardize his life's long work for someone like her? The sun was already bearing down this morning so she coaxed Casey to hurry up so she could go back inside to the comfort of the safe house and its air conditioning. Once she was back in the house she picked up her phone and texted Dean.

I need some time, must figure things out. I will only be available by phone today, so text or call me if you need me. It was wonderful to have you near last night, but I cannot continue to put you at risk. It felt like a dream. ~Jess

Dean once again got in late and was up early to work out at the gym with his crew. Tim, Adam, Derek, Ninja and Dean met twice a week to have their morning meetings and work out at 5:00 a.m. However, this morning Dean couldn't sleep and was back up again at 4:00a.m. so he went on over to the gym to get started early and found Tim already there looking like he had slept there.

"Man what are you doing here so early? Did you get evicted?" Dean inquired.

"Ha-Ha. I wish. Getting evicted and having all my worldly possessions dumped in the front yard would have been fun compared to what I have been dealing with the last eight hours." Tim said laying on the floor throwing his arm over his eyes to block the overhead lighting.

"What happened? I thought you were going to pick up that witness and drive her to Charleston to catch a plane? In and out right?" Dean asked starting up the treadmill to warm up.

"Well I got the call she was ready when I was at the safe house with Jesse, so I already had drama going on which I hated to leave in the middle of, since I think I was the cause of that one. Sorry man. Then I had to change cars, pick up the Charger to pick up the package. She was supposed to be ready when I got there, and well she was gone. Nowhere to be found. So I tapped into Adam to find out where in the heck she was, and apparently she had placed a call to her boyfriend to say goodbye which she was *NOT* supposed to do, so he came and got her to talk to her. Well, then all his undesirable friends showed up to also try and convince her that she needed to rethink her decision. She managed to make it into the bathroom and called Adam freaking out realizing they were planning to kill or torture her, who then tracked the GPS on her phone to determine her location then sent it to me. So here I am the lone ranger walking in to pick this girl up not knowing what in the world I am getting into... with no back up." He stated with a sigh.

"Oh my God Tim, you should have never been put in that position, that's not your job. You are the driver not extractor. Did you request back up?" He stated angrily to think that this really could have gone south.

"Well yeah, but the Columbia team was unprepared for what we were trying to do, but did their best in a pinch. Anyway to make a very long story short, after some gun fire, punches thrown, and one hysterical witness I was able to get her in the car and take off. One of the baddies had escaped the backup team and proceeded to follow/chase us. Thank God that is my area of expertise, and after about thirty minutes we were in the wind and he was nowhere to be found. Then I had to contend with an overzealous High Way patrolman that finally Adam was able to get to stand down, he tracked us for nearly 40 minutes. I handed her off to our guy in Charleston at the airport, then headed home. By the time I hit town it was nearly 4:15 so I figured I might as well come here."

"Man I am so sorry. We'll make this short today so you can go take a power nap." Dean said sympathetically.

"So how is our girl?" Tim asked through a yawn.

"She had a meltdown last night after you left. So I rode out there to just check on her, not engage her, and I no sooner arrived when she flew out the French doors on the patio, in the dark, straight for the ocean like the house was on fire or something. I followed her to the water's edge where she just stood there and screamed at the ocean or God I don't know which and then she fell like a heap into the water. It was killing me Tim, so I came up behind her, pulled her out of the water and just sat and held her trying to soothe her."

This caused Tim to sit straight up. He bent his head down and paused for a moment to make sure he selected the right words before speaking to his best friend.

"Dean, man, you cannot do this with her. You are going to lose everything. Director Johnson is already pissed you put her at the safe house without prior written permission. The fact that Jerry threatened her life, is the *only* reason he didn't throw the book at you. I know you know this, and I also know what she means to you, but you have to know that Dean and Jesse can never be together. Look I think she is great, I want nothing more than to see both of you happy. Please just be careful man. If you go down it's not just you that it affects. You and I have been together a long time, and we have done some great stuff, I will never have that kind of history or rapport with another leader. I'm sure that sounds selfish, but it's true, and it's not just me, but Ninja and Adam too."

They heard the latch click and realized more of the team was arriving. Dean got off the treadmill, walked over to Tim and extended a hand to help him up off of the floor. They both leaned in and hugged. Ninja was the first to make it through the door and see this momentary display of affection.

"Ok you bunch of girls, break up the romance, we have business to discuss." She said offering a sly grin.

"What? What did we miss?" Derek asked coming in behind her. Adam came in last and upon seeing Tim said, "Dude, heck of a run last night, hate you got your panties in a twist but it all worked out, glad you didn't get shot." He said grinning.

"Shut up Adam, next time make sure my package is secure or I'm gonna come back and kick your tail." He said levelly.

"Wow, being up 24 hours, and getting shot at makes you cranky Tim, Dean I think he needs a nap or a time out. " Adam said playfully punching Tim in the arm.

"Let's get started everyone. Good morning. Adam, Tim has a point, please don't let it happen again, I am not willing to risk one of our team on a simple in and out like that, lets discuss the particulars in my office later. And for the record he will be taking a nap as soon as we finish here." He stated with a grin.

He opened up the floor for updates on projects they were working on, and then updated them on the Beta project he was working on. Ninja and Adam were part of the Alpha escalation team, and Derek was an interrogation specialist and Handler, like Dean. They were at the half way mark with the Charges and so far things were going really well. Dean and Jesse were at the top of the Leader board with the most reports and reports that lead to escalations. Derek was in second place, then Ann, Craig and Homer. Now this was not a contest, but merely a tracking tool to determine where most of the leads are coming from, the effectiveness of the Handler to guide his Charge and discover patterns if any. Once the meeting was finished, Tim and Dean both skipped the work out part, Dean went on into the office and Tim went home to shower and sleep.

Dean had a 7:00 a.m. meeting with the director on the Beta program and to present the mid-way point progress assessment. The director tried not to let on, but he did have a soft spot for Dean, he saw the potential, but also saw that passion that when channeled properly yielded great results. It's when the emotion combined with the passion collided together that the Director had to rein him in. It was not often that Dean ever allowed his emotions to override his duty or logical critical thinking and the director had only seen Dean get like this one other time, and it was when Tim was in jeopardy.

Tim had been part of another CIA ops team at the time, he had received bad Intel and was compromised. Dean found out that Tim's life was on the line then proceeded to break every rule in the book, called in every favor he had and then some to rescue him, nearly losing his life in the process. That is why to this day he allows them to be on the same team, there is a bond between those two that is incredible, and if he were to put Tim on another team, Dean would just be sticking his nose into other projects he was not in control of to make sure his friend was safe. Easier just to let them be together, not to mention they had a level of non-verbal communication that had been deftly used in missions that provided favorable outcomes. Plus it was easier to keep an eye on the two of them if they were together.

By the time Dean got back to his version of the 'war room' where he did all of his monitoring of the Charges and projects he looked down and saw that he had missed a text from Jesse. He had to read it twice to make sure he understood her. At this point, he was going to have to give her a bit of space, whether it was a couple of hours or a couple of days, but it still stung his heart a bit. That combined with what happened to Tim last night just brought back all kinds of emotions.

It wasn't that Tim could not handle himself in a fight, he was skilled, but Tim is not a warrior at heart. Tim was quick on his feet and his sense of humor often kept him out of the fire, but his forte was that he was brilliant at all things vehicles, driving them, fixing them, understanding them, and setting them up for missions and his work for the team was invaluable. He was not just a lowly mechanic, he was a master at his craft. No doubt Tim would fight for who he loved and would fight to the death, but he was not a soldier, at least not in the typical illustration of a soldier.

Jesse was sitting on the deck under the umbrella thumbing through a book she found on the bookshelf in the living room. It was a murder-intrigue-mystery type of book and she thought it ironic to find a read such as this in a safe house. She thought she heard her phone ring and realized she had left it on the kitchen counter, she quickly got up to answer it but by the time she picked it up the call had gone to voicemail. It was her sister Susie. *Great.* Best to go ahead and get it over with she thought. She picked up her phone and sat on the leather sofa in the living room, Casey curled up at her feet.

"Hello?" Susie answered.

"Hi Sue, I was outside and didn't get to the phone it time."

"Hey that's fine, are you home? Why aren't you at work? Are you sick, do I need to come by? Bring soup?" She quizzed.

"Well I have a bit of news…" She started.

"Oh no! You've been fired, oh sweetie I am so sorry! What can I do?"

"No, thank goodness I have not been fired. Are you sitting down?"

"You are sick aren't you? It's the cancer isn't it?" Her voice rising now in a panic.

"Sue, please let me finish. You are all over the map." Jesse stated flustered.

"You are right I am sorry I won't say another word until you are finished. Go." She said biting her tongue trying to remain silent until the beans were spilled.

"Saturday after our shopping trip I found out Jerry was having a long term affair, and he kicked me out of the condo. I also found out that he is having a baby with this woman. It's over. He has filed for a divorce and I am now on my own." She managed to get out without being interrupted.

"Ok. Wow, didn't really see that coming. Jesse, for you my love, I am on the one hand heartbroken that your life has been turned upside down. But on the other hand, he is a piece of crap, evil snake, good for nothing, lying, horrible man that I hope the Lord or Karma blesses with hot coals upon his head and or festering boils all over his body. What can I do? Do you want to come stay with us? Samantha is still so little she can stay in our room, Matty wouldn't mind, he loves you." She offered.

"Um thank you for your support...I think." She said laughing secretly loving the hot coals and boils comment. "With the help of some friends I have managed to secure an apartment, and Jerry did agree to buy me a newer car, and give me some relocation money. So I am going to start moving either late today or tomorrow. It's a great place Sue I can't wait for you to see it. Perfect for me and Casey."

"Well I am stunned to hear he is helping you out. Oh sweet Jesse, I am so relieved you have found a place so quickly, if you can wait until tomorrow I will see if Tori can sit for Sami and come help you." Sue offered.

"That would be great Susie. I miss you and I would appreciate the help. I'll text you later and give you the details, ok?"

"Yeah please do, hey Sami is crying let me go see what's up. Love you."

"I love you."

Well that went better than I expected. I knew she would be happy that Jerry is out of my life, they never thought him good enough for me anyway and merely tolerated his existence. I guess they picked up on things I never noticed.

She pulled out her laptop and found the vehicle she had bookmarked and planned to send it to Dean for his review and opinion. She prepared her email then attached the picture with the stats and information then sent that to Dean. Then went back out to the refuge of the back deck with it's fabulous views, she was doing a lot of just sitting this morning, praying and trying to bring some order to her emotions and life.

Dean heard the familiar ping of his Outlook alerting him to a new email. He had various people set up with their own ping tone so that when he received emails or texts without looking he knew who they were from. This ping told him it was from either Jesse or Tim, and since Tim was more than likely sleeping he was hoping it was from Jesse.

Hi Dean,

I hope your morning has gone well, here is the car I found. I know it's not new, but this car purchased as new is crazy expensive. So I am fine with it being a couple years old. I love the medium blue color and it's fully loaded. I really like this one since it will give me the space I need to get things from the wholesale club for Reed's when I need to. Have you ever tried to put a case of 12oz Styrofoam cups into a Ford Escort? I'm here to tell you it can't be done. Ridiculous. Tim said at one time he would look at it for me, if he is *still up for that? I don't have an email for him so if you could forward this for me? I think it will work with the amount Jerry said he would pay, they are asking $21,500 I think, I don't know if that is a good price or not? Just let me know if you think this will work or if I need to look at something else. Again thank you for everything you do and continue to do. Love Jesse*

He finished reading the email then located the website for the vehicle. It was at a local dealership only had nineteen thousand miles and appeared to be in decent shape. Dean had already received the twenty eight thousand dollars from Jerry and it was sitting in an account for Jesse. His goal was to save her as much money on a vehicle as he could so that she would have some padding in her account for the unexpected things life throws at you.

Providing Tim gave his blessing this could work out nicely. Dean forwarded the email to Tim and said 'Let's make this work, check it out and it out then let me know. Thanks brother.' Then he went back to analyzing the latest bit of data that had come in from a report.

Tim rolled over in bed then looked at the watch on his arm which read 11:47 a.m. slowly he sat up and then stretched. His long legs lifted him off the bed and he meandered into the bathroom. Taking stock of his appearance with his shaggy layered collar length hair and five o'clock shadow that had now turned into a four day homeless man look, he determined he needed to hit the barber's shop sooner than later, but doubted it would be today. He brushed his teeth, applied deodorant then checked his phone.

He reviewed the email from Dean first then, read the other twelve that were sitting out there for him. Tim grabbed his keys then headed for the dealership to check out Jesse's choice and then would report back to Dean.

He showed up on the lot and inquired if the vehicle was still available, the salesman indicated it was still for sale, Tim looked under the hood, crawled underneath it, quizzed the sales guy on why it was traded in and then asked to drive it. It drove well and other than needing to be detailed it appeared to be in great shape. Tires still had a decent amount of tread left, the sunroof worked and the leather seats were intact. There was one scratch on the passenger seat but that could be treated and was nowhere near being a rip in the leather. After taking it for a quick spin, he called Dean and asked him to come take a look, so he asked Derek to drive him down to meet Tim.

The sales guy could smell a sale but had no idea what he was in for when this dynamic duo began to tag team him during the negotiation process. Even when he called in his sales manager, they were still no match for this well-crafted team who when they wanted something, usually got it. Since they were paying cash they had a little more leverage and walked out with the vehicle for several thousand less than the advertised asking price. Dean was pleased he could save Jesse some more money and still get her in a decent ride. Dean followed Tim back to his shop so Tim could really dig into the SUV and then get it detailed properly. They were in between mission jobs at the moment and were only doing routine maintenance on the fleet, so the timing was perfect.

Dean shook Tim's hand and left him with it. He could see the giddiness in Tim's demeanor at the prospect of getting to play with a new toy. He was such a kid at times, and Dean let him enjoy his moment. Meanwhile Dean has some work of his own to do and needed to focus on some hand off assignments to the Alpha team. He was going to need some concentrated time to devise the plan and implementation for this recon mission. So he set out the photos and notes then began the tedious task of planning the plan and backup plan B and C. He turned his phone to Do Not Disturb.

Jesse texted Reed to give him an update then stood to stretch squinting in the bright sunlight. She called Casey outside and then walked her around to the grassy area, it was there she realized she was hungry. No starving. So they went back inside and she heated up the shrimp fajitas that she had originally made for supper last night but was too upset to eat. Turned out to be just what she needed, and it made her think of Wex, so she stopped and said a quick prayer of healing and protection over him.

Now that she was full, had gotten plenty of vitamin D outside, her eyes were starting to get heavy so she laid down on the sofa to take a quick nap. This was exactly the kind of drama free day she needed. No café work, no report details, just her and Casey being lazy and getting to take a nap. If she wanted to eat, she ate, she was not relegated to any kind of a time schedule and certainly not one for someone as ungrateful as Jerry. Jesse drifted off to sleep imagining a different kind of life on the horizon, and it was good.

Dean had been at it for hours and needed to stand up and move around to get the blood circulating that was now pooled at this feet. He walked down the hall to get a fountain drink from the canteen and stretch his legs. Once he was back at his desk he decided to check in on Jesse since he had not heard or spoken to her all day aside from the one text and one email she had sent. He was thankful for the workload today as it helped keep his mind off of her for a change to give her the space she needed.

He tapped into the monitoring system at the safe house and immediately found her lying on the couch with her tanned legs peeking out from under her sundress crossed at the ankles, and Casey sleeping watch at her feet. He felt a warmth rush over him at the sight of her and just sat there staring at the screen for several minutes taking in a peaceful serene moment while he watched her sleep. He had met a lot of women in his time...a lot. Why was it this one that caught his eye, and made his heart stir like none other? Sure she was cute, really cute, but not beautiful. He loved her heart shaped face and blue eyes along with her dimples and lips that always seemed to lean towards the curve of a smile.

In a lot of ways, her personality reminded him of Tim. Always ready to help, tender hearted, funny, and at times silly even when they were trying to be serious. There was also a vulnerable side to her that she was able to embrace and work through that he envied. She was very kind to people, even ones in his opinion that did not deserve the kindness she bestowed and he found that appealing. The biggest thing that he thought about with her is that she doesn't have an agenda, she is not a schemer, she is not trying to one up the person next to her, she is content where she is and is just a good person who keeps trying to do the right thing.

It was refreshing, because the women at the agency who were single, were focused on jockeying for positon to put them in the best light for the next big assignment or management roll. Women outside of work that he met seemed to be looking for the next sugar daddy or husband that would pay for their Botox treatments, Jimmy Choo shoes or Coach bags. Sure some of the ones he dated were beautiful, but would sleep with your best friend in the blink of an eye, and steal your wallet while doing it. Jesse didn't want anything from him other than to be his friend. She wasn't demanding, so it made him want to do all the more for her since she was not greedy or unkind. Plus she felt perfect in his arms, she was the glass slipper that fit Dean.

A knock on his door stirred him from his thoughts so he killed the feed showing the safe house and told them to enter. It was Tim grinning like a fool and all but dancing a jig.

"Hey man, I've got the car ready and I was able to mend the passenger side seat so it looks perfect now, and I got her new floor mats for the front, a new cargo net and cargo cover shield so if she wants to put things in the cargo area, this will shield people from seeing what she has back there. It's ready to deliver, have you spoken with her today?" He said making himself at home sitting on top of Dean's desk.

"No not really, she wanted a little down time today, so I was trying to honor that, plus I have been slammed. I did check on her a few minutes ago and it looks like she has fallen asleep on the couch so she is there..." Dean offered.

"Ok well if you are ok with it, I am going to ride out there and deliver this bad boy? Ok?" He said almost giddy again. Dean just shook his head at his friend, cars were truly his love and he was so excited to be able to share with this someone he cares about and someone who will truly appreciate it like he does.

"Of course, get out of here and let me know what she says. Or keep your ear piece open." Dean said with a smile. Tim bounded out the door then quickly returned, "Oh yeah, guess what I did and all by myself?" Tim said beaming with pride.

Dean shook his head laughing, "What did you do Timmy? All by yourself?"

"I went to Director Johnson and told him I wanted to buy an undercover car, and it would be great because it was *really* an undercover car, no one would *ever* think that an agent would be in a sixteen year old *Ford Escort*! I told him I could jack it up and make it super-fast and so it would be to spec, but it would have the real element of surprise. And he said YES. Gave me a voucher right then and there to cash it out and buy it. So now I have an additional thousand dollars for Jesse to put in savings or where ever she wants to do with it or if she wants to blow it! I did good, right?"

"That is awesome, great job man, I can't believe you sold him on it." Dean said standing and extending his fist for a knuckle bump.

"Hey I did not question his good mood or my excellent timing, I just thanked him, took the money and ran. Who knows maybe he thinks that will be the punishment car, when we screw up, we get stuck in the Escort for a few days." He said laughing at himself, then turned to trot down the hallway to the exit.

CHAPTER 12

MOVING

J esse had just started to stir, and couldn't believe she had slept so long, she must have needed it. She went to the bathroom, then brushed her teeth to refresh herself and to shake off the slumber that was still clinging to her frame. She had just wiped her mouth on the towel when she heard Casey barking up a storm. She cautiously came around the corner, not remembering if she had set the alarm before her nap causing a momentary fit of panic to engulf her body.

Then she heard a familiar voice that was Tim's and let him inside. He scooped her up in a big hug, then drug her over to the sofa, it was hard not to get caught up in his exuberance, and she immediately started smiling.

"Hey you, gosh girl, you look great today. All refreshed and relaxed." He said grinning as he mussed with her hair.

"Hey it takes time to create this look mister. Like two hours asleep on the couch and don't you forget it!" She said teasing right back.

He leaned in and kissed her on the cheek then jerked her up off the couch, "Gotta show you something, come with me, and close your eyes." He encouraged. She slid her sandals on then made her way out the door with him guiding her. "What is it with all you CIA spooks wanting us regular folks to keep our eyes closed?" She asked as he guided her down the walkway. He just smiled and admitted she had a point.

"Ta-Da!!" He said removing her hand from her eyes.

"Wow you brought the car for me to test drive? Oh Tim thank you, what did you think, I mean is it a good car? Or can you tell yet?"

"Girl, you *own* this bad boy. It is all yours, Dean and I went and picked it up today, I had it detailed and went through it with a fine tooth comb. It's in great shape and what wasn't up to my personal standard I fixed, so now it is. We were also able to get it at a good price so the extra is pocket money for you honey. Here get in and let's go for a ride." He said handing her the keys.

"It's mine? Really mine?" She said dancing around and then flung her arms around him and he spun her around.

"Get in let's go!"

"Ok, ok... I am so excited. It is sooo beautiful, more so in person than even the picture showed. I can't believe it! Oh look, and a full tank of gas too. Wow." She said getting settled in the driver's seat. He came around and showed her some features about night driving, the sun/moon roof and the security system he tweaked. Completely in his element. Then he ran around to the passenger's side and buckled up.

"Please text Dean right now and tell him I said thank you and I love it and I love you both for doing this for me. It drives so dreamy, and I like sitting up higher, I feel like I can see better now. This is so cool, right?" She said opening up the sun roof as they cruised down the coastal highway towards town.

"Heck yeah it's cool." He said grinning from ear to ear, knowing she was pleased and oh so excited over the vehicle in general. That was all the thanks he required. He continued to give her the rundown on some other features and told her about the cargo net and cover. She insisted on trying to pay him for it and he refused saying he happened to have them lying around and it was no big deal but thought she would like to have them.

She drove around the cove, then into town past Reed's, and then to the new apartment and sat in her new parking space for a moment letting it all soak in. "It's gonna be ok, isn't it Tim?" She asked quietly.

"Yeah, Jess, it is. You are going to be ok." He said holding her hand this time.

"Well it's due to you and Dean there is no denying that, I'd be living in my sister's nursery sharing a room with a 3 month old if it weren't for you guys. I just don't know how I can ever repay all the kindness and attention to detail you guys have done for me. Not only that but I feel like I have made two really good friends in the process. I am so blessed." She stated earnestly.

"There is nothing to repay, we didn't do this so that you would owe us or be indebted to us, we did it because we care about you and you are a good person who got a raw deal, plus we did it cause we can." He said unleashing his magnificent smile.

"Well you guys aren't CIA spooks anymore, not to me, you are like angels walking among us." She said sweetly. "Hey do you still have the key? I'd like to look at a couple of things first before I start moving in tomorrow, if we can?"

"Yeah I still have it, let's go look and see what's going on." He said getting out of the car and opening up the entrance for her. They both bounded up the steps like a couple of kids, silly with excitement. That was one thing about Tim, dealing with a job that could be life or death caused him to really enjoy the little moments. Whereas Dean tended to hunker down and be the man with the plan. That's why he was the Handler. Smart, dedicated, a master at problem solving and a geek techie at heart. He was always uber prepared and had a plan A, B, C and even a D sometimes. Tim wanted no one else to have his back on a mission but Dean and that was a fact.

They entered the apartment and began to measure and mock place furniture based on the pieces she had tentatively selected. The bedroom was definitely big enough for a king sized bed, but did she really want to go that route? Sleeping at the safe house had her spoiled with that little perk. At least she knew it could hold one and she would still have room to move around and not be wall to wall bed. Then she started going through all the cabinets in the kitchen, mentally trying to figure out what her essentials would be and what the wish list would be, while she was under the sink they heard a knock on the door. Tim told her to stay put, and then checked the peep hole in the door.

She heard the door swing open and then heard Tim invite someone inside. It was Carter from downstairs, he heard the commotion upstairs and just wanted to check it out. *Great. My hair looks like a chicken attacked me. And no lip gloss. Ugg.*

"Where's our new tenant?" Carter asked looking around. She tried to gracefully crawl out from under the sink and compose herself.

"Here, I'm here under the sink." She said trying to scrunch her hair back into place looking sheepishly.

Tim stood behind Carter imitating her fixing her hair, and laughing at her, while she was trying to smile and have a normal conversation with her fabulously handsome neighbor to be. *I think I'm going to kill the tall lanky dark haired man. Yes, he just may not make it home.*

"So when are you moving in? This weekend?" He asked as he moved, now looking down over the balcony. She walked over to see what he was looking at and they both kind of got stuck in the doorway at the same time. She noticed that he smelled remarkable and somewhat familiar. It was comforting.

"Yes. Oh excuse me, um you smell really nice. What is that? That you are wearing I mean? I'm sorry is that too forward? I hope I didn't make you uncomfortable." She said now turning bright red at her rambling nonsense.

Which of course gave Tim even more ammunition. *What the heck girl, get a grip.*

"Oh it's Nautica. Blue, I think." He said trying not to grin at her, furthering her embarrassment.

"Hey that's what I wear sometimes, it has a clean scent that doesn't scream 'I'm trying to hard', ya know?" Tim piped up, trying to get the conversation back on track. Then she attempted to answer his original question.

"You asked when I was moving in, and I'm starting tomorrow. I just got a new car and so now I can go pick up some things I need, plus my sister has a babysitter and can come tomorrow to help me." She stated smiling sweetly.

"Well I am off tomorrow, so I will be around if you guys need any help. Just holler at me I can help you ladies with some of the heavy lifting." He said his steely blue eyes penetrating into her soul.

"Thank you so much, how kind of you. We may just do that, since you are offering." She said smiling as her stomach fluttered.

"Sure, well listen I'll let you get back to....whatever you are doing here. See you tomorrow." He said waving as he exited the apartment.

Jesse finished up her mental decorating for the moment and then insisted on buying Tim dinner for all his work on the Highlander, and for just being a good friend in general. They stopped in at China Palace then decided on the buffet. They had the best Cantonese boneless chicken and their wonton soup was probably the best in the state. Light delicate wontons and a light broth that was perfect if you were under the weather or had a cold. Tim plated up like he was feeding a family of five, and she was thankful for once that he wanted buffet and not off the menu. Wex was right, he could eat you out of house and home.

"So there will be you, me, your sister, and Captain America if he shows up, do you think we will need any additional hands on deck? I can try to rustle up some if you think we will need it?" Tim asked.

"I wish Dean could be there, ya know. To see the new place first hand, I mean I wouldn't be there if it wasn't for him. Makes me sad." She stating taking a sip of her soup.

"Oh he'll be there..." He started.

"He will? Oh-my-gosh that is great, I can't wait to see him!" She interrupted.

"No baby girl, not *there* there, but in spirit. You know you can't see him." He stated sympathetically, wishing he could get his big foot out of his mouth.

"Oh yeah, silly me, what was I thinking? Um, can you excuse me for a moment." She said through a forced smile, and exited to the ladies room.

"Tim, dude you are *killing* me." Dean tapped into his ear piece after over hearing their conversation.

"Ugg, I know... diarrhea of the mouth, what is wrong with me lately? Please don't suit me up for any hard missions any time soon, I am apparently not at my best game. It's so hard to lie to her Dean, do you see those baby blue eyes? I feel like Jesus is going to smite me if I lie to her. Seriously man, it's hard." He whispered.

"I'm going to smite you if you make her cry again! On task man, get on task." Dean strongly encouraged, but deep down he knew exactly what Tim was struggling with, and if the roles were reversed Dean would be in the same boat.

She returned back to the table looking like she had just washed her face. They continued to eat and Tim attempted to keep the conversation light and asked about her sister.

"Oh Susie is great. She is tall, fit and so beautiful. Great naturally curly, wavy strawberry blonde hair. Unlike me, she is a fireball, fiercely loyal and so witty. That's who I want to be when I grow up. She is always fighting for the underdog, ya know? I remember one time in school that I was wearing a dress my momma made me, it was really cute, not to mention mom had worked really hard on it. I was proud of it until I got to school and this girl Alyssa Cumberband started making fun of me. It was horrible, everyone started laughing and taunting me. Well Susie, who was a couple grades ahead of me, caught wind of the taunting and not only did she verbally slay the dragon on the playground, she beat the crap out of her when Alyssa slapped her face. She said it was worth every minute of the suspension she got for fighting." She shared as she retold the story proudly.

"Man where was she when I was getting my tail kicked at school? She sounds awesome." Tim said finishing his plate.

"Oh yeah she is pretty awesome. No one at school ever messed with me again. She has this mean girl face that she does, even now and people just start backing away from her. It's that 'I'm crazy and not afraid to use it face' ya know? Now she is a stay at home mom. Matt is her husband, he is a great guy, a real teddy bear, so they make a great couple. You would love her." She said wistfully.

"Well I can't wait to meet her, and if she is related to you, I know we can't go wrong. Hey are you full?" He asked leaning in towards her.

"Why?" She replied with a grin.

"Cause I'm thinking we need to end this day on a double scoop waffle cone. Are you in? Come on... say you are in." He said giving her his best boyish smile.

"Let's do it. New car celebration, new apartment celebration, new life celebration. I'm in, ice cream makes everything better." She replied.

After splurging on waffle cones she drove him back to work so he could get his car. She pulled up to the front of the building and looked at all the windows and wondered if Dean was still in there somewhere. Tim saw her gazing outward and told her he had already gone home for the night. That he didn't *get* to take a nap today.

"Ha-ha. Ok, well get some rest friend; oh and by the way if I gain ten pounds it's *your* fault. I have never eaten this much in my life until I started hanging out with you. At this rate I will never get a date and be an old spinster living at Apartment 1A." She said laughing.

"Well if that happens, you call me and I will come get you and take you on a date, miss pitiful. We'll go to the I-hop or S&K Cafeteria." He said then busted out laughing at his own joke. She attempted to swat at him, but he slid out of the car and was out of her reach.

"Hey thank you again so much, I love this car, so much so that I might sleep in it tonight." She said grinning.

'Happy to do it, be safe going home. I'll see you tomorrow. Text me what time we need to gather and what the plan is, ok?" He said with a wink then walked through the building to the special car park that they had set up for the teams.

Minutes after she was back on the road Dean rang her phone and the next thing she knew he was coming through the speakers in her car. She was stunned and tickled to think she had 'hands free' communication in her new car. Immediately she began gushing about the car, and the apartment and how much she wished he could be there to see it all since she would have none of it if it weren't for him. He spoke to her all the way home, then told her to give him a call before she went to bed. It was so good to hear his voice and she realized how much she had missed him in that moment.

She got home then took Casey out, then walked to the beach once again. Tonight she was much calmer and the ocean was soothing her soul once again. She stood out there and instead of screaming she began praying and thanking God for peace, and provision and prayed that he would keep Dean and his team safe from harm. She walked up and down the water's edge only the length of the safe house not knowing what really laid beyond it and not wanting to wander out of range. Once she felt she had sufficiently covered all the prayer topics, she slowly walked towards the house, rinsed off her feet then went inside. She locked up everything tightly then got ready for bed. The walk on the beach was twofold, it allowed her to commune with God uninterrupted and also walk off that ice cream she and Tim indulged in.

She hopped into bed and put her ear piece in, then tried to see if he was on line. He was and they began talking about their day, he too laid in his bed in the dark focusing on her voice as she went through the events of her day, listening to the her voice as it lilted when she said certain words and then when she giggled. She told him about Carter the new neighbor and about how Tim acts like a crazy person when he is around and refers to him as Captain America. Dean laughed and said that it sounded like Tim, always joking around.

She continued to talk and talk until she eventually fell asleep on him and he didn't have the heart to wake her up. He was able to secure her list of furniture she wanted including the sofa she wanted so badly, so by tomorrow she would have a bed room set, with a king size bed, the French country cottage looking sofa, and a matching TV table along with a 46" Television, and a blue ray player, that he and Tim decided for her that she needed, so it was being delivered in the afternoon. The unit already came with appliances including the washer and dryer so she was good there. She had located four bar stools for the kitchen she really liked but unless they came into the store over the weekend they would have to be ordered. That is if he could keep Tim from driving to Charleston to pick them up for her.

He finally tried to shut his mind down for the night since tomorrow was going to be busy.

Jesse woke early and laid there for a minute once again watching the sun stream in through the blinds in the room. She rolled over and texted Susie to see when she was going to be ready. She wanted to clean the apartment first, before they started moving things in, and so she needed to run by the store and pick up some cleaning products, and sponges and a mop. There are a million little things that you take for granted after collecting them a little at a time, that you need to set up a new house again from scratch. She also wanted to make sure the water was turned on and the ice maker was ready to go. She thought there was ice in there, but in these wee hours of the morning thinking back, she was not sure.

Susie texted back that she would be there by eight and would bring breakfast. Jesse jumped up and took Casey out, then hurried back inside to get a shower. Just before sticking her head under the spray she remembered her ear piece, so she had to remove that and laid it on the counter. *That would be a horrible start to my day, ruin an expensive piece of equipment. Dean would kill me.*

After blow drying her hair and donning a pair of jean shorts and a tee-shirt, she was ready to check in, finish loading her clothes in the car, and hit the store.

"Report." She stated.

"Good morning Charge 25. I guess we have to get back into the swing of normal things again don't we?" He said smiling.

"Yes... I guess we do. I am ready to go to the apartment and start cleaning, you know give it a once over before anything new goes in, not that it's nasty or anything. Just to freshen things up. So I am headed over to the store now to pick up things like soaps, sponges, hangers, a mop, toilet paper, and a few other items. Sue is going to meet me there about eight. Tim wanted me to let you know, so you could text him, do you mind?" She asked sweetly.

"Of course, and I saw him this morning and he told me he gave the key to your neighbor in 3A. He might not be over there until nine or so and didn't want to hold you up. He had a meeting he could not get out of, but once that is finished he's yours for the afternoon. Most of the furniture is being delivered, so the work load should be light. The bedroom set is being delivered first at ten, then the sofa around noon. The TV stand and television won't be delivered until this afternoon between two and four." He stated absentmindedly as he went down his list.

"What TV? I'm getting a television?" She asked incredulously.

"Shoot... My bad. That was supposed to be a surprise. Tim and I decided that there was no way you could move in and not have some kind of television available. So we bought you one, and a blue ray player so you could rent movies if you like. Consider it a house warming gift from your two favorite spooks." He said grinning.

"Dean, you guys are gonna make me start crying again! You are both entirely too sweet to me, and I have no idea why someone like me has gotten the attention of two great guys like you. Thank you *so* much." She said trying her best not to tear up.

"Jesse, please don't refer to yourself like that, you are an amazingly kind, funny, generous woman and you deserve to be spoiled, pampered, and doted on. Just because Jerry was a first class jerk who made you feel less than special, does not mean that is how Tim or I, or the world sees you. The next fella who gets to spend time with you is going to be thanking his lucky stars, believe me. You are a catch Jesse Hardin, and don't you forget it." He stated earnestly.

They disconnected and she locked up the safe house and put Casey in the kennel crate. She grabbed her new keys and scampered down the walkway to her new car. She had her list with her and was ready to get started. She moved through the aisles in the store like a woman on a mission, soon her buggy was full of cleaning staples and a few snacks and drinks for later in the day. Then she realized she didn't have any glasses, so she swung through the 'home' department and picked a set of twelve glasses and a couple of double insulated tumblers for herself. She picked up some plastic heavy duty knives fork and spoons until she could decide on a silverware pattern and grabbed a buy one get one free deal of Chinet heavy duty paper plates. *Ok that should get me started.*

Jesse arrived at the apartment, her mind going a mile a minute with everything that needed to be done. She inhaled deeply closing her eyes then exhaled slowly. *You can do this Jess. It's gonna be great. Nice neighbors and Tim is around the corner.* The tap on her window startled her and she nearly screamed.

"Hi, you ok?" Carter asked waving at her. She smiled and opened her door.

"Yes. You scared me. Just mentally preparing for a new life, that's all." She said trying to smile.

"Can I help you carry anything up yet? I just pulled up myself, had to run a few errands this morning. Oh and I have your key, your friend stopped by last night and asked if he could leave it with me since he had to work this morning."

"Well I have a few bags to take up, and thanks for holding the key for me. I appreciate it." She slipped out of the car then walked back around to the tailgate and lifted it up. He started snickering and she turned to look at him.

"What?" She asked.

"Women. You guys crack me up. You will have six different kinds of soap to do one job. You have hand soap, body soap, facial soap, dishwashing liquid soap, foaming soap... Guys buy one and use if for everything. I just think it's funny how differently our minds work is all." He said trying not to make fun of her.

"Humph. Well…" She started to defend her choices when he interrupted.

"Hey it's no judgement. I have women in my life, it's the same with them too. I helped my little sister move last year and it took four boxes to pack up her bathroom. ONE bathroom." He said flashing a brilliantly sexy smile. *Ok… You are forgiven. Swoon.*

"Here is the envelope he dropped off last night, I think there are a couple of things in there, not just a key." He said handing her the manila envelope and grabbing several of the plastic bags out of the cargo area.

"Oh ok, thanks. Why don't I run up and unlock the door so we can carry all this in?" She offered,

"I'm right behind you."

She trotted up the steps opened the sealed envelope and located the key on a new key ring that said home sweet home. Then she found her diamond engagement ring, with a note in there from Tim. *So sorry I have been carrying the ring around in my pocket and forgot to give it to you. I picked it up with the flowers the other day. T~*

She walked into the apartment and laid the items on the granite breakfast bar counter top. Carter walked up behind her and asking where he should put the bags for now, and she told him to just set them down there next to the kitchen bar.

"What's this?" He asked picking her ring up off the counter and eyeing it.

"It's a trinket that used to have emotional and sentimental value, now it's just a painful reminder of broken promises and lies. I'm going to see if I can take it into a jeweler and trade it in then buy something else. Something that won't make me sad." She said not making eye contact then stooping down to rummage through the bags to find kitchen items.

He also stooped down and put his hand over hers to stop her rustling, she stopped then looked up at him, their eyes locking and he said to her, "Jesse, I know I don't know you that well, but whoever this man is, he is an idiot."

"Thank you for saying that Carter. I'm going to be ok, it's just that this is still really new for me. This time last week I was married and had no clue my husband was a lying conniving cheating creep." She said softly.

"Jesse? Where the heck are you honey?" Susie came hollering up the stairwell. Carter winked at Jesse and they both stood up almost bumping heads.

"Here Sue, we are in here." She answered back grinning.

"Hey I brought some food. Well…hello there handsome, I hope you are part of the moving team." She said flashing a flirty grin at Carter. Who immediately smiled back, amused by her entrance.

"Susie this is Carter, a new neighbor of mine who lives below me, and *please* behave!" Jesse chastised.

"Hi Carter, I'm just teasing, I'm a happily married person and big sister here to Jesse. I'm a harmless flirt, pay me no mind. Susie Maxwell." She said grinning and extending her hand for a shake.

"Nice to meet you Susie. I'm Carter James. You sound a lot like her other friend, Tim. He'll be here later, I can't wait until you two meet." He said laughing as he went back out the door to get more bags.

"Oh Jesse. You didn't tell me that you had a Mr. *Fabulous* living below you. Holy Cow girl he is super fine, seems nice, love his laugh and smile. This new apartment may be just what you are needing." She loudly whispered.

Susie set out the small breakfast buffet of sausage biscuits, bagels and cream cheese, and some cut up fruit for Jesse. She also bought some individual bottles of juice and set them on the counter top too. Carter bounded up the steps with the last of her bags from the store and set them near the other ones.

"Carter, please take a biscuit or a bagel. Help yourself." Susie offered.

"Thank you I am a sucker for a sausage biscuit, I think I will have one." He said smiling.

Jesse busied herself by putting the soaps away in the various bathrooms and in the shower, then placed the toilet paper in the holders storing the extra under the guest bathroom sink. She walked back into the main area and saw Sue and Carter just chatting up a storm. She laid her list down and took half of one of the bagels and spread some of the blue berry cream cheese on it, Sue remembered that was her favorite. Carter looked at her list and then remarked that the first delivery should be here any minute, and excused himself to go downstairs and wait for them.

The girls meanwhile were making quick time of wiping out the cabinets, and under the sink and continued to add things to Jesse's list they still needed for the apartment like a trash can. She bought liners, but forgot the can. The bedroom furniture arrived on time and the delivery crew along with Carter had it set up in under an hour. The mattress arrived at the same time, so the bedroom except for linens was complete. The furniture was a rich maple color with clean classic lines and simple pulls adorned the drawers. Susie set up in there and began hanging up all Jesse's clothes and arranging her drawers for her.

A short thirty minutes later the truck with the Cottage style over stuffed sofa arrived along with the white distressed television stand. Tim pulled in right behind the delivery truck, so he showed the movers where to bring it. Once they had it in place, Carter helped her remove all the protective plastic so the sofa could breathe. The television stand looked amazing, and not like a mere TV stand it was a nice piece of furniture. It was approximately five feet long, with a shallow shelf directly below that could hold various components like a DVD player or low profile receiver, with storage below for movies or books or Knick knacks.

The next delivery wasn't for a couple of hours, so they decided to recess for a bit, Carter was going back to check on some things in his apartment, Susie and Jesse were on a mission to find bed linens, dishes, possibly end tables, and a couple of lamps. Tim double checked on the bar stools and two out of the four arrived, so he was going to go over and pick those up for Jesse. They were to all meet back at the apartment by 2:45 to be there in time for the Electronics delivery, and Carter and Tim stated they could have that up and going within the hour. Cable had already be run into that unit, and was turned on the day before, so it was live.

Jesse and Sue headed over to the Home Store and proceeded to find a bedspread, sheets, extra pillows, throw pillows, and sleep pillows. Sue went to get another buggy, then together they located bathroom rugs, a mat for the kitchen floor, and a welcome mat for the door. Jesse came across an area rug for the living room that she absolutely fell in love with and decided to splurge on it, since it would match the sofa perfectly. They stopped by a thrift store that was nearby and found two matching end tables that were a grayish blue distressed shaker style that would match the sofa and tie in with the television stand. They also found in the very back of the store, a similar style coffee table and purchased it as well, but were going to have to come back for it since it wouldn't fit in the SUV with everything else they had purchased.

There was one last specialty store Jesse wanted to stop by and they had only about thirty minutes left before they needed to be back at the apartment. That is where she found her Fiesta ware dishes and serving pieces. Sue located two lamps that would be perfect in the living area and one she thought might work in the bedroom. Jesse liked the lamp but chose a different lamp shade. They pulled up back in front of the apartment with minutes to spare.

They started carrying their treasures up the stairs, garnering Carter's attention. He came back out of his place shaking his head and grinning from ear to ear.

"Man you ladies are something…I am stunned with everything you found in under three hours. This place is going to look amazing Jesse." He said.

"I am so excited, and I'm running on pure adrenaline I assure you." She said with a smile.

"Here let me help you guys get this stuff upstairs." He offered.

Tim pulled up about ten minutes later with two of the four bar stools, and the biggest grin on his face. He hollered up the stairs and asked for Carter to come downstairs to assist him. While picking up the stools he also came across a small apartment sized gas grill, so he bought one for Jesse's balcony area. While they were inside washing the new sheets, towels, and washing the new dishes, the guys brought up the stools and then set up the gas grill. The doorbell alerted them that the television must have arrived, however, it was Mrs. Smith from downstairs, with a homemade lemon pound cake.

"Hello dear, I'm Janie Smith and I live across from Carter over there. We are so excited you are here, and if you ever need anything, I have taped all of our contact information to the bottom of this plate. If you ever just want to sit and talk, or go for a walk, please tap on my door I would love to go with you." She stated sweetly.

"Oh Mrs. Smith how wonderfully kind of you! This smells delicious, and let me introduce you to my sister, Susie. This is a good friend Tim, he also lives here, back in unit 6."

"Lovely to make your acquaintances. I don't want to distract, I just wanted to drop this off so you and your friends could help you enjoy this. Take care, and welcome to your new home." She said giving her a quick hug before heading back to her apartment.

"Now that is going to make me cry, how sweet was she?" Jesse gushed. She set the cake over near the stove as they continued to dry the dishes and put them away. The next tap at the door was the television delivery team. Once it was in the apartment and delivery paperwork signed off on, Tim and Carter immediately went to work, Carter had brought his tools from his place up in anticipation. The two of them worked together like they had been a team their whole life. Neither one really having to speak to the other to get the job done.

"That's crazy, look at the two of you go? Man what a team?" Jesse remarked.

"It's a man thing. Men instinctively know all things TV and movies. I'm pretty sure it's genetic." Carter said with a smile.

Sue and Jesse had just finished the dishes when they heard the flat panel TV come to life. Tim located the sports channel then sat on the sofa acting like he was going to settle in for the night, so Carter took the remote from him and located the romance channel for her, then winked as he handed her the remote. Tim busted out laughing. She sat on one of the stools just beaming as she looked around at her new little home. Just a few days ago she was distraught thinking that she did not own a single stick of furniture, now she had a bedroom full of furniture including a king size bed, and a beautiful comfortable sofa and end tables with matching lamps that softly lit the space. *If only Dean could see this, he would be so pleased.*

Carter checked his watch, then announced that if everyone was game, that he had taken the liberty of making hamburgers to grill out, since they all had been working all day, and hadn't eaten since Susie so graciously brought breakfast. They all looked at each other and agreed they were starving. Jesse had drinks that she could contribute, and the paper products. Carter indicated that he had the rest of the fixings along with chips that they would just keep it simple. He excused himself to go and fire up the grill, so that they could eat and finish up. Tim showed Jesse the grill and she teared up at his thoughtfulness and gave him a big hug.

Sue walked out onto the balcony and also gave Tim a hug and thanked him for being such a great friend to her baby sister. Jesse heard the dryer buzz and left to pull the sheets out and make the bed. Sue and Tim stayed on the balcony chatting and laughing. Jesse was thrilled they were getting along so well, it was nice to see two of her favorite people laughing and talking. It took her a minute to get ahold of the fitted sheet for the king size bed and figure out how to make the bed all by herself. It was tempting to call Sue in to help, but realized she could not call her sister over each time she needed to change the sheets.

Finally it was secure, and she moved on to the top sheet then the pillow cases then she placed the Laura Ashley cotton quilt in a soft pink over the bed along with the matching pillow shams and the whimsical throw pillows with bright bursts of color to finish it off. She stood back in the door frame, her chest swelling with pride at how wonderful and inviting *her* bedroom looked. It would indeed become the sanctuary that she envisioned.

"Jesse?" Dean asked softly.

"Hi, oh Dean, I really wish you were here. I just finished making the bed. My very own bed. It's so beautiful." She gushed.

"Where is your camera pin? Put it on and give me a tour." He requested.

"Yes! Of course." She paused for a moment to retrieve the pin and clipped it into place. "Ok this is my new bedroom. I think it looks serene. Don't you?" She anxiously asked awaiting his approval.

"It looks really nice Jess. The furniture looks great, and seems to fit the room well, can you move around in there?"

"Yes there is plenty of room. I think I am really going to be ok here, and you guys were too sweet to get me a television and blue ray player. Tim and Carter were able to get it put together in a flash, it was amazing. Must be a guy thing? Then again Carter is in I.T. so it's kind of up his alley. I could have made due until I could have afforded one, but it will be so nice to come home now and have a distraction. Thank you again."

"Jesse it was our pleasure. Tim told me he bought you a grill. He is so kind hearted and he loves surprising you." Dean said sincerely.

"He is so sweet. He and Sue are on the balcony laughing up a storm. I shudder to think of what or *who* they are talking about." She said laughing.

"What are your plans for tonight?"

"Oh, um, Carter invited everyone over to his place for an early dinner since we all skipped lunch. He's grilling out hamburgers, and actually I am starving. That's nice of him isn't it? Also Mrs. Smith downstairs made a homemade lemon pound cake that I am dying to try."

"Well I will let you go, eat a piece of cake for me that is one of my favorites. My mom makes a mean pound cake. Have fun Jess. We'll talk later."

Tim announced that Carter had waved them down to come and eat, so she grabbed the sodas and the bag with the paper products, and Sue grabbed the cake. Carter's apartment was similar to hers when you first walk in, except he had a larger black leather L shaped sectional with a matching leather ottoman. In his dining area he had a large dining room table with a bench seat on one side and several chairs on the other side. He had a black and white abstract piece of art hanging above the couch and the apartment appeared to be tidy. He was very welcoming and dinner was laid out well and very tasty. After they had almost finished eating, Jesse saw that there were several burgers left over, so she asked if she might have an extra burger to which he said of course.

They watched as she made a plate, with chips and a pickle spear, then she wrapped it in clear wrap and walked out the door. Tim and Sue continued eating, but Carter walked to the door to see where she was going, his eyes followed her upstairs to her neighbor's door. She knocked lightly and much to Carter's amazement the door opened.

"Hello my name is Jesse and I am moving in next door, you may have heard us banging around in there today? I just wanted to introduce myself and say hello, we grilled out burgers and had an extra so I thought I would bring it up to share with you." She stated handing the plate over.

"Hi, my name is Andrew. Andy. It is nice to meet you, Thank you very much for the food..." He stated thankfully, now looking self-conscience about his sloppy *I just rolled out of bed* appearance.

"Ok, well, I'm sure I will see you around. Have a good night." She said smiling then turned to head back downstairs.

"Well that was mighty nice of you to include Andy, I'm sure he appreciated that plate. I guess I should have thought of that." Carter said as she ducked under his arm to enter back into the apartment.

"Well this way I had an excuse to meet him and he got a home cooked meal." She said nonchalantly. Tim was the first to excuse himself, he claimed he had an early morning appointment coming up and needed to prep some things and so he needed to take off. Jesse walked him out the door to his car, she stood on the stoop talking to him for a couple of minutes then gave him a great big hug and a kiss on the cheek. She waved as he pulled away.

Susie had started helping Carter put things away, when Jesse came back in to see what she could do to assist. "Carter, you have been so gracious to not only help with moving and setting my apartment up, but then you fixed dinner too? I definitely owe you a nice home cooked meal one night once I get completely settled in, ok?" Jesse said searching his eyes.

"You're on." Carter replied with a smile. Between the three of them his kitchen was back in tip top shape in no time. They thanked him once again, then headed upstairs to get their pocketbooks, Sue needed to head home, and Jesse had to get back out to the safe house and get the last few items she had there and pick up Casey.

Jesse locked up the apartment then made her way to her car, she cranked it up and rolled back the sunroof. She took her time driving back to the safe house her mind lost in thought. It was going to be bitter sweet coming back to the safe house, and the beach to gather her things and leave for good. It truly was the break and rest that she needed to gather her thoughts and collect her emotions. The sea to her represented God's enormous power and sovereignty over this world and her life. The sea had the power to take away and destroy, and also had the ability to soothe and heal. This visit was one fraught with turmoil, but this place brought about soothing and restoration to her mind and emotions. Above all she was so very grateful to have had the opportunity to stay here and recover.

She pulled up and punched in her code then brought Casey out for a walk. Jesse then made one last sweep through the house to collect any of her items she was not able to get this morning. Once they were loaded in the car, she cleaned out the refrigerator and started the dishwasher. She also stripped the bed of linens and put them in the washing machine, and removed any trash and put it in the can outside. The flowers that have been sent to her were still so lovely, so carefully she also put those into the car to take back to the apartment. She had really enjoyed them this week. Then she just sat there in the middle of the floor with her eyes closed and prayed. Prayed for all the new people she had met this week, for the staff at Reed's and for her sister.

Dean just happened to pass the monitor for the beach house and she caught his eye, he had forgotten he had the cameras cued up. He sat down for a moment and just watched her as she sat there praying. A warm rush washed over him, and he put his head in his hands and said a prayer or two of his own. Finally she scooped up Casey, locked up the safe house and got back in her car. She drove in the direction of her new life, with the breeze blowing her hair and a smile on her face. *I'm ready Lord. For whatever you bring me.*

CHAPTER 13

BACK TO NORMAL

J esse awoke early Thursday morning having slept fairly well in yet another new setting in the course of a week's time. She threw on some shorts to take Casey outside to check out the new grassy area. It was nice and quiet back there, with the exception of some light traffic sounds from the highway muffled through the trees. From back here she could actually see Tim's building and they were actually much closer than she realized. She felt her stomach rumbling since they had eaten such an early supper the night before, so she jumped in the shower and then headed over to the I-hop for some pancakes. She still needed to buy some serious groceries and began to devise a list.

After breakfast she went back to the thrift store to pick up the coffee table they had purchased yesterday. It fit nicely in the back of her car. Then she drove over to a strip mall that had a local family owned jewelry store. Mr. Timms the owner was there, along with his son getting set up for the day. She walked in and meandered around, then finally got up the nerve to ask if they took trade in's. Mr. Timms Sr. took the lead and asked to see what she had to trade. She pulled out the ¼ carat diamond engagement ring, along with the 4mm gold band and set them before him.

He took his time eyeing the small diamond engagement ring, and gold tested the band. Then he looked at her and asked why she wanted to turn it in, making sure in a subtle way that these items weren't stolen. After she gave her brief but blunt explanation, he asked her what did she have in mind, did she want cash for the items or to purchase something else or to perhaps have the diamond reset in another setting?

She looked around and found a lovely white gold band with seven small sapphires deep set running through the middle of the band with accent diamonds following the length of the sapphires on either side. It was a little more expense than what she was turning in by about fifty dollars, and the owner filled with compassion, decided he would do an even swap for it. He took the new ring and buffed it then placed it on her right hand, third finger.

"It looks lovely my dear. I hope it brings you happiness and better memories." He stated sweetly.

"Thank you so much Mr. Timms. I think it will. I've never really had a nice piece of jewelry like this, so I will certainly cherish it. Have a blessed day." She said walking out of the store with her head held high.

Jesse then went to the grocery store to pick up some staples for the new apartment and decide on her meals for the week. She came to the conclusion long ago that if you plan your meals that you tend to spend less, and then she also remembered she needed to get her coupons going again. She decided to just get enough food for the weekend and that she would regroup back at work on Monday. She called Reed while she was thinking about it and thanked him for the week off, and assured him she was fine to go back to work on Monday. He stated that everyone missed her but overall they had a good week, he also gave her permission to hire another kitchen assistant to help Johnny since business has increased so much. He didn't realize how slammed they were back there trying to get orders out. This was very welcomed news and she was excited to start interviewing immediately.

She headed home to put the groceries away, and let Casey out. Once the items were stored, she decided they would go for a walk to check out their new surroundings. She traded her sandals for tennis shoes, hooked up the leash and they were out the door. First they walked down to where building six was located, then turned came back up the slight incline back to building one, then beyond to the main road which led out to one of the main veins that led into the downtown area. They walked for several blocks, then turned back around to head home. She loved that the road to the apartment was secluded and honestly unless you were looking for it you would drive right past it.

As they turned the curve Casey started barking and pulling on the leash, when Jesse looked over to see what she had her eye on, she saw Carter sitting outside on his patio area. He looked up from his project and waved. She slowly cut through the grass to where he was sitting.

"Hi there. Whatcha doing out here?" she inquired looking at the hardware assembled on the table.

"Oh just cleaning my guns. I have a 9 mil. and Sig Sauer P229. I've been to the range lately so I need to get these cleaned up. I should have done it a week ago." He said focused on ramming the cleaning cloth through the barrel.

"I didn't realize you had guns." She said kind of nervously.

"Don't know a military guy active or inactive that doesn't have at least one. I have my conceal carry permit. Since you are single you ought to look into getting your conceal carry permit. If you wanted to pursue it, I could help you." He offered.

"Thank you for the offer, let me think about it." She said watching intently as he worked to put the 9mil back together without missing a beat.

"We could go to the range and I could teach you to shoot, whether you get your permit or not. At least you would know the proper way to handle a gun, it's not like it looks on the television. That's for sure." He said with a sly grin.

"Um sure, that would be cool. I'd much rather go with someone who knows what they are doing, and has experience. Well… we are coming back from a long walk so I need to get her inside and water her. Have a good rest of your day." She said smiling sweetly.

"Hey wait!" He said calling after her.

"Yes?"

"What's on your hand? Come here lady, and let me see that thing." He said with a smile.

"Oh, yeah. Do you like it? I went today to a local jeweler and turned in my wedding set and bought this ring. I thought it was pretty, something I could dress up or down and wear it every day. Ya know?" She said beaming extending her hand to show him the sapphire and diamond band.

"Very nice, I like it. I think it suits you. It caught my eye as you were walking away, so I wanted to see it up close." He said with a smile.

"Why thank you. Talk to you later." She said waving goodbye.

Jesse climbed back up the stairs and then opened up the apartment. She found a note slid under her door, and waited until she was inside with the door shut before stooping to pick it up. It was a basic thank you card type envelope, and once she opened it was a very simple but sweet note. *Thank you so much for dinner last night, that was very kind of you to include me. I hope you like your apartment. Andy.*

She took that note and dated it then placed it in her night stand near her bed. *Bless his heart. Must try and remember him more often. Maybe I can bring him dinner home one night?* She kicked her shoes off then sat on her new sofa, leaning back and taking in the new smell. Reaching for the remote she turned on the romance channel to see what was on, thankfully one show was almost over before a new one she hadn't seen was on.

It was kind of surreal sitting in her own new space, with her own television and having control of the remote. No one to storm in and demand to watch his shows regardless of what you were in the middle of, no one to taunt you about what you were watching, and no one to have to make dinner for when she wasn't hungry. The flowers dotted throughout the apartment on the end tables and in the kitchen reminded her of people's care and affection towards her and it lifted her spirits. Casey was relegated to her doggie bed at the foot of the sofa since she was not allowed on the new sofa.

Jesse enjoyed staying in and popping popcorn and watching her new television. Her mom called to check on her, and so did Susie. Susie had spilled the beans to mom, which Jesse didn't have the courage to do just yet, but was going to, and again her parents took it remarkably well. They lived in Florida now along the panhandle and enjoyed the waters of the Gulf of Mexico. She hoped to be able to go down later in the year hopefully before hurricane season. Her father took a position down there a few years ago, and didn't worry about leaving the girls since they both had responsible husbands to take care of them. They were planning to come back up for Peter's wedding in July, so she would definitely get to see them then.

Dean rang her cell phone about 9:30 p.m. and it startled her. "Hi Dean, is everything ok?"

"Yes, just checking on you since I haven't heard from you all day. Did you have a good day?" He asked sounding tired.

"It was productive. You sound really tired, are you ok?" She inquired concerned.

"Yeah, just a few late nights in a row and some 4 a.m. starts are catching up to me. I'll be fine." He assured her.

"I took my wedding set today and turned it in on a beautiful new sapphire band. I'm wearing it on my right hand. And I picked up my coffee table from the thrift store, which reminds me I need to see if one of the neighbors or Tim can help me carry it up. It's solid wood so it's kind of heavy. Oh anyway, sorry I got distracted. Are you sure you are ok, have you eaten? Getting plenty of fluids?" She quizzed.

"Yes ma'am, I promise. Listen I just wanted to hear your voice before I hit the hay tonight. Sleep well Jess."

"You take care Dean. Sweet dreams." She replied.

She grabbed her lap-desk and some thank you notes she had picked up at the home store, and began to write thank you notes to everyone who helped make this new life she was living possible. She started with Ninja, then Tim, Wex, Carter, Mrs. Smith, her sister and last but not least Dean. Dean and Tim's were front to back long and once she had finished them, she put them in the same manila envelope Tim had put her keys in, then she hand delivered Mrs. Smith's and Carter's by dropping them in their mail slots. She decided to mail Wex and Sue's since it's always exciting to get real mail instead of bills all the time.

She decided to close the books on this day and go to bed early. Hard to believe that tomorrow was Friday, then the weekend would be here and then back to work on Monday. She took Casey out one last time noticing a dim light emanating from Carter's bedroom window. She felt safer knowing he was downstairs. Even though she really didn't know him that well, it still made her feel like in a pinch he could handle anything that came through those doors.

Just as she was dozing off she got a text from Tim. *Feels weird not to have seen or spoken to you today. Everything cool? T~*

I agree, hope your day went well. Everything here is good, going to bed early, but thanks for checking in. Sleep well. ~ Jess

The weekend went smoothly and she was starting to really get into a good routine, she continued walking and resting, even managed to experiment in the kitchen with a few new Food Network recipes. If she was going to be entertaining at all or having Carter over for dinner she wanted to be on her game. She even managed to use the grill on the patio which turns out to be a pretty sweet set up. She woke up Monday morning with a renewed outlook and was up, dressed, ear piece in and broach in place in record time. She wanted to get to Reed's early and see what kind of condition the store was in since she had been away.

She and Johnny arrived within seconds of each other, and he gave her a big ole bear hug after congratulating her on the new vehicle. Dean was tapped in and happy to have her back to work and was ready for them to resume their daily schedule. Libby and Hannah both arrived squealing about her new car and demanded to go for a ride after work, to which she readily agreed. It was Hannah who noticed her new jewelry, and when she had a moment took Jesse off to the side to inquire as to what was going on. Jesse felt it best to go ahead and hold a quick staff meeting to discuss recent events. She explained that she was recently single, had a new apartment, and of course a new vehicle but that she was good, it was all going to be fine. She also let them know that Reed had approved some help in the back for Johnny who nearly fainted when he heard the good news.

Customers were thrilled to see her back and she thanked the ones who had sent cards expressing her deep appreciation for their thoughtfulness. It was around 11:45 when a patron came up to the counter, his presence and demeanor completely unnerved Jesse. She had just come back up front to bring a Take Out order to the register and there he stood. The man from the Chinese Bistro, the one with the gun. Trying not to panic at the mere sight of him in her store, she reached out to Dean.

"Boy, we need to make sure we get a *Report* for tomorrow's weather." She said trying to act nonchalant.

"Charge 25? You have a report?" Dean asked confused.

"Yes sir, Here look here, uh here's a menu if you need one." She stated trying to talk in code, handing the man at the counter a menu, hoping Dean would catch on. Dean finally caught a glimpse of the man at the counter then understood her fear.

"Jess, he doesn't know who you are, he is only wanting a sandwich. Calm down, way down, ok? You've got this, he's hungry and he's buying lunch. That's all that is going on here. Ok?" He said in his calm tone.

"If you have any questions about anything on the menu, I'll be happy to answer them." She said trying her best to steady her voice and look normal.

"Ok." The stranger muttered.

When he finally spoke up, she nearly jumped out of her skin. "Ok, I need a special sandwich, and then I'll have a number two on I-Talian." He stated in an odd accent. Russian? German? She wasn't sure, all she knew was that he was *not* a South Carolina native.

"Ok, what is your special sandwich?" She said taking notes, while listening to Dean reassure her she was doing fine.

"Ok, I need whole wheat breads toasted, with the spicy mustard, the Swiss cheese, a layer of ham, then turkey, then pepperoni, then the provolone cheese. Got that? Has to be in *THAT* order." He stated emphatically. She imagined him shooting up the joint if she mixed up the cheeses. *Chill Jesse, come on now.*

"No problem, I will make it myself. Now on the bread does that need to be a crisp toast or a light toasting?" She asked because to some people this made a difference especially someone who had to have a sandwich layered that specifically.

"Breads. Both pieces toasted. Do medium." He stated firmly, then attempted a smile.

Breads?? Of course toasting *both* pieces was on her agenda, but if it made him feel better to be that specific, then O-kay…who toasts only one piece of bread on a sandwich? How odd she thought, but then killers for hire were an odd bunch and who knew what other eccentricities they had?

"Yes of course. Please have a seat and I'll be right back with your order." She said managing a smile. She sped off to the back and was panting as she laid the order down on the work station sandwich bar. Johnny went to take the order and she nearly tackled him explaining that she had to fill this one personally. He just shrugged and let her do it and moved on to the next order.

"Jesse, you are fine. I told you, he is just hungry. He has no idea who you are, do you understand? Please relax and treat him like anyone else, this could be a great break, but only do what you are comfortable with and please *breathe*." He encouraged.

She took great pains to make sure the sandwiches were perfect and completely to his specification. She wrapped them in the white paper and then bagged them.

She made eye contact with the stranger and nodded that it was ready. He stood up and walked back over to the counter and pulled out his wallet.

"Will this be a combo with chips and a drink?" She asked sweetly.

"No. No combo. No. Just sandwich." He stated in his somewhat limited command of the English language.

"So tell me… where are you from? I hear an accent and I know you are not from around these parts." She stated pouring on the southern charm as she ran up his purchase.

"I am, um from the Ukraine. Do you know this place?" He asked again attempting a smile back at her.

"Well I have certainly heard of it, so you are here on business here in the park? We get a lot of international folks here during the summer season." She stated trying to keep him talking.

"Business, yes. Summer is hot here, too much sand." He stated off handedly. "Here, keep change." He said handing her a five and a ten dollar bill.

"Oh thank you so much, please enjoy your stay. Bye now." She said giving a slight wave as he walked out.

Once he was down the street she flew back to her office and shut the door. Johnny just shook his head and kept making sandwiches.

"Dean, did you get all that?" She whispered loudly. Nothing…. "Hello?? Are you there?"

"Charge 25, I have the information you provided, good job. Please let me know if there is any more information you need to turn in today. Dean out." He stated in a formal tone.

Humph. Well *that* was anticlimactic she thought. She went back out into the fray of the front and helped the girls get all the customers taken care of and lunches served. Once the lunch rush was over, she went back to the office to prepare for the next day's order and plan out for the next week's menu. She looked down at her phone and saw she had missed a text from Dean.

Had company could not really chat but you did one heck of a job, off to a rocky start but stellar finish. That's my girl. –Dean

Thanks, was beginning to think you had been kidnapped by aliens. Totally get it. TTYL ~Jesse

Feels that way some days, sorry for the confusion. ~ Dean

Well that explained a lot, she had to remember that the protocol was to be formal, what she and Dean had been doing although effective, was really bending the rules. She finished up the menu, the bread and deli order for the upcoming week and called it in, then prepared the ad for the local paper for the new position.

She came out of the office and the girls had already started cleaning the front, and tallying up the till for the day. The rest of the afternoon was slow, and only one or two stragglers came in, one for a drink and one for a Meatball sub to go. Since it was so slow Jesse let Hannah and Libby go home early promising a ride later in the week, and Johnny was finishing cleaning the meat slicer then he would be leaving too. The deposit was finished, and although today's head count was lower, the total sales was right on up there. Good solid day.

"Bye Jesse, see you in the morning." Johnny called as he walked out the door.

She walked back out front and locked the doors again and went ahead and wrote up the chalk board with tomorrow's specialty sandwich the Chicken Club Panini. As she walked back through the kitchen into the office to retrieve her purse and deposit, she heard a noise outside like someone was banging the trash cans around. She thought maybe Johnny had forgotten something then realized it was not him. She stepped outside and looked around the building and noticed that the lids on the cans were askew. The only people she saw anywhere remotely close were a couple of unkempt looking teens on skateboards. A teenage boy who had shoulder length dingy brown hair, and the girl, whose hair was a mix of synthetic reds and purple. Even from the distance Jesse could see their eyes looked hollow and untrusting.

Her heart went out to them, she had a hunch they were looking for food. The realization of this broke her heart, so she went back inside, found a box then made two basic sandwiches with turkey and ham threw in a couple bags of chips and two bottled waters. Then she wrote a note to put into the box.

I can't do this every day, but when I can I will leave food in this box for you. Please go home to your families, or seek assistance. God Bless you. Be well.

She set the box on top of the trash cans, then locked up the store and walked over to the bank to make her deposit. Once that was in and credited to Reed's she left the bank and sat out on the short wall near the small garden area of the courtyard. The sun was ebbing back and the light breeze that filtered through the courtyard was a welcoming feeling that caused her to close her eyes and just let it flutter over her.

Jesse got up from her perch in the park then walked over to the CIA office and made her way to the second floor. That is where she dropped off the envelope for Dean that had the thank you notes in it for Tim and Ninja and him. Ms. Lane manning the front desk was stoic as ever and merely nodded an affirmation that these would get to Dean. Jesse just smiled and said "Have a blessed day." Then proceeded back to the elevator to head home.

CHAPTER 14

WAVES

J esse arrived home, took Casey out and then checked her mail. Still nothing of substance yet, since the forwarding address was still new, mainly just advertisements. Mrs. Smith happened to arrive home just as Jesse closed the mailbox.

"Oh hi dear, thank you for my sweet note. How are things in the new apartment? Getting all settled?" She asked, checking her mailbox now.

"Oh yes ma'am. I love it. Getting used to all the new sounds that a home has, ya know?" Jesse stated with a smile.

"Oh indeed I do. We have lived here about five years now, and we love it. When Mr. Smith retires we may move to Charleston. We have a son there and our grandchildren, well most of them live in the Summerville area. But for now I am completely content to be here." She said patting Jesse's arm then reaching to pet Casey who was dancing a jig at her feet.

They both smiled then turned to go their separate ways. Jesse began preparing Shish Kabobs to put on the grill. She layered the yellow bell pepper, red onion, steak, mushroom, shrimp and more veggies onto the metal skewers. Then she slathered it in an Italian dressing type marinade. Then she turned on the grill, came back and salt and peppered the kabobs and then prepared to put them on the grill. The smell was heavenly, and she closed the lid on the grill to let the four kabobs cook on low. Once she was back inside she turned on the instant Yellow rice, which she knew was a cheat, but she was in a hurry tonight, and the rice was really an afterthought. Once that was simmering in the pot, she took it off the heat to let it finish.

She carried a plate back out to the grill, with Casey weaving in between her legs as she walked. She lifted the lid on the grill and the steam billowed up towards her face, she took her pot holder and began picking up the skewers laying them on the plate. She was balancing the plate on her arm as she attempted to turn off the grill and shut the lid, then Casey jumped up on her knocking her off balance sending a Shish Kabob over the railing.

"Oh- my- gosh! Casey! Really?" She said peeking over to see where it landed. She rushed back inside setting the plate on the counter, then threw open the door to head downstairs to retrieve her skewer, and there stood Carter.

"Strange dinner invitation. I thought I was being attacked by a lawn dart with food attached." He stated with a smirk on his handsome face.

"Oh heavens. Are you ok? It didn't stab you did it?" Looking at his fantastically tanned biceps.

"No. It landed on end amazingly about two inches from my arm. Thank goodness I have cat like reflexes." He said grinning at her.

"Well, please come inside, and here I will take that... I can't believe Casey did this, she never jumps up on me, so I never saw it coming. When she hit me, it threw me off balance and the skewer rolled right off. I am lucky I didn't lose the whole plate." She said exasperated.

"Uh, I think *I'm* lucky you didn't lose the whole plate." He said now laughing at her expense.

"Ha-ha. Can I get you something to drink to take your mind off your near death experience?"

"Do you have any lemonade? If not I'll just have some water." He stated sitting at the bar watching her bustle around.

"Have you eaten supper yet? I have plenty, I made four and I can only eat one. Plus I have some rice, you are welcome to stay." She said sweetly.

"If you are sure, that would be great. I haven't eaten yet."

She fixed him a glass of lemonade, then scooped some yellow rice onto a plate and laid a skewer over the rice. Then handed him the plate and set a knife and fork on the countertop for him. Then she plated up her dinner and sat down next to him. She asked if he minded if she offered up grace, and he smiled and said sure.

Carter took the first bite and was pleasantly satisfied then complimented her on the deliciousness of the meal. They chatted all through dinner discussing their days, and what the upcoming week was going to look like. Once they finished eating, Jesse offered him some raspberry sorbet for dessert. They took that over to the sofa and finished their conversation. Carter didn't want to overstay his welcome since it was rather impromptu, so he started cleaning his dishes and rinsing them in the sink.

"Oh hey, I've got this, seriously. You are my guest; and for the record *this* doesn't count as my 'repayment for your kindness' meal. I am still planning that, ok?" She said smiling setting her plate in the sink along with her dessert bowl.

"Oh that reminds me, that was a very nice note you wrote me, and you are very welcome. I really didn't do that much."

"You are welcome, and yes you *did*. It made me feel very welcome and comfortable here. I was very nervous, first time on my own and all." She said softly.

"Hey I think we need to come up with some kind of signal or something if you are going to be grilling out in the future." He said seriously.

"What?" She stated, her eyes opening wide.

"You know, so I can get my gear and hard hat on, in case you decided to fling more food over the balcony." He said grinning. He leaned in and gave her a quick kiss on the cheek, then smiled as he headed down the stair case.

She had one skewer left over and about a serving of rice left so she made a plate and took it next door to Andy.

"Hi Jesse. Wow, thanks. That is so nice of you." He said sheepishly.

"Well I had some leftover tonight, and I have plans tomorrow night, so I wanted to share. Have you had a good day so far?" She asked sweetly.

"Yeah, I guess working on a project that is keeping me up at night, but overall I can't complain. I bet you think all I ever do is eat?" He said self-consciously.

"Heavens no! I just know men tend to not cook for just one, and well, it's my nature to feed people, I work in a restaurant." She said laughing.

"Hey listen I know you have a dog, and if you ever need help walking her or anything I will be happy to walk her for you." He offered.

"How sweet of you to offer, I may take you up on that. She loves to walk. Well you enjoy." She said waving goodnight.

Jesse locked her door then proceeded to clean the kitchen. Once that was all finished she took Casey out for one last potty break before she headed off to bed. Her phone started buzzing, and it was Dean.

Got your very sweet note, and once again you are so welcome. I think you almost made Ninja cry. Almost. Tim took his and I'm sure will read it within the week. Ha-ha. ~Dean

I am in a good place emotionally and physically, and it's all due to you and your wonderful friends. Sleep tight. ~Jess

Her dreams were pleasant and filled with images of her handsome downstairs neighbor. She awoke fresh and wide awake and rushed through her morning routine. Just as she was walking out the door, she received a call from Susie. She and Matt wanted to have Jesse over for supper tonight and insisted that she come. Jesse assured her she would be there and would bring a dessert.

The crew was in early and bustling this morning, it was *Ruben day* which meant they were going to be slammed, so everyone was prepping and gearing up for it. Much to their surprise Reed showed up about 10:30 to help out and boy was he a sight for sore eyes. He hugged Jesse, and they got busy, it was just like old times, working together the team handled the lined up out the door crowds that lasted until after 2:00 p.m. Reed helped Johnny clean up in the kitchen while Jesse and Hannah cleaned the front, Libby started tallying the register, to get a head start on the deposit. They had a couple of orders after 2:45 but for the most part the store was quiet.

Reed took that opportunity to talk to Jesse in private about the future of Reed's. He was wanting to retire and sell the store, but did not want to do so and displace all of the staff who had been so loyal. He wanted to give Jesse the opportunity to buy him out first, before he considered putting it on the market. She was honored that he thought of her, and there was a part of her that wanted to take on that challenge, but there was a part of her that hesitated. He stated that he would not be putting it up for sale until late November so there was time, but if this was not an opportunity she wanted to pursue, to please let him know sooner.

They hugged and he went out to say goodbye to the staff and head home. Jesse said she would take the main deposit over now, and wanted Libby to walk with her, they had a huge day today and she was nervous carrying that much money by herself. After they dropped off the deposit, Libby went back to the café and Jesse stated she had to run a quick errand.

"Dean? Report." She stated softly.

"Charge 25 go ahead." He stated somewhat distracted.

"Nothing really to report, busy day, nothing out of the ordinary, and no new sightings of our mobster friend." She stated levelly.

"Ok, thanks for the report, have a good afternoon and be safe." He stated as a matter of routine.

"Um, ok... bye." Jesse said, sounding dejected.

Jesse knew he must be under scrutiny by his boss, and so she had to be understanding. It was just throwing off her balance, and she felt like their rhythm was off. She wondered if he felt the same way. She returned to the café then told the rest of the staff they could leave that they were closing in minutes and didn't expect a rush.

She locked up and then made her way to her car, she decided to go to Stefani's Bakery for tonight's dessert. Something Chocolatey would be nice. Sue tended to cook Italian when she had company, like Lasagna or stuffed shells, with a salad and bread which was fine with Jesse. She tended not to cook those items because it made so much that she would have left overs for a week, but now that she had Andy and Carter she may have to reconsider.

She entered the bakery and her sense were assaulted with all kinds of smells. At the door they had a Rum pound cake sampler tray along with a fruit sponge cake concoction. However, behind the tall carousel she spotted it, a yellow cake with fancy chocolate frosting with white and dark chocolate shavings adorning the top. *Yep. That's the one.*

Jesse ran home to let Casey out before she headed over to Susie's house. While she was walking up and down the side walk, a car whipped in behind her car parking all caddywompas. She was startled until she saw Tim's lanky body unfold out of the sports car. He rushed over all smiles and lifted her up giving her a giant hug.

"Hey sis! So are you and the super dog patrolling the neighborhood?" He said setting her back on solid ground.

"Hey, I have missed you buddy. Where have you been and are you ok?"

"Oh yeah, I'm fine. Dean is not in a good place but he will be fine. Hey thanks for the super sweet note. You know I love ya girl. I'm here if you need me." He said kissing her on the cheek.

"I know, same here. I am worried about Dean. Are you sure he is ok?" She said concern shrouding her delicate features.

"Yeah, Dean's a fighter and not one to give up easily. That's why he's the brain of the operations. Mr. Planner. He's a fixer, and he is really good at what he does. It's not just the beta program that he's working on, that's in addition to his regular job. So he's just under the gun right now, he will get his bearings and level back out, he is just in uber focus mode right now." Tim said reassuringly.

"Ok, so it's not me then, I haven't gotten him in trouble then?"

"Nah, that's all good. He is just juggling a lot right now. Give him some time." Tim stated as he hugged her then kissed her on the top of the head.

"Will do, and I am so happy you stopped by, I am on my way to Sue's for dinner." She said looking up at him.

"Cool tell the old gal I said hello. Where does she live?"

"They live on the other side of town, you would drive out like you are heading towards Wex's place and when you see the big Park Place Villas sign, turn right there and it's in a neighborhood down that road on the right. Willow Run subdivision, fourth house on the right, in the cul-de-sac."

"Ok yeah, I know right where that is, I looked at a house in that area once, and drove all through there. I remember seeing that neighborhood. They were still building in there when I was looking. Well ya'll have fun." He said patting Casey on the head and then trotting off to his car. She stood there and waved until she could no longer see him. Carter stood at his window watching them, so he decided to walk out to his car to get a CD and say hello to her.

"Hi Carter." She said smiling and waving.

"Who was that in the sports car? Was that Tim?"

"Oh yeah, I never know what he is going to pull up in, he's a car nut." She said walking up closer to him.

"So are you guys an item?" He asked leaning against his car.

"Who me and Tim? Lord no." She said laughing and waving him off.

"No? You guys just seem really close. So you don't have feelings for him?" He asked staring at her intently.

"Well sure I have feelings for him, he is fantastic. He is the big brother I always longed for and never had. I would do anything for him, and I think he would for me, he is a great friend. But I don't have *those* kind of feelings for him, not like romantic feelings." She stated earnestly.

"So you don't find him attractive?" He said still prodding.

"Well heck yeah, I mean he is extremely good looking, but again, I don't look at him and think hubba- hubba, it's more like *awe isn't he precious*. Totally different. Like when he looks at me or touches me, I don't have those pit of your stomach quivers like I do when you...I mean like other people, you know make me feel, um well...?" She stammered looking down realizing what she just said. He caught what she said too and inwardly smiled but did not want to embarrass her further so he did not let on.

"Oh ok, well I was just curious. I was thinking maybe we could go out some time, but I did not want to tread on another man's territory. Especially someone as big as he is and who lives in the same complex." He said tentatively.

"Well there are no toes to step on here. Tim is like a best friend and big brother all rolled up into one. Now he and my sister are another story, if she were single, I think he would be all over her. But me, I am definitely not his type." She said smiling.

"Hey what's in the back of your car?"

"Oh yeah, I totally forgot about it. It's my coffee table I purchased the other day, but it's too heavy for me to carry up the stairs. I meant to ask Tim if he could carry it up for me, and forgot."

"Well unlock your tailgate and I'll carry it up for you. I don't mind."

"Really? Thanks Carter." She stated, unlocking it with the key fob. He followed her up the stairs and placed it in front of the sofa.

"This looks really nice, your place is really coming together nicely. I like your taste in furniture." He said smiling.

"Thanks, I am kind of coming into my own. It's a little terrifying, but nice at the same time." She said with a smile.

"Well I guess I'll let you go…" He said hoping she would invite him to stay.

"Ok, Thanks again for carrying that up for me. I have to scoot off to Sue's house now, she is fixing supper for me, and I have the dessert in the car. It's a fabulous chocolate covered yellow cake. I'll bring you a piece back if we have any left." She said with a smile.

"Sounds good, have fun." He said with a smile.

She put Casey away then walked down the stairs with him waving as she got into her car. She put the sun roof back and proceeded in the direction of Susie's house. Jesse was missing Dean and just wanted to say hello so she called in, "Report" and he answered.

"Jesse? Go ahead."

"Hi Dean. Just wanted to say hello, Tim stopped by and told me how very busy you are, and well I just wanted to say I will try to keep things professional so you can do what you need to do." She offered.

"Jesse, I have missed our chats. I'm sorry I have been distant lately, but it can't be helped. Are you ok? I am still here if you need anything, you know that right?"

"Oh sure, no worries. I just wanted you to know I am doing ok and that I miss you." She stated sadly.

"I know, I miss you too. Hey I have a meeting in five minutes, can I call you back?"

"No, it's ok. I'm going to Sue's for supper tonight. We can talk tomorrow. Goodnight Dean."

"Night Jess." He stated sadly.

CHAPTER 15

WATCHING

Dinner with Susie and Matt was great, she got to spend quality time with baby Samantha who if she got any cuter would send you into cardiac arrest. She was starting to smile and coo which thrilled Matt to no end. Jesse was content to hold, coo, play and rock Sami while she was there, which gave Sue a nice little break. Susie was a great mom and wife, but since she was not working at the moment, her interaction with adults had become limited. While she would not trade this time with Sami for anything, she did long for meaningful conversation with people whose IQ's were not still developing.

Sue surprised Jesse with spaghetti with meat sauce over angel hair pasta, and homemade ranch dressing for the salad. Jesse used to wonder when they were younger if they were part Italian, since her mom regularly fixed Italian dishes for supper each week, and by regularly she meant three or four times a week. Every now and then they had cubed steak or fried chicken, but now as an adult, Jesse rarely ate it unless she was with Sue. They ate, laughed and talked getting all caught up on the new apartment, new neighbors and work.

Jesse told her about Reed's plans for the café and she was really torn. Matt took Sami after dessert and got her ready for bed so the sisters could continue talking. Jesse felt loyal to Reed and part of her wanted to stay and try and keep the legacy going since she had helped create a solid steady business but since she was now single there was a part of her that thought she should go back to school. It was a lot to think about, and she wasn't twenty years old anymore, and being on her feet like that all day was getting harder.

It was getting close to eleven and both girls needed to hit the sack, so Jesse took a piece of the cake home for Carter, and hugged Susie and Matt extra tight as she got ready to go home. She wanted a relationship like they had, strong and solid. Matt was crazy about Susie and treated her like a princess.

Jesse loved her new vehicle and loved that it had this moon/sunroof, every time she was in it that top was back. She noticed a car, a mid-sized sedan following her turn for turn as she left Sue's. At first she didn't think anything about it, but a gut instinct caused her to make a turn not in the direction of her home and it continued to follow her. Immediately she tried to raise Dean on the channel, "Report" She stated her voice elevated.

"Report, Dean are you there? This is real. Please answer." She stated trying not to allow the full blown panic she was feeling to overtake her. He didn't answer, so she tried to call him, again no answer. *What the heck??* *Come on Dean.* So she called Tim.

"Hello? Jesse?" Tim answered confused.

"Tim, I'm really scared, I'm in my car and I'm being followed. What do I do?" She shouted into the phone.

"Where are you and why do you think you are being followed?" He stated throwing on his pants then looking for shoes while trying to keep her calm.

"I left Susie's about 11:05 and started home, immediately I noticed that a mid-sized sedan was right behind me turn for turn. So I made some turns left and right that I normally wouldn't take on my way home, and they are still on my tail. I tried to reach Dean but he didn't answer. I'm sorry Tim but I don't know what to do. Can you please help me?" She said speaking ninety miles an hour.

"I'm on my way, listen I am going to put my ear piece in, reach into yours and click the switch one time downward that will put you on my frequency. I need my hands free and so do you. Do it now." He commanded.

"Ok, can you hear me now?" she stated.

"Yes, we are a go, I am in the Porsche that you saw me in earlier. I am going to come up behind you and then I am going to get between the sedan and you. When I do, you take off and head for the apartment complex, but not your unit, go to mine. There is a garage there, park in there until I get home. Got it?" He rattled off at her.

"Yes. Will you stay on the phone with me?" she asked now almost in tears.

"I'm not going anywhere baby, I am on the road now. What street are you on?" He asked as he pealed out of the parking lot.

"I'm back on Highway 17 south, just past mile marker 62. Tim, I'm really scared, who would be following me?"

"I don't know, but we will find out. I know you are scared, I'm on my way, about 7 minutes out, so hang on sis. I'm coming. Keep your speed level, and don't go faster than 55 mph ok?" He instructed as he put the Porsche through its paces, downshifting as he weaved in and out of traffic racing to get to her. "Honey, hang on, Dean is beeping in, just give me a sec."

"Ok." She replied. After a minute he came back online.

"Ok I'm back, I'm close now and I'm getting the plates on the car, is it a dark blue Chevy Malibu?" He asked.

"Yes I believe so, I couldn't tell if it was black or navy blue."

"Ok I am right behind him, I want you to keep going straight ahead, I am going to pass him and get in between the two of you. When I do, you take the next left, and turn back toward home and punch it. Got it?"

"Yes, got it."

"Ok here goes…" Tim said as he shifted and punched the gas to accelerate the Porsche Cayman around the Malibu, sliding right in between Jesse and the sedan. Then he flashed his beams at Jesse signaling her to turn around.

She slowed slightly and made a U-Turn, and then pressed the accelerator taking off in the other direction. Based on Tim's maneuver, and then him flashing her, the driver in the car realized the gig was up. He then slowed down and turned off on a residential road to the right, parked and waited. Tim drove about another quarter of a mile, then turned around to catch up to Jesse and escort her home. He passed the car again and it was just sitting there, and Tim wondering *what* he was waiting on. He could not investigate anymore at this point he had to stay focused on catching up to Jesse, Tim kept looking in the rear view mirror for the car, but he never saw it again. He called the plates into Adam and told him to start running them.

"Dean?" Tim raised him on the ear piece.

"Go. What happened?" He asked anxiously.

"Jesse is on her way to my place, I did an intercept maneuver allowing her to get away, and then the other driver realized he was busted, then pulled over on the side of the road and waited me out. He did not attempt to follow her again. I have already called the plate into Adam."

"Good job, thanks man. Is she pretty freaked out?" Dean asked concerned.

"Well yeah, what do you think man? She couldn't raise you, so then she called me, I didn't know what else to do. She's not a trained driver, at least not for evasive driving, plus if I know her she is terrified to do anything that would jeopardize her new car. I had to go get her." He stated almost perturbed.

"I'm sorry, I had just gotten home and jumped into the shower. I didn't see I had missed a call until after I had gotten out, by that time you were fully involved. I'll try her now, do you have her in sight?" Dean asked.

"No! Don't you dare call her while she is driving? Seriously Dean? Right now I have her dialed in and if she hears your voice she'll start crying. Hold up until we get home. OK?" Tim implored.

"What is your ETA?" Dean stated levelly.

"About four minutes out." Tim replied.

"Jess, hey it's Tim, are you still with me sis?" He stated calmly.

"Yeah, I'm here. Is that you behind me now?" She asked nervously.

"It sure is baby. Head on to your place since we are not being followed at the moment. I finally reached Dean, he had just gotten into the shower that is why he didn't answer. He feels like crap that he wasn't there for you and that you had to call me. Honestly it's probably best you did call me, he's not a bad driver, but I am *sooo* much better." He stated laughing trying to lighten the mood.

"I am just so grateful you answered. I guess I would have driven clear to Charleston if I hadn't reached anyone."

"Ok, we're here, so pull in and park so we can talk." Tim stated pulling in right behind her.

Jesse parked but did not immediately get out of the car and Tim realized her adrenaline rush was probably crashing. He walked around her vehicle then opened her car door and all but lifted her out of the SUV. She hugged him so tightly that it was hard for him to speak, then she started crying. Which he was expecting, so he just held her closely and rubbed her back allowing her to get it all out. Then he walked her up to her apartment, her hands were shaking so badly she could not get the key into the lock. Once he got her inside he fixed her some juice then sat at the bar with her.

"Listen, sweetie, I am going to let Dean conduct the debriefing, ok? He knows what to ask you to get the right data, since that is his area of expertise. I am going to run with the data I have and update him in the morning. If you see or hear anything unusual tonight or in the morning you call Dean or me, I don't care which. I'll do what I can, you know that, right?" He asked brushing the hair out of her eyes that were still filled with tears, tugging at his heart.

"Yes. Thank you." She said with her lip quivering. He kissed her forehead and then started to leave but remembered about the note she sent to Wex.

"Oh hey, Wex got your thank you note, and you nearly made the man cry. He says if I don't marry you I am out of the will. So thanks for the added pressure sis." He said grinning at her.

"Oh I am so glad he received it, I thought I had the address right but I wasn't sure." She said finally smiling. Once he saw her smile he felt like he could leave, so he gave her one last hug, then left the apartment.

Dean called shortly after and started to debrief her on what happened during the day, and could she have missed anything? They went step by step through her day, and she only noticed the car once she left her sister's house. Dean immediately started running queries on Matt to see if he was involved in anything that would jeopardize his family. At first glance there was nothing, Matt was a solid honest business man, so Dean would continue to investigate and then would know more after receiving Tim's report and the detail on the plates that Adam was running. Maybe then it would make some sense. He placed her on high alert tomorrow until they had some answers. God how he wished he could be there with her to hold her and reassure her. After taking down the details, he spoke softly to her for a little while trying to get her mind off what had happened.

It was during this time that she told him about Reed's plan to sell the store. She shared her thoughts and dreams about maybe pursuing a degree and doing something truly meaningful with her life. She stated she was going to really be praying over this and hoped that God would be very clear and specific in what direction she should go. Dean agreed that going back to school or getting a technical degree would be a great idea. When he could tell she was winding down, he told her he would speak to her first thing in the morning and that he was going to sleep with his ear piece in and recommended she do the same. Finally she brushed her teeth and fell into bed still fully clothed.

Jesse slept fitfully through the night waking several times, it was around 4:00 am that she finally fell asleep soundly sleeping right through her alarm. Dean was up at 5:00 a.m. and out the door shortly after, but he was going to let Tim sleep in since he worked on his data until after 2:00 a.m. However, Tim was also awake at 5:00 a.m. and worked on a few things from home, and then started to the office around 7:00 a.m.

As he pulled around the driveway in the complex, he noticed Jesse's car was still there and should not have been. He pulled in Carter's parking space and parked. He tried to call her first, but no answer. So he quickly trotted up the steps and knocked on her door, which sent Casey into defense mode. This is what finally woke Jesse up. She felt disoriented and wasn't sure where she was for a moment, then she heard the knock on the door, and reached for her phone. *Missed call from Tim. Missed call from Johnny.*

She jumped up and ran to the door then looked through the peep hole. *Tim!!*

Jesse unlatched the door and he came busting in. "Girl you are giving me a heart attack this morning... and weren't you wearing that last night?" He said smirking realizing she had just overslept and was not in any real danger.

"Um hey, I think I overslept and um, yeah I slept in my clothes. I guess I need a shower?" She stated still not fully awake.

143

"Look… I think you look *fabulous*, but you might scare the patrons with the wild child hair thing you have going on and the Goth girl eyes. Look I'll take Casey out to do her thing, while you hop in the shower. Deal?" He stated grinning trying to pat her hair back down into place.

"Yes, good plan. Thanks. Ok, here is her leash." She stated with a weak smile.

Tim took off downstairs while Jesse prepared to get into the shower. She was about to step inside when she heard, "Take the ear piece out please" from Dean. He had heard the whole interaction between her and Tim and he was partly jealous and partly amused.

"Oh yeah, thanks Dean. Wow. That would have been a disaster." She stated as she removed it and laid it on the counter.

Meanwhile Tim was back inside and feeding Casey for Jesse. He turned on the television and then grabbed Jesse's phone and texted Johnny back. *Sorry overslept be there shortly. Jesse*

Then he reached out to Dean to let him know where he was and what was going on. Dean said that he understood and would see him shortly. Jesse finished showering and then dried her hair. She dressed quickly and when she exited her bedroom there stood Tim.

"Ok, dog has been watered, fed and has done her bid-ness. Your work has been notified that you overslept and will be there shortly. Anything else we need to do before we get you out of here?" He said grinning. "Whew, now I know what it's like to get kids out the door in the mornings for school." He said dramatically, then laughed.

"Ha-ha Mr. Funny pants. Ok, I think that's it. Thank you for tending to my furry child. I'm ready, let's go." She stated smiling grabbing her purse and keys.

"Come on and I'll follow you in, ok?" Tim said with a wink. She nodded then got into her car and he followed as promised.

Jesse arrived at Reed's with the crew in full tilt and she felt horrible for being late. They were all doing fine, and cut her some slack since she usually opens and closes and is never late. Today's business was slower, and she was thankful since she was still so very tired from the night before. She went into the small office and shut the door to chat with Dean.

"Report."

"Go ahead charge 25, how are you this morning?" He asked.

"Tired. This spy business is crazy. You guys must mainline coffee with these crazy hours." She said laughing.

"Some days it feels like that, I have some data on the car following you, and we are escalating it to the Alpha team. Just know you will be under strict surveillance for the next couple of days. More than likely my team will be driving dark navy blue chargers, a Tahoe or there is a black mustang in the mix too. If you are unsure, tap in and call me or Tim we can confirm who is who, ok? I'm really sorry you were so scared last night." He said sincerely.

"It was just so unexpected. Thank God Tim answered the phone. What should I do in the future?" She asked.

"Best thing to do is call 911 and drive to the police station or a fire station, but that doesn't always work. We can go over evasive driving later, and bring Tim in, he's our expert." He stated.

"Ok, well I am going to church tonight, then home. Just so you know."

"Thanks Jess, I'll be in touch." He stated signing off.

She finished out the day, and Johnny took the deposit to the bank for her today. She tidied up the small office and then checked her email. *Great another email from Jerry.* In it he accused her of all kinds of philandering and was threatening to sue her to get his money back. She pressed the forward button and sent it on to Dean asking if he knew of a good attorney. She really did not have the emotional energy for this garbage.

This divorce could not happen soon enough for her. She never realized what a selfish evil person he was and she was grateful to now be away from him, but actually pitied his mistress and the baby she carried. Even if she never found love again, she would have good friends and her family, and for now that was enough. Dean emailed that he was on it and for her not to worry. This would all be over soon enough.

CHAPTER 16

KISSES

The next couple of weeks went without incident and Dean early on determined that Jesse was being followed by a Private Investigator that was hired by her soon to be ex-husband. Dean once again had to step in and let Jerry know he was not happy with the latest turn of events and that it had better stop or he would arrange a meeting. The Alpha team confirmed that the P.I had been pulled off and Jerry was behaving for now. Charge 25 was out of immediate danger.

Andy the next door neighbor had started taking Casey out at least once during the day, which helped Jesse but also was healthier for him. He appeared to be vitamin D deficient and needed to get some sunshine and exercise or he was going to have a heart attack at the ripe age of thirty five. She would bring him home sandwiches occasionally or fix him dinner, as a gesture of friendship which he obviously appreciated.

She was downstairs checking her mail, when Carter stepped out of his apartment. "Hey I'm glad I ran into you, I was going to walk up later but this will save me a trip. I have a couple of steaks I was going to grill out this afternoon, so I was wondering if you would like to join me." He looked a little disheveled but still magnificently handsome, and she just stood there taking in his image. *Tan. Muscular. So fine.*

"Jesse?" He said smiling trying to get her attention.

"Oh Yes, food. That would be great. I would *love* that, what can I bring?" She said snapping out of her catatonic gaze, causing him to grin at her response.

"Nothing I have it all, just come hungry. How about 4:30 or so?" He asked.

"Sure, that sounds great, I have a couple of errands to run so I will go and do those now." She smiled.

She went back upstairs to get her purse and keys then quickly went down the steps and out the door. She called Susie while running errands to let her know she was having dinner with Carter at his place. Grilling out steaks, and won't that be fun...

Sue screamed so loudly into her phone, Jesse nearly wrecked. She and Matt had gotten a sitter and were also having a date night themselves. So they talked wardrobe and hair, when Jesse realized she was in desperate need of a trim. She hung up with Sue stating a hair emergency, and called Tiffany her friend and trusty hairdresser. She stated the nature of her emergency and Tiff said she could work her in, to come on by the salon.

Jesse arrived at the salon, and Tiffany was finishing up a regular who was in for a high and tight military cut. She browsed through the salon hair design books, and flipped through a few pages looking for something new and fresh to replace her wavy chin length bob. Tiffany spoke reason into her life and they decided a new doo would require thought and preparation. For now she would trim her hair, which would breathe life back into her existing cut and look perfect for her date. Jesse finally agreed with her friend's professional opinion and stepped off the new hairdo ledge and back onto safer ground.

Now that her hair was back on track she went to the mall for a quick trip to the makeup counter to get more of her moisturizer and dark brown eye liner. She also passed by the junior department and found a really cute sundress that was mid-calf length and willowy. Jesse made the impulse purchase deciding that with the right shoes she could also wear it to church. The blue and purple hues made her eyes just pop, along with her blonde hair, the dress was a win-win. Her last stop was to the grocery store to pick up some fresh fruit and yogurt.

She arrived home with her arms loaded down, then took Casey outside. She came back in and freshened up with a quick shower. The she slathered herself in lotion and lightly applied some makeup. When she looked down at her phone it was 4:27 p.m. she was right on time. She slid on her sandals and proceeded downstairs. She knocked lightly and a few seconds later, Carter opened the door barefoot, in jeans and a snuggly fitting black pocketed tee-shirt.

"Wow, you look amazing Jesse. Please come in." He stated obviously pleased with the afternoon's errand run.

"Thank you." She said stepping into his apartment. He was busy in the kitchen preparing the salad and the steaks were marinating.

"Here please have a seat, can I get you something to drink?" He asked.

"Sure, what do you have?"

"I have Lemonade, Coke, sweet tea, water or a beer, but I don't think you drink, do you?" He stated eyeing her.

"Not alcohol no, but the lemonade sounds great. Thanks."

"One lemonade coming up then." He stated pouring it in a fancy glass then setting it down in front of her.

"Please let me help you do something, I can chop veggies for the salad if you like?" She stated taking a sip of her drink.

"If you insist, chopping the yellow and orange peppers would be a big help." He stated smiling getting her a knife and a cutting board.

They stood there in close proximity preparing the salad, chatting, he was really enjoying her company and she smelled heavenly. He excused himself to start the grill since he was using charcoal today not the gas grill. After a few minutes he reappeared and they continued their conversation. She was telling him about her arrangement with Andy, and that it seemed to be working out well. He was intrigued and just listened to her as she spoke about work, and her baby niece and about the possibility of her going back to school. Once again he excused himself to check the grill, and decided it was time to put the steaks on. She stated she liked hers medium and he preferred his medium-rare.

After placing the steaks on the grill he came back inside and washed his hands. He had soft music playing in the background and Jesse was finally relaxing, just now getting a handle on her revved up emotions. She had just taken a sip of her drink and was standing near the sink when he came back inside he leaned in and kissed her gently on the lips.

She froze. The moment she had been dreaming about was happening and she was paralyzed. He of course could tell she was not responding to him, and so he slowly pulled away with his head down, and murmured something about checking on the steaks as he turned to walk away. She was completely mortified.

"Carter wait." She called softly after him.

"I'll be back in a sec." He replied as he shut the door to the patio area, trying to recover his ego.

Jesse seriously? You are blowing it! What is wrong with you?

Panicking, she left his apartment so quickly that she left the front door wide open. She ran upstairs to feed Casey and to take a moment to compose herself, then she was going to go back down there and try to act like a normal person. Her door was cracked so Carter slowly walked through and stood up against the door jam.

"Were you going to come back?" He asked quietly.

"I just forgot to feed Casey and I...I just needed a moment." She stammered slowly standing up to face him, tears filling her eyes. His face was etched with concern. He walked over to where she was standing near the bar then realized with their height difference she could potentially feel intimidated by him standing over her, so he gently lifted her onto the countertop. Now she was sitting nearly eye to eye with him.

"Did I do something wrong?" He asked as he stepped closer to her taking her hands into his.

"No, Carter. I mean it's me, you make me *so* nervous. On the one hand I am *very* attracted to you, then on the other hand you have this intense stare, and when you look at me so intently I can't decide if you are trying to see through me and into my soul, or if you are some kind of closet serial I.T. killer plotting my demise." She said letting out a long exhale. He couldn't help but smile at her admission.

"But the real reason is, well you know I was married up until recently, and not once during my entire marriage did my husband ever make me feel inside like you make me feel. When I am around you I can feel the blood actually coursing through my veins, my stomach does flip flops and I feel like I can't breathe. But in a good way you know? You convey more intimacy in a single touch of your finger to me than he did in eight years of marriage. This may sound crazy, but I have not been kissed, *really* kissed in so many years I can't even count. I'm nervous and feel so inadequate." She said casting her eyes downward.

Carter let out a sigh, his heart going out to her. He reached in and took her face into his hands, which caused her to look into his eyes. "Thank you for sharing that with me Jess. I'm so sorry." He stated softly.

"If you want to run out the door, I would not blame you."

"Jesse, first of all, I am *not* a serial killer. I promise." He stated with a wink, trying to get her to smile.

"I know." She whispered looking up at him.

"I know I can be intense, it's just that I have such strong feelings for you, but I know you are somewhat fragile since your separation. I just don't want to move too quickly and scare you away." He said coming in even closer. She bit at her bottom lip as he spoke softly to her.

"Can you do me a favor? Will you trust me for a few minutes?" He asked taking her hands back into his. She nodded, so he started with a hug, he wrapped his arms around her and she laid her head on his shoulder putting her arms around him too. He just held her quietly for several minutes, until he could feel her relax, his thumb lightly stroking her shoulder. Once she relaxed a little more, he slowly took his hands and placed them on either side of her face and gently began kissing her with light butterfly kisses over her forehead and cheeks. She closed her eyes allowing herself to enjoy his experiment.

By the time he made his way to her lips, she was ready. His mouth came down gently on top of hers, and slowly she responded. It took her a minute to find his rhythm, but he was patient with her and they finally synched up. He kept it at a passionate but sweet level, and he did not escalate it although everything rising up within him was fighting for more of her. He knew if he pushed here, he would lose her trust. His hand still cupping her face ever so lightly, and her hands were now pulling him in closer. Slowly he pulled his lips away from hers but kept his face very close. Heavy breaths escaped both of them, as they still clung to one another. Finally he pulled back, then kissed the tip of her nose.

"Dinner is ready if you still want to eat?" He stated cautiously trying to gage what was going on in her mind.

"That was amazing." She whispered dreamily her eyes still half closed.

"Well, we have plenty of time for more of that… but I am starving." He said with a wink.

"Oh yeah, sure. Food. Food is good. We can go eat." She stated still a little dazed. He smiled and lifted her off the counter, and held her hand as they both walked back downstairs to his apartment.

He had taken the steaks off the heat and were letting them rest, so he served her first then himself. He placed salad in the bowls and then presented her with two types of dressing, a homemade ranch and a store bought Italian. She asked if he would cut her steak in half, that there was no way she could possibly eat that entire thing, it was enormous. So he cut her a section of the steak and saved the rest for later. They sat on the bench side of the table close to one another instead of across from one another, and he tried to keep the conversation light.

She ate her steak and finished most of her salad, as her stomach was still topsy turvy from the kiss. The kiss apparently threw gasoline on his appetite since he all but inhaled his steak and his salad. He insisted on cleaning up the kitchen, requesting that she go rest on the couch and enjoy the soft music.

"The steaks were fantastic Carter. So tender and the flavor was amazing. Thank you so much for cooking and having me over, not to mention I still *owe* you dinner." She said sincerely.

He dried his hands then walked over to the sofa where she sat, he leaned back and pulled her back with him, and they sat there listening to the music and he gently traced her arm with his finger. They sat that way for a long time, then slowly he bent down again to kiss her and this time she was ready for him. He shifted and soon was laying length wise on the long sofa and she was tucked in beneath him. He was careful about his space, and was very gentle and tender with her. At one point although they were fully engaged in kissing, he could feel her trembling beneath him. He propped up on one elbow and rested his head in his hand, and his other hand was stroking her arm and cheek.

"Are you cold?" He asked since her trembling had increased.

"Um, no." She responded, confused by his question. He could see by the look on her face that she didn't even realize she was shivering. Again his heart went out to her, here she had been so honest about her feelings towards him, and her insecurities, and then he places her in a position of uncertainty. *Idiot!* He leaned back in and began gently kissing her again, and he could feel her trembling so hard it bordered on being a shake. Slowly he rose back up again, lightly kissing her nose, and forehead, then took his finger and gently traced the outline of her face.

"You know I would never hurt you, don't you?" He asked searching her eyes for a response.

"Yes." She whispered. He leaned in and nuzzled her with his nose, lightly kissing her lips.

"I will never go further than you want to go, I will never force myself on you. Ok? I want to go at a speed you are comfortable with, and I will wait as long as you want to wait. You set the pace." He said in a soft tone back to her. She finally exhaled, and slowly nodded that she understood.

He leaned back down to kiss her and this time she raised up to meet him, so he wrapped his arms around her and held her firmly. Her trembling had subsided and now it was his turn to have his stomach do summersaults, she had an effect on him that he had not experienced in a very long time, and from where he was sitting it was way overdue. Jesse was someone he could definitely see himself spending the next forty years with. He decided to end this intimate time together or else he would not be able to make good on the promise he had just pledged. He rolled back a bit still holding her close to him, her head was now about even with his chest, and she rested her ear against him listening to his heart beat.

He wanted her so badly, but knew he was going to have to seriously pace himself. She was not a one night stand kind of girl, or one that would be comfortable with a booty call. She was classy, sweet, and sincere with her emotions, and he would do his dead level best to protect her. *Breathe Carter, just breathe.*

"Want to go for a walk?" He asked needing to divert his energy in another direction.

"Sure, where?" She replied casting her big blue eyes in his direction, causing his heart to melt.

"I was thinking the beach, since the sun is waning, it won't be hot and the crowds should be thinner. I know a place, that's fairly private." He said sitting up lifting her gently up with him.

"Sounds perfect." She smiled.

Jesse slipped her sandals on and he slipped into a pair of Vans. He grabbed his keys then they headed out to his car. It was a five speed mustang Cobra with black leather seats and tinted windows. He checked the trunk to make sure towels were in the back and they were, in case they got wet. He opened the car door for her, then came around and slid into the driver's seat.

The car came to life then purred under his authority.

"So what is it with guys and fast cars?" She asked curiously.

"Ah, I don't know. It's just fun I guess." He said grinning. He pulled out and headed in the direction of the highway, as though they were going towards Sue's house. They made several turns and he drove a lot like Tim, fast, but in control shifting and putting the car through its paces.

They arrived at an area that had a very small parking area. He pulled into the first spot and parked. He got out, then came around and opened her door. Once again he held her hand and they walked past rows of tall sea grasses that lined the way to a long wooden planked path that led to the sandy area, then to the water. She stopped momentarily to slip her sandals off and walk barefoot in the sand.

They strolled up the beach hand in hand just taking in the scent of the ocean and sound of the waves crashing and the gulls squawking in the distance. She was relaxing now becoming a little more animated in her conversation and he was content to listen to her tell her stories. They came across a private party where the small group had a bon fire and music playing. As they were passing by the group he took her hand and twirled her around, several of the other people stood to dance and said they could join in.

They stayed, dancing a few dances then waved goodbye to the friendly group as they continued up the beach stopping occasionally to look at shells that had washed up on the shore. Suddenly she released his hand and ran forward at the water's edge then stooped down to pick something up.

"Look Carter! It's nearly perfect. A sand dollar." She said with a childlike expression on her face that caused his chest to swell.

"Nice find. I say we keep it." He said smiling sweetly at her. She stayed near the water to rinse it off, then walked back over to where he was and slid her hand back into his. He bent down to kiss her, his lips seeking the warmth hers provided, he pulled her close and they were lost in one another in this perfect moment. The vast expanse of the sea as their backdrop and the gentle lapping of the tide as their special music.

He felt her shiver and so he began lightly rubbing her arms with his hands, then once again slowly tore himself away from her.

"Missy you are going to get me in trouble." He stated lost in her big sky blue eyes as they gazed up at him.

"I like kissing you." She replied innocently.

"And I like kissing you…maybe a little too much." He stated with a smirk. They turned to head back in the direction from which they had come. The party was still in full swing and they once again waved as they walked past.

"Hop on." He stated and they neared the wooden pathway.

'What? I have a dress on."

"Shift it up, and hop on." He directed as he bent forward.

She complied and he carried her to the walkway so that she wouldn't sink into the softer sand with her wet legs, she would have been covered in sand otherwise. At the top of the landing there was a water spigot and he used that to help rinse her calves and feet off. Then she slipped her sandals back on and they walked the short distance to the car. She still held onto the sand dollar as though it were gold, treasuring her beach find memento. He drove slower going home not wanting the night to end, he knew once they were back at the apartment he would have to walk her to her door and leave her there, since it was becoming apparent that he was falling hard for her.

He looked over at her and smiled seeing her leaned back with her eyes closed, the breeze blowing her hair gently back, and she was humming ever so slightly to whatever he had on the radio. He reached over and placed his hand over hers, and she opened one eye to look at him and smiled. Finally they pulled back into his spot at the complex and he parked then came around to open her door. He walked her upstairs and neither one of them spoke, he took the keys out of her hand and unlocked her door for her. They saw a note taped to the door stating that *Casey was out at 10:05 to go to the bathroom since your date was running long. Andy.* She leaned back against her door and looked up at him, "Carter, this has been so wonderful. Thank you for a perfect evening." She said looking up at his chiseled features and his eyes were gentle now, and crinkled in the corners when he smiled.

"No thank you for indulging me. I have been wanting to spend more time with you getting to know you better. I had a great time tonight." He said leaning in for one last kiss. He was now convinced after just one night that he would never tire of kissing her sweet perfectly shaped lips. *Never.*

"I will see you again, right?" She asked in earnest.

"You can count on it." He started to kiss her again, and diverted to her cheek. "I really need to go…." He said with a chuckle.

"Ok, goodnight Carter."

"Night Jess."

CHAPTER 17

UNCERTAINTY

J esse got undressed and took a quick shower to get all the sea salt off of her. The warm water felt wonderful over her skin and she loitered there day dreaming about the evening she had just spent with Carter. She turned off the water and reached for her fluffy towel and patted herself dry then found her night shirt to slip into.

As she was getting into bed she heard, "Jesse?"

It was Dean. All at once she felt guilt, remorse, and uncertainty wash over her like a tidal wave.

"Hi." She said softly forgetting that she even had her ear piece in all night. *Please tell me he did not hear all of that tonight. Please no!*

"I haven't heard from you all day, did you have a nice day?" He asked.

"Yes, Carter asked me over for dinner. He grilled out then we went for a walk on the beach." She stated feeling honesty was best. He was in the spy business after all, it's not like he couldn't find out or didn't already know.

"How nice, did you have a good time?" He asked.

"Dean, I now feel weird and conflicted." She stated honestly.

"Jesse, please don't. You have a right to have a life, and I/Dean can't stand in the way of that, it's not fair to you. Please don't let your loyalty to me keep you from a real relationship with a real person." He stated softly.

"Dean you mean so much to me, and you have done so much for me. I had a wonderful time tonight with Carter but now I feel like a horrible cheat. Just like Jerry." She said tearing up.

"Oh Jess please don't say that, you are *nothing* like Jerry, not in a million years. Listen what I did was so selfish on my part and unfair to you. I am the one who crossed the line. I want you to have a normal life, with a real guy

154

who will treat you like a princess. I do not regret anything I have done to help you or the time I have spent with you. Some days honestly it's all that gets me through the next 24 hours. But I know I can't be with you like this, it's just not possible and again I want you to have a real shot at happiness. It's ok that you had a great time with Carter tonight. Really. Please promise me you will not feel guilty or upset. Promise me." He gently commanded.

"How do I do this Dean? I don't want to hurt you, it kills me to think I have disappointed you or ..."

"Jesse, I am fine. Truly. I will always be here for you. Always. Even if you marry Carter and have ten kids with him. If you ever need anything I will be here for you. If you are ever in trouble, I will find you and save you or die trying. Please do not hesitate for a moment if you have feelings for Carter, or if it turns out to be someone else...please live your life. That is the best way to make me happy." He said sincerely.

"I love you Dean." She whispered. Relieved yet saddened that it would never be him, but that he was giving her the freedom to let it be Carter.

"I know Jess. I love you too. Get some rest, ok?" He said.

"Sleep well."

"You too honey."

With that she removed her ear piece and laid it on the charger. She flopped back on the bed and felt like crying. This night had been a roller coaster of emotions, from the beginning to the end. She was really bewitched by Carter and prayed that they would get to spend more time together. Although he could look intimidating, he was actually so very sweet and gentle which she appreciated probably more than he would ever know.

She heard her phone vibrate against her night stand and looked to see who was texting he at this hour. It was Carter.

Getting ready to take a shower to see if that will relax me enough so I can get some sleep. Still very stirred up from our date tonight. Just wanted to say again, how much I enjoyed our time together tonight. I can't wait to see you again. Sleep well. –Carter

I was just laying here thinking about every detail of our time together tonight...I know I will have sweet dreams. Thank you for being such a gentleman. ~Jess

Jesse woke the next morning and got ready for church, she walked Casey early then got into the shower, dried her hair and got dressed. Word had gotten out at church about her and Jerry, and for the most part people were very supportive of her. There were a few whisperers and that was to be expected, but she had hoped for more from church people, and at the end of the day, people were people and human nature took over.

Her friend Sandy asked her to lunch after services, and Jesse accepted. They had not really gotten to see each other much lately with everything going on with Jerry, and work. They went to a local bistro and sat outside enjoying the weather. A storm was forecasted for later in the day but for now the weather was gorgeous. They laughed and got caught up with one another that is one thing she liked about true friendship, even though they had not really seen each other in weeks that they could pick up right where they left off and it was as though they had never been apart. They made plans to go see a movie or go shopping soon, and hugged as they said goodbye.

Jesse felt restless and decided to go for a ride. She drove back out to the safe house and slowly crept down the long driveway, just in case it was occupied. It was not. She parked then walked around to the deck. She sat under the umbrella for a long while just looking out over the water. Dean was alerted by sensors the minute she turned down the road to the house and cameras went into full on mode watching her as she sat quietly on the deck.

Dean just sat quietly in his dimly lit room with all the monitors watching her to see what she was going to do there. He watched as she once again found the welcome mat and got down on her knees to pray. He wondered what was going on in her mind, but did not dare interrupt her quiet special time communing with God. He actually had to tear himself away from his monitors and his special room to go spend time with his family today. It was his father's birthday and he was expected to be there for the celebration. He pulled himself away from her, turning out the light as he left his room and drove to his parents' home.

Jesse stayed at the safe house for about an hour, then the storm started rolling in and she felt like she needed to leave. Part of her wanted to reach out to Dean, but she did not. She drove home, getting inside just before the bottom fell out of the sky. Part of her longed to text Carter, but again she was not going to chase him. His car was not there when she arrived at home. She ended up curling up on the couch and fell asleep.

A couple of hours later a light tap at her door woke her up, she sat up then walked over to check the peep hole.

"Hey sis!" Tim said grinning from ear to ear.

"Hi, come in." She said sleepily. The weather was still dark and cloudy but the rain had stopped for now.

"Oh did I wake you baby? I'm sorry." He said giving her a quick squeeze and mussing with her hair.

She swatted him off and smiled. "Would you like something to drink?" She offered.

"Nah. Hey Wex was feeling lonely and invited us for dinner, do you have plans?" He asked.

"No not really." She stated a little disappointed she hadn't heard from Carter.

"Come on, let's go see the old goat, he said he's making fried shrimp and hush puppies." He said grinning.

"So why bring me? Trying to get back into the will?" She said teasing him.

"Pfft. You know it. A guy's gotta do what a guy's gotta do." He said putting his hands on his hips.

"Ok, can you give me ten minutes to freshen up?" She asked walking towards the bedroom.

"Only ten?" He smarted off at her. Then he quickly ducked to miss the pillow she winged at his head, then burst out laughing.

He took Casey out for her then fed and refilled her water dish. Then he sat on the couch and turned on the weather channel. He pulled out his phone and called Wex to tell him that he and a plus one were coming for dinner. They would be there within the hour, Wex was thrilled and said he would be ready. Jesse emerged refreshed and hair somewhat combed into place. She had changed from her Sunday dress into a pair of Bermuda shorts and a sleeveless button down shirt that tied at the waist. She slipped on her Converse tennis shoes then grabbed her purse and phone. She kissed Casey goodbye then locked up the apartment. Carter's car was still gone, so he definitely was not at home.

Tim was driving the Porsche again today, and it prompted Jesse to ask about this new vehicle.

"Oh it's the agency's car. I've been working on it. It's due to go undercover soon, so I am just testing it out. Perks of the job. Somebody's gotta do it." He said unleashing his boyish smile.

"Wow, cool. So the only car you really own is the Bronco, right?" She quizzed.

"Lord no, however I won't bore you with my menagerie of vehicles. I have one like this but a couple years older and it's white. I also have a Mustang, a vintage Camaro, oh yeah and a truck. I'm car insurance poor that's for sure." He said laughing.

Her phone started vibrating and beeping to alert her to a text. *Hi Jesse, I hope you have had a good day. I am stuck at work, a server went down and one of the drives won't come back up. Ugg. This storm caused additional problems. If I get home in a bit, maybe I can walk up? -Carter.*

Hi Carter, I am so sorry you are having to work today. I am actually out with Tim for an impromptu dinner with his family. He didn't want to face them alone. Ha-ha. Not sure what time I will be home, but would love to see you. ~Jess

> *Gotta scoot, I'll text you later. Tell Tim hello. CJ*
> *Will do, Talk to you soon. Jess*

"Hey...hey... what's up with all the texting? Are you talking to Dean?" He nosily inquired.

"Um, no. I had a date last night, and he was just saying hello." She said coyly.

"Whoa, wait one minute. A date? With who pray tell?" He said with an English accent, giving her the *eye.*

"Carter." She said looking straight ahead.

"Captain America? Girl, I am *proud* of you. Nice catch." He said raising his hand for a high five.

"Stop it. He is a very nice person, and I like him." She said laughing as she gave him the high five.

"Seriously, though, did he try to put the moves on you? Kiss you?" He asked in mock concern.

"You are incorrigible. Stop it." She said grinning.

"Oh he did, I can tell. Hmmmmm girl. So there is no hope for you and me then, right?" He said pouting.

"What am I going to do with you? I know you don't *like* me that way, plus you would never do that to Dean. He is your best friend and he loves you. I told Dean about last night. It's hard Tim, and so confusing. So many feelings swirling around in my heart that sometimes I feel like I might suffocate. He wants me to be happy and be with a real person. That's how he put it, like he's not a real person." She said her voice etched with melancholy.

"Jess, honey he's not, he's a ghost. Heard but not seen. That is the life he chose, and he is damn good at it. Dean can never be with you, or anyone for that matter. It's just the way it is, but I know he will see to it you are taken care of one way or another. If he cares about you, he is loyal to a fault. Remember, it was him who found you your apartment. If you like Carter, then I say go for it. Dean and I have checked him out and he's clean." He stated honestly.

"Just makes me so very sad for him. He is such a good person." She stated.

"He is an extremely complex person that is for sure. Many, many layers." Tim stated off handedly.

The time passed quickly and soon they were pulling into Wex's drive. Godiva met them at the gate wagging her tail so hard her whole body wagged with it. Tim got out and then helped Jesse out then patted his four legged sibling on the head.

"Where's daddy Diva? Where is he?" He asked sending her into a wiggling frenzy.

"Did you bring that girl you are not dating?" They heard him bellow from the canteen. Tim started laughing and reminded Jesse, *you love me and can't live without me, be sure and tell him that....* Wex came around the corner and gave Tim a big bear hug and patted his back roughly. Then he spotted Jesse, and walked up and took her hand and kissed it. Then she threw her arms around him giving him a kiss on the cheek.

"You kids get in here, we have a few more guests. I hope you don't mind. Marie heard you were coming over, and she was begging to see you. Then there's Sid and Carrie Ann, you remember them, don't you Tim?" Wex asked as he pointed out the people for Jesse's benefit.

Tim walked around shaking hands and hugging on the women. They were pretty sure Marie was sweet on Wex, and Sid was an old fishing buddy that sometimes helped Wex with the boat if he was expecting a large catch. They pretty much had dinner ready by the time Tim and Jesse arrived, so they all sat at a long table and visited as Wex and Marie served everyone. They had fried shrimp, macaroni salad, coleslaw, hush puppies, and Carrie Ann had baked a cake for dessert. Wex said the blessing then they all dove in like it was their last meal on earth. Everyone was telling stories and laughing, and of course everyone assumed that Tim and Jesse were an item. For tonight, they just let them believe that and it made Wex happy to see Tim content and with someone he cared about, even though he knew deep down they were just friends. It still gave him hope, that one day that his boy would settle down and have a family.

They stayed for a piece of cake, but then left soon after stating that Jesse had to open the diner early Monday morning. After saying goodbye for nearly thirty minutes and hugging everyone at least twice, they were back on the road. Tim reached over and picked up her hand and kissed the back of it.

"Thanks for going Jess. It makes him happy to see me with a nice girl." He said grinning.

"Hey, I love Wex, I think he is terrific. Anytime you need a plus one, I'm your gal if we are going to Wex's." She said smiling.

Tim wound up the Porsche and showed her what it could do, he loved showing off, but had to stay off the radar of the local police. Literally and figuratively. They made it home in record time, he pulled in and Carter's car was finally there. He decided to drop her at the door, and let her go up alone. She waved as he pulled away, then she walked inside. She decided to go get Casey first to walk her then would see if he was still up.

She turned the corner to walk towards the back grassy area, and found him sitting outside on his patio.

"Hey you." He said softly as she started to pass by him to the grassy area.

"Hey, you are finally home! I'm sorry you had to work today." She said walking over near where he was sitting. He reached up for her hand and she placed it in his, he seemed to really crave a point of contact with her, even if it was as simple as holding hands.

"Did you just pull up in a Porsche?" He asked a little surprised.

"Oh yeah, Tim's… well his company owns it and he's working on it. You know he's a mechanic, right?" She said swaying ever so slightly back and forth while she stood there talking to him.

"I'm not sure I did know that, he may have mentioned being good with cars. How was dinner?" He said in a serious tone.

"Oh it was fun. Wex is a surrogate father to Tim, he's really a sweet older man and he had invited some of his close friends for dinner to see Tim and the girl who is *not* his girlfriend. That is how he refers to me. It's actually hysterical. Tim told Wex the first time I met him that we were just friends and I was not his girlfriend. Apparently Wex is not going to rest until he gets Tim married off. So it's gotten to be a joke." She said smiling.

"Oh I see. Well I'm glad you had a good time." Once again he stated in a somber tone.

"What's wrong, you seem really sad tonight, is everything ok?" She said squatting down near his knee.

He reached up and moved her bangs out of her eyes, then leaned forward resting his elbows on his knees. "I don't know, just feeling really melancholy tonight, I feel like the weekend went by too quickly and it's back to work tomorrow."

She reached up and kissed him, it was long and slow, and he lifted her into his lap as they continued to kiss. She pulled away and whispered to him "I missed you today."

"I missed you too, I was hoping we would get to spend a little more time together today, but it just wasn't meant to be I guess."

"Well we will just have to try and carve some time in this week then, right?" She said with a smile.

"Yes we will." He said trying to pull himself out of this funk he was in.

"Please don't be worried about Tim, Ok? We cut up a lot, but he is really like a brother to me. I mean he is way too handsome for his own good, but I'm not attracted to him in that way. Now you on the other hand make me crazy." She said smiling and nuzzling him, which finally got him to smile.

"I guess if I'm honest it hurt seeing you pull up with him knowing that he got to spend the whole evening with you, when I was dying to see you." He said finally being truthful about what was going on inside.

"I'm so sorry, but I swear on my life that he is just a friend, and he feels the same way. He is not attracted to me in any way. So please do not worry about him, he is harmless, truly." She said lightly running her hands through his hair, and he close his eyes, enjoying her gentle touch. Once again she leaned in to kiss him and he eagerly sought her mouth, he needed her tonight and was grateful for this late night interlude.

It was getting late and she really needed to get to sleep and so she slowly pulled away and stood up, leaving him wanting more of her. He stood up and said that he would walk her upstairs, so she reeled Casey in on the leash and they walked upstairs to her door. She let Casey off the leash in the apartment and stood in the doorway.

"You have been the very best part of my weekend that is for sure." She stated looking up into his sad blue eyes.

"And you mine. Sleep tight Jess." He said trying to smile then brought her in close for one more lingering kiss. Finally he released her and turned to go downstairs. She waited until she heard his door close before she shut hers.

CHAPTER 18

ADVENTURES

Jesse was finally happy to get back into rhythm with Dean, their reports were back on track and mini conversations throughout the day kept them connected. He seemed to be in a better place than he had been previously. Things were also going very well with Carter, they spent every spare minute they had together until it was time for bed, and then they would pull themselves apart and retreat to their separate bedrooms.

Thursday at lunch time was a zoo at Reed's and her infamous table of eight showed up right at 12:30 p.m. in the crush of the lunch crowd. They had to wait a few minutes to get their table but waited patiently for Jesse. Doc was the first to give Jesse a Hug as she cleared their table and brought the menus. She got them seated then took their drink order. Yoshi was the one that noticed that her ring was gone, and began grilling her. Mack told Yoshi to tread lightly sensing that although this development was probably for the best, it still stung and he was not to be irreverent. Doc agreed and Jack apologized for Yoshi's lack of tact. She smiled and appreciated their concern. She left to get their drinks and as she walked past the counter she saw Carl come in. *Ok my day is complete.* He smiled and took a seat at the counter so she stopped to get his drink order.

"Hey Carl, thank you for the sweet card while I was out. That was thoughtful. What can I get you today?" She asked.

"I'll have a diet soda." He replied with a smile.

"Hey-hey look at you stepping outside of the box. A diet soda coming right up." She said smiling.

She whipped up the drinks for her table of eight and walked them back out setting Carl's soda in front of him, promising to come right back and get his order. She passed out their drinks and began going around the table getting their food order. Today's specialty sandwich was the Philly Cheese Steak and all but Duke were getting that, he selected the club sandwich on whole wheat.

"Thanks guys for making this easy for me today. Hey have ya'll heard of the band March Daze?" She said grinning.

Leo and Joe-Bob chimed in that they were playing at a local warehouse bar at the beach on Friday night and that they were all going. The band was a new South Carolina phenomenon reminiscent of Hootie and the Blow Fish. They were playing on home turf and a huge turnout was expected. Libby and her boyfriend were going and had invited Jesse. She was curious but was not into club scenes, however she had heard really good things about the band so she was tempted to go. Knowing that the table of eight and their significant others were going made it even more appealing. Maybe she would ask Carter and they could all go.

She came back to get Carl's order, he also ordered the special of the day nearly sending Jesse into happy dance mode. She grinned and patted his hand then disappeared into the back to help Johnny. A new kid, Rob had started on Monday and was doing really well. He had just finished high school and was going to community college at night.

"Eight Philly's and one club on whole wheat please." She called back. Then went back out front to refill drinks and clean off tables. When the order came up, she took Carl's his first and then took the group theirs. She stood there chatting with them about Friday night as she refilled their drinks, and by the time they had left, she had pretty much decided to be adventurous and go see the band. She exchanged numbers with Doc and Mack and said she would try to find them once they got there. *It's a date!*

They had a couple of sandwiches that were made incorrectly and were put in the refrigerator so at the end of the day, Jesse put them in the box for the homeless looking kids, wondering if they were doing ok. She locked up and made the deposit at the bank. On the way back she strolled past the Chinese Bistro and almost fainted. She saw Jerry and his new gal, now looking a little pregnant eating at an outside table. She saw the mistress lift her glass to take a drink and noticed the huge diamond engagement ring on her finger. Jesse felt as though she had been pierced right through the heart remembering her much smaller token of love he had given her. She immediately bolted from there to her car and drove straight home.

Dean tried to raise her on the ear piece and she finally answered. Tears rolling down her cheeks. He did his best to console her, but unfortunately this one would have to run its course. Jerry was a jerk and there were some hurts that were bound to crop up and regardless of how badly he wanted to wipe them away, some things he just couldn't fix. She made it home safely and ran upstairs to the safety of her bedroom and just cried.

Carter called when he got home and wanted her to come down but she said she wasn't feeling well and was going to go to bed early. He could tell something was wrong but she wouldn't say what it was. She did ask him to come out with her and the group to go dancing on Friday, but he explained that he had to work. He was doing a server migration starting that night after work that would most likely last the whole weekend. After she explained who all was going, he encouraged her to spend time with her friends and that he would make it up to her. The fact that she would not get to see him all weekend now added to her angst. She finally said goodnight, rolled over and cried herself to sleep disappointed on all fronts.

From where he laid in his bedroom he could hear her muffled sobs above him and it ripped at his heart. He could tell she was upset but she wouldn't say why, which disappointed him that she didn't feel she could confide in him. He laid there looking at the ceiling tiles trying to take his mind off the countless items that were swirling through his restless mind as he tried to psych up for the weekend project ahead of him. At some point he finally drifted off to sleep.

Friday came early and Dean was up and at work by 5:00 a.m. he and the team had a mission planned for this weekend, it was off of one of the leads Charge 25 had turned in. The one she called in from the Bistro, turns out after further investigation that they are suspected in promoting human trafficking. They were running a sting operation at one of the main sights of the suspected activity. Dean had been pouring over surveillance data and Intel collected by the Alpha team. He had Adam, Ninja, Tim, Craig, and Derek assigned to the detail and they were being briefed on plans A, and B this morning. Dean would be calling the shots and everyone had been given their assignments.

Jesse closed out her work day at Reed's and made plans to get picked up by Libby and her date. Then they were going to hook up with Doc and the guys at the warehouse club called Cubby's. She was nervous and excited. This was truly stepping out of her comfort zone, but with the safety of her friends she was starting to get excited. The dress code was beach comfy and pretty much anything goes. Jesse asked Andy to please take Casey out if he could and he readily agreed. He was really enjoying the feeling of almost having a pet. She brought him a sandwich and chips as a down payment for his dog sitting services. He just laughed and told her enjoyed it and he had already lost seven pounds. She went inside and changed her shirt and shoes deciding on the converse tennis shoes and loose flowy shirt over her Bermuda shorts. She carried her id and ten dollars in her pocket and took only her house key and her phone in a small wristlet carrier. Libby and Eddie were to pick her up right at six.

She texted Carter before she left. *I'm sorry about last night. Saw Jerry and his new fling out together and caught a glimpse of the huge engagement ring and well it just threw me. So wishing you could come tonight, missing you already. Love Jess.*

I'm so sorry to hear that. I miss you terribly, just trying to get through this project. Hope to see you at some point this weekend. Have fun and be safe. –CJ

Libby and her date were right on time and she sat in the back of his Honda Civic. They chatted all the way to Cubby's and even though the band wasn't set to play until 8:00 p.m. the place was already packed. They hooked up with the table of eight and their significant others, luckily they found two large tables and claimed those for the group. They had a DJ playing music while the band was setting up and so Mack, and Yoshi both had asked her to dance, and she accepted. She hadn't danced since the prom aside from the dance she shared with Carter at the beach.

It felt good to let go and dance and laugh, she hadn't had this much fun in a long time. Mack offered to get her a drink, and she requested water. She enjoyed meeting Doc's wife Karen, and Leo's wife Elle. They were very nice and easy to have a conversation with, she felt like she knew them as well as she knew the guys she saw nearly every week. Between Mack and Leo, they kept Jesse hydrated with water. They said it was their turn to serve her since she always took such good care of them.

Karen commented on Jesse's pin and she explained it was her grandmother's and she always wore it...She couldn't very well tell them it was a spy camera. The band started and played one set and the crowd was incredible. The warehouse was packed and people were milling around outside at the beach, near the parking lots and inside it was almost to capacity. During the set break she and Mack had taken another turn on the dance floor and then he excused himself to go to the 'head' so she made her way to the bar to get some more water.

"Hey can I please get a water in a glass?" She said waving down the bartender. He smiled and said he hadn't seen her before and asked if it was her first time at Cubby's?

"Yes and how could you possibly know everyone who comes in here?" She said amazed. He poured her a water then proceeded to squeeze limes into it and stirred it up. "Here you go, enjoy this." He said with a smarmy smile placing a straw in it for her.

"Thanks." She stated gulping down half the glass since she was so hot and thirsty.

Meanwhile on the drive out to tonight's mission location Dean had received news that Tim was out, a family emergency and so Ryan was going to sub in as driver if they needed it. Ninja was in place and Adam was in the crow's nest manning all the electronics and surveillance from the van. Dean was on the floor calling the shots as the rest of the team found their strategic positons.

"Boss, code 1." Adam hailed.

"Go."

"Dude we have a problem, Charge 25 is in the house."

"What? Repeat." Dean commanded, trying to hear over the din in the warehouse.

"Charge 25 is in the house and I think she's been roofied. I thought I heard her voice so I turned up your monitor, and then I saw her camera pin pick up the bartender making her a drink. He put a clear liquid in her drink, squeezed limes in it and gave her a straw. I don't feel good about it."

Dean swore under his breath, when she said she was going out with friends, it didn't even occur to him that she would come here, since this is so outside of the norm for her. Dean raced through the crowd trying to see if he could find her, there were throngs of people everywhere and he was wasting precious time trying to locate her. He finally raised Ninja on her ear piece and told her to look and see if she could spot her anywhere. They both methodically moved through the crowd as Jesse's time clock ticked away, minute after minute as they searched. If she had been slipped something he didn't have much time to get to her and get her out of there.

His mind raced as he tried to stay focused on the mission at hand and find his charge in the process. Finally as a last resort he texted Duke who was one of theirs but on loan for an undercover assignment.

Duke...Dean here, I need you. One of my charges is in your group tonight. Jesse. We think she has been compromised by the bartender. Please find her and get her out of here ASAP.

Boss, I am on this. Will report once we have her secured.-Duke

Dean struggled to get back to business and had to trust that Duke or someone in his group would find her, he had to redirect his attention back to his team. From across the room he saw Duke stand up, then go to Mack and Doc. Immediately they began searching for Jesse, they enlisted their whole table of men, and half went outside and the rest were combing through the warehouse.

Doc and Mack shot out the back door, finding two men on either side of Jesse all but dragging her to an out building at the back of the warehouse near the beach. It looked like a shipping container. Mack stepped in front of the two men, and demanded they let her go.

"Hey man, she is just drunk and we are helping her walk it off. No worries." He said trying to pass by the formidable Mack.

"She is not drunk, she has been with me all night and has not had anything to drink other than water. Let us have her or you will have a bigger problem than just me." He menaced. Both men looked at each other then looked back at Mack, then finally looked around them realizing they were surrounded by eight buff service men who were not afraid to fight.

Begrudgedly they finally handed her over, claiming they didn't know anything about her being drunk but that the bartender had just told them to get her some air. Mack lifted Jesse up and carried her to Doc's SUV. Doc got his medical bag out of the back and grabbed his stethoscope to listen to her heart and to her breathing which was labored. His wife Karen came running out to see what was going on and insisted they take her to his office on the base and check her over. The rest of the crowd went back inside, and so Doc, Karen and Mack drove Jesse back to the base. Karen called Leo's wife and told her to tell Jesse's friends that she had gotten sick to her stomach and was being taken home.

"Boss?" Duke called in.

"Go."

"It was close." Duke relayed.

"Did you find her, please tell me you found her." He said anxiously awaiting his answer.

"Yes, Dr. David Stewart has her and is taking her to his office at the base to check her out. Her breathing is labored and he fears its GHB, the date rape drug. It can adversely affect the lungs and breathing if she was given too much. That is in line with your mission tonight, yes?"

"Affirmative." Dean said swearing under his breath. How could he have missed this in their conversations this week?

"We will see that she gets treated and home safely." Duke replied.

"Copy that." Dean replied.

Knowing she was now off the premises he kicked the operation into high gear, and within the hour had arrested the bartender, four other perps and rescued two women who were found bound up in the out building drugged out of their minds with johns lined up ready to pay for their turn with them in the shipping container. Once they were all rounded up and the club shut down for the night, the team was called back to base.

Now the interrogations and investigation were going to get real. Dean's stomach lurched at the thought that Jesse was being dragged out to that container to endure God knows what? He was grateful that the two other women were rescued in time, but how many had been violated that he had not gotten to in time? This was truly a nasty horrible business and he was proud to be a part of any team that would help bring this type of human cruelty to an end.

Around 1:30 a.m. Dean received word that Doc had treated Jesse and she was coming back around so he, his wife and Mack were going to take her home and put her to bed. Doc explained that she would be very groggy and most likely would not remember much if anything that happened. When they arrived at her apartment, Doc and Karen helped get her into her bedroom. She looked dazed and pitiful, Doc was furious that this had happened, and he too was sickened to think of what could have happened if they had not reached her in time.

They were instructed to write her a note explaining partially what happened to her and to please call Dean when she woke up. They left her there sleeping in her bed, and then headed back to the base.

Jesse woke up with a start reeling from a massive headache. She was stunned to find herself home and in her own bed. She looked at her phone which read 2:48 a.m. then she looked at the note on the table. She was horrified to read what had been explained. She tried to get up, her limbs felt heavy and awkward. Jesse grabbed her keys stumbling down the stairs, got into her car and took off into the night.

"Tim check in please." Dean requested.

"Tim here." He stated sounding exhausted.

"Report?" Dean asked.

"He has a nasty gash on his palm that nearly took his thumb off. They took him back to surgery kicking and screaming about 9:00 p.m., but he's out now in a room now resting, fully sedated. I'm sorry Dean, but I am all he has, I had to come." He said trying to explain.

"Tim please. I know this, I just wanted to make sure he was ok, and that you are ok. Mission was a success." Dean stated levelly. He didn't want to tell him about Jesse and freak him out on top of all this business with Wex.

"I'm glad I didn't leave the team in a bind. I'll call you tomorrow and check in ok?"

"Affirmative." Dean said signing off.

"Boss we have a development." Adam came on the head set.

"Go." Dean replied.

"Goldilocks is sleeping in your bed, or couch I should say." He replied.
"Put it on screen." Dean demanded, feeling like he was the leader in a three ring circus tonight.

The next thing he saw was Jesse back at the safe house asleep on the couch. *How did she get back inside and not set the alarm off?*

"Want me to send people out to retrieve the wayward package?"

"Negative. I've got this, find out what code was used to get in." Dean said grabbing his keys and running out the door.

He was almost to the safe house when Adam tapped back in to Dean's ear piece. "It was Tim's sir."

"Roger that." Dean responded.

He parked next to her then looked in the windows and realized she had left her keys in the ignition. He pulled his side arm and checked the premises first. The safe house was out of commission for renovations, and an eventual sale. A new safe house had been purchased in a completely different location. Since it was still an asset it was still being monitored and tracked. The perimeter was secure so he quietly entered the house through the side door. She lay motionless on the couch and for a moment with the way the moonlight was eerily streaming in she looked grayish and dead. Dean's heart leaped into his throat and his pulse was racing.

He slowly came alongside her and checked her breathing. It was shallow but she was breathing. *Thank God.* Dean attempted to wake her, he was dressed in all blues, blue cotton tactical work pants, matching blue button down shirt that said CIA on the pocket and a blue baseball cap turned around backwards. She tried to open her eyes they fluttered momentarily, then they closed again. He sat on the couch next to her and she literally crawled up into his lap like a child and laid her head on his chest. He wrapped his arms around her and exhaled slowly.

"I prayed you would come." She whispered, her eyes still closed.

"What are you doing here honey?" He asked slowly rocking her, and enjoying holding her close.

"I'm scared. *This* is my safe place." She stated almost inaudibly.

"I've got you baby, and you are safe now. Let me take you home angel." He whispered in her ear.

She was out again. He kissed her forehead, and then lifted her up and carried her outside. He placed her in the passenger seat of her car, and then he went back inside to lock up the safe house. He was absolutely amazed that not only was she able to drive here but that she could remember a code to get in. He drove towards her apartment, occasionally looking over at her, his heart sick at the thought of what almost happened to her tonight. What if

Adam hadn't been alert? What if they hadn't done the sting operation there tonight but at the other suspected site? What if she had wrecked driving in her current condition? What if…. He looked upward towards the sky and said *Thank you Jesus for sparing her. Thank you.*

He pulled into her spot and then proceeded to carry her back upstairs to her apartment and laying her back in her bed removing her shoes then tucking her in. He removed the note Karen had written, and replaced it with one that simply said *Please call Dean.*

He locked up her apartment, then walked down to Tim's place and took one of his cars back to the office. He would have someone give him a ride back to the safe house later to retrieve his vehicle. Once he was back at the office, he texted Tim.

Took your Camaro. -Dean

It was nearly 4:30 a.m. now and he was still running on adrenaline. It was a good solid bust tonight, but that wasn't the goal. The goal was to get the bigger fish, and he prayed the smarmy bartender would give up the tools that were running this wicked operation. Ninja and Derek were doing the interrogations, and they played an awesome game of good cop bad cop. She was not to be under estimated, she was smart, fierce and fearless. Which sometimes caused Dean to almost have a coronary. She was not only an agent but a lethal weapon. He for one was happy she was on their side, and more importantly on *his* team.

He went back to his office and started writing up his report. Adam walked in and sat in the chair across from his desk. Dean looked over his monitor at him and cocked an eyebrow.

"Want the footage at the safe house scrubbed?" He asked his boss. The whole team was pretty jaded with all they had seen and done over the years, but Adam was actually kind of touched to see Dean treat his goldilocks so sweetly. He of course would take that to his grave, but he felt it none the less.

"Just give it to me, and fill it in with loop footage." He responded unemotionally.

"Yes sir." He replied.

"I need to get my car out of there."

"I can assist you sir."

"Give me ten minutes and we will head out."

"Copy that." Adam stated getting up to attend to the taped footage.

They first returned Tim's vehicle to his garage, then drove out to the safe house so Dean could get his car. After that they went their separate ways home since they had to reconvene again at 10:00 a.m. Dean got into the shower and turned it on as hot as it would go. He stood there leaning against the wall letting the cleansing water rush over his now tired aching body. He was officially physically and mentally tired.

He placed a fresh ear bud in and collapsed on the bed falling asleep almost instantly.

CHAPTER 19

UPSIDE DOWN

J esse woke back up in her bed and was completely confused. She remembered getting ready to go to the club, thought she had danced but after that it was a blur. She dreamed she spent time with Dean at the safe house, it was so real she could still feel his arms around her. She looked over at her phone and the time said 11:42 a.m. She attempted to stand and felt a little shaky. She saw the note on her nightstand that said *Call Dean please* and she was still dressed in the clothes from last night. *What in the world happened to me?*

She got up and brushed her teeth and then put her ear bud in the charger and placed a new one in and then tried to hail Dean. She crawled back to the comfort of her bed and waited for him to answer.

"Hey Jess. Are you ok this morning, can you tell me how you are feeling?" Dean asked concerned.

"Fuzzy, and clumsy. I got up and brushed my teeth but got back into bed. I'm still in my clothes and who put this note on my night stand. What happened last night?" She asked confused.

"You did go to the club and were there with your table of 8 friends, but the bartender there slipped you a drug called GHB, which is often used as a date rape drug. Thankfully Doc and Mack found you in time and took you back to the base to medically check you out, then they brought you home. At some point you woke up, then drove out to the safe house and fell asleep on the couch. I saw you on the monitors, so I went and picked you up and brought you back home. I left the note for you." He stated carefully.

"I don't even know the bartender. Why would somebody do that to me?" She asked innocently.

"Honey there is a lot of evil in this world, and you were spared incredible pain this time around. We also found two other women who were tied up in a container that we were also able to rescue last night. Anytime you go out please let a male friend or date that you trust get your drinks. Even if it's water. Stay with people you know, like your table of 8, which in this instance saved you. Jesse I want you to kind of stay close to home today honey. I think the drug is out of your system now, but I want you to eat and rest, ok?"

"Dean did I do something wrong? Is this why these things are happening?" She asked tearing up.

"No baby. You haven't done anything wrong. He picked you because he knew you were innocent, they hone in on that with women and try to exploit it. There is nothing wrong with you, you are just fine. I promise." He said reassuringly.

He continued to talk calmly to her, while looking over data gathered last night. Finally she agreed to fix herself something to eat and rest. He then turned his focus to these new developments and plan the new step in bringing this group down.

Jesse stayed in bed for another thirty minutes or so then slowly walked into the kitchen to see what she had in the refrigerator to eat. Nothing in there seemed appealing, and so she rummaged through the cabinets. Casey was doing her doggie dance so Jesse hooked up the leash and walked her outside, noting that Carter's car was still not there. She rushed Casey and wanted to get back inside quickly. She felt conspicuous and awkward like anyone who saw her would tell what happened to her last night. Once back inside the safety of her apartment, she looked up some restaurants that delivered and ordered some take out. She opted for hamburger steak with mushroom gravy, mashed potatoes, and green beans. They indicated it would be there in 10-15 minutes. She sat on the edge of her couch nervously awaiting the arrival of her lunch. When the doorbell rang, she leapt to her feet and paid the driver, shutting the door a little too hard then flipped the locks.

She devoured her meal and then retreated back to the safety of her bed. She laid there wondering if paranoia was an after effect of this drug, because she was suffering from a severe case of it at the moment. She wanted to talk to Dean again, but didn't want to bother him. She wished that Carter was home, but on second thought was glad he was not. Jesse could not stand the thought of him seeing her like this, knowing what almost happened. *Will he think less of me? Will he think I am a tramp or promiscuous?*

Eventually she fell asleep again and her dreams were frightful. At one point she must have called or screamed out, because Dean came on line in a panic. After speaking with her for several minutes he realized that she had been having a nightmare and was not in actual danger. He tried to talk to her about normal things to take her mind off the dreams and her miserable night last night. He longed to be there with her and hold her once again. Once he felt like she was calmer, he encouraged her to go watch some television, something light to take her mind off of everything. She stated she would.

An hour later, she received a text from Carter.

Still in the throes of this project. Decided to take a break, and I was just wondering how your day is going? –Carter

I'm ok, just watching some television. ~Jesse

If I get out of here at a decent time do you want to go grab dinner somewhere? –Carter

I don't know. ~Jesse

Ok...are you sure you are alright? You don't sound like yourself. –Carter

Just call or text me later, ok? If you can get away. ~Jesse

Carter was confused and disappointed in her response and it made him it want to see her face to face all the more. He was exhausted and ready to be home. Maybe it was just him, and he needed a nap?

Tim called Dean to check in and make sure his Camaro made it back home safely. Dean assured him it did, then he asked after Wex. Tim explained to him that he would be heading home tomorrow or the next day, but that he wanted to stay an extra day or so to clean up around Wex's house to make sure he was set on a few things since he would not be taking the boat out for a while. Finally Dean told Tim about the mission and what had happened to Jesse. Tim was livid. He was ready to drive home, find the bartender and his friends and bust some heads. Dean had to repeatedly talk him out of this and kept telling him that they got to her in time, and that she was fine.

This mission from the start was one they all felt passionately about due to the horrific nature of the crimes, but when it hits a little too close to home like it did with Jesse, the commitment to it was even greater than before. Dean encouraged him to rest while he could and enjoy the down time with Wex.

Jesse drew herself a bubble bath and stayed in there until the water was ice cold, then she let some of the water back out and refilled it with piping hot water again, and repeated this process two more times before finally pulling herself out of the tub and putting her sleep shirt back on.

Carter arrived home, but went straight upstairs first. He lightly knocked on her door and waited. He was almost ready to go back downstairs when the door slowly opened. He saw Jesse standing there all pink and flushed from being in the hot bathtub for so long and when she went to take a step forward crumpled to the floor. Carter tried to catch her but it all happened so fast. He scooped her up and then carried her back to her bedroom laying her on the unmade bed.

After a couple of seconds her eyes fluttered and she looked at him startled. He started to ask her a question and she just burst into tears. He sat on the edge of the bed trying to hold and console her.

"Baby what in the world is going on, you scared me to death. Are you sick?" He asked trying to soothe her.

"No, some bad man drugged me last night and strange people wanted to have sex with me, and thankfully Doc and Mack saved me... but now I am just ashamed and feel dirty, I never should have gone out last night." She said through her sobs.

"What the ..."He started, furious to see her this upset.

"The bartender did it. I'm scared Carter. Do you think less of me now that I went to that place and this happened?" She asked tears still streaming.

"Oh baby, whatever happened was *not* your fault, and of course I don't think less of you. There are a lot of predators out there, and I am just sick I was not there to protect you from this horrible experience. Are you ok, did they hurt you?" He asked holding her closer.

"No...no. I'm ok, just scared. My friend Doc, is a real doctor and he made sure I was ok and that the drug didn't hurt me and then him and his wife brought me home. I don't remember any of that but they left me a note." She stated trying desperately to get her breathing under control.

He kicked his shoes off and leaned back against her headboard, throwing his legs onto the mattress holding her close to his chest. She crawled back under the covers and wrapped her arms around his mid-section, clinging to him. They laid like that for several minutes before they both dozed off. It was nearly 7:30 p.m. when he awoke with a start and checked on her lying next to him. He sat there gently stroking her face as she lay facing him, thinking about what terrible things could have happened to his sweet Jesse, and now this event has caused her to reel in insecurity and self-doubt.

Carter checked his phone, no new messages which was a good sign, since he had kind of gone off the radar for the last four hours. He checked his emails quickly and responded to a couple that needed his immediate attention. He knew he was going to have to go back into work soon but did not want to leave her unattended. He gently started stroking her arm and she murmured and stirred slightly.

"Jesse, baby. Are you awake?" He said softly.

"Ok." She replied sleepily.

"Honey I have to go back in to work shortly to try and finish up this project. I received an email that the other crew that was working in another area is finished now and I can get back in to do what I need to do. But I don't want to leave you. Are you hungry? We can grab something to eat if you want?" He asked still trying to get her to wake up.

"I look terrible and I don't want people to see you with me like this." She stated softly.

"How about I order a pizza, and we can eat here? I just want you to get some more food in you ok?"

"Ok, pizza is good. Will they bring it here?" She asked confused.

"Yeah baby, I'll order it and they will bring it here. Why don't you go wash your face and get some water? You need to stay hydrated, ok?" He stated picking up his phone to order the pizza.

He got up and walked into the kitchen and got himself a soda out of her refrigerator. He badly needed a dose of caffeine. Casey was laying at the foot of Jesse's bed just watching them both move about the apartment, like she wasn't quite sure what was going on.

Jesse came out of the bathroom and grabbed the leash, then called Casey to go outside. Carter was trying to order the pizza but was waving her off from going outside. Jesse looked at him perplexed standing there in her short sleep shirt. He finished the call then took the leash from her, and said he would take the dog outside since she had failed to put on pants.

Jesse poured herself a glass of water and sat on the couch. She still felt odd and agitated and wasn't quite sure why. Carter returned, then about ten minutes later so did the pizza. They sat on the floor and ate, making light conversation. He could tell she was still out of sorts, but at least she was not hysterical. So that was an improvement. As terrifying as the whole ordeal was for him just to imagine what could have happened to her, he could only try to imagine what was swirling through her mind. He sat close to her while they ate and found himself touching her leg or arm while they talked and ate.

He put the left overs in a container for her and then sat back down for a minute before he had to leave to head back to work.

"I really hate I have to go back, I wish I could just stay here." He said solemnly.

"I know, its ok. I understand. I will be fine, I am feeling better now. The food is helping." She lied to keep him from feeling so badly. Well it wasn't a complete lie, but she hated seeing him look at her with his beautiful steely blue eyes looking so sad. She knew he had to be exhausted pulling the hours he had over the last few days and he didn't need to be worrying about her.

"Ok if you are sure. Call or text me if you need anything ok? I'll see you tomorrow if you are up for it ok?" He gave her a kiss on the forehead and then put his shoes on and left.

She went back into the bathroom and put some eye cream around her eyes to minimize the puffiness and swelling, because at this rate the .15 ounce jar was not going to be enough and she wondered if they sold it in a Mason jar size. It was starting to help a little and she was starting to look normal again.

She heard her phone ring and ran to pick it up.

"Hey Sis!" Tim said joyfully.

"Hey where are you, you sound far away." She replied.

"I am down at Wex's house, not the restaurant and I need a favor." He stated.

"Sure, from me? What can I do?"

"In my apartment is a tool kit I desperately need. I left in such a hurry the other night I walked off without it. Can you bring it to me?" He said feeling her out. He wanted to see for himself if she was ok.

"Um sure. How do I get into your apartment? Is there a hid-a-key somewhere?" She asked.

"No I have a keyless entry. When you get over there call me and I'll give you the code. Are you ok, can you drive it out here to me?" He asked, now questioning his impulsiveness.

"Yeah I mean if you need it, how come you didn't come home to get it?"

"Wex is being released now from the hospital and I can't leave him just yet."

"What? Oh-my-goodness, what happened? Is he ok?" She stated alarmed.

"He nearly cut his thumb off and had to have emergency hand surgery. He is an old stubborn cuss and Sid could not get him to the E.R. so I had to get down here and take him. It was really bad, but he's doing better now. Marie and I have taken turns sitting with him, and cleaning up his house. But there are some things I need to fix and I want my tools. I can't find what I need in his mess and I'm under the gun. Can you help me Jess?"

"Of course, I'll throw on some pants and come on down, so text me his home address. I'll call you back when I get to your apartment." She stated then hung up.

She quickly threw on a pair of denim shorts and slipped her tennis shoes on, grabbed her purse and locked up the apartment. She drove down to his building and then walked over to his apartment, it was in the same place as Carter's. She called him and got the code and he directed her to where it was on an end table and then to a duffel bag he needed that had a change of clothes for him. Once she had both she exited the building and got into her car and punched in the address on the GPS. His house was not far from the shop where the boats were stored, just a few streets over in the other direction.

She put her sunroof back and made her way down the highway.

It was around 9:30 p.m. when she pulled up to the small framed house painted a taupe color with black shutters. She could tell some serious yard work had recently been done and Tim's Porsche was in the driveway along with a small compact car which must have been Marie's. She pulled in behind Tim and then grabbed his bags out of the back, by the time she shut the tailgate, he was at the door waiting on her.

He met her half way in the yard and picked her up and spun her around giving her a big bear hug and kissed her check. He could see that she had been crying at some point, but he tried to keep things light. He was always the one that could take her mind off things and make her smile. Finally, he set her down and took the bags from her. They walked in and Wex was laying on the couch covered in a crocheted blanket. Marie was in the kitchen making coffee and waved as she walked in. Wex's face lit up at the sight of her and she immediately walked over to hug him and kiss his cheek. Tim was grinning from ear to ear, so happy she was here.

"Well what are you doing here darling?" Wex asked his voice still a little weak.

"Well I heard my favorite fella was down, and I had to get here to see for myself if he was being properly taken care of." She said smiling sweetly. Which caused his eyes to light up and a broad smile broke out across his unshaven face.

"So you didn't come to see this tall drink of water over here?" He asked with a wink.

"Well, maybe him too." She said grinning back.

"Son get her something to drink and let her sit down." He barked at Tim in his affectionate way. Tim grinned and showed her to the oversized recliner and then left to get her a soda. Marie begged off for the night since Tim was staying and said she would see them all for breakfast since she was making homemade biscuits and gravy. Tim locked the door behind her and then came and sat next to Jesse in the giant oversized recliner. He put his arm around her and kissed the top of her head.

They all chatted for a bit, and Tim told on Wex regarding his antics at the hospital trying to garner sympathy for his rough weekend. They laughed and it appeared it was good for Wex to have some company. While he cat-napped on the sofa, Tim turned inward towards Jesse and spoke softly to her about her ordeal on Friday night. He had to really temper his emotions as to not upset her, but he was still furious this had happened to her. He was also a little miffed at Dean for not catching it sooner, there is no way she should have been anywhere near that operation. Especially since they knew the scope and breadth of what it involved.

"So is this you're new look now? I'm just curious cause you are starting to look a little like me except without the 5 o'clock shadow." He said with a wink mussing her hair again. She huffed at him pretending to be mad, then smiled.

"Maybe, but I make *this* look good." She said gesturing with her hands. He threw his head back and belly laughed at her. *God I needed this tonight. I would die if anything had happened to her.* She was indeed the sibling he had yearned for his whole life. A little sister to pick on, to love on and look after. Sitting here in this little two bedroom house across town from where his parents lived in an upper class neighborhood gated community, he was reunited with his real family. Life was good.

His phone started buzzing and he saw that it was Dean. He excused himself and went outside to take this call. He had a hunch there was going to be yelling, and he was ready for it.

"It's Tim." He stated as his long legs paced back and forth in the freshly cut grass.

"What the heck is Jesse doing at Wex's and please tell me she did *not* drive there." Dean demanded, furious that she was that far from home in her condition.

"Look Dean I know you are angry right now, but I'm mad too. Did you think I wouldn't find out? I can't believe you let this happen to her. You are her handler! How did you miss this man? Seriously? I know you love her, but I love her too, do you ever think about that?" He stated nearly in tears he was so frustrated. Dean could hear the anguish in his friend's voice and immediately backed down. Dean stopped to think about the fact that Wex was badly injured, then Tim finds out that Jesse was nearly compromised, and then here I am yelling at him, pushing him to his limit. It took a lot for Tim to fight back with Dean, so Dean knew he had to be distressed.

"Tim, look man I am sorry. You are right. I screwed up. I have been racking my brain trying to figure out how I missed this with Jesse. I know you have been stressed out with Wex. Playing nurse to that old man who is like a father to you, I know how much you love him. I'm sorry I yelled at you. You know I love you man. I'm just concerned about Jesse's safety, she's been through a lot in the last 24 hours and I'm not sure how steady she is at the moment." He stated apologetically.

"I know Dean, and I would never do anything to put her in danger, but I had to see her after I found out what happened. I had to see for myself that she was ok. Do you understand that?" Tim asked.

"Yeah I do. Listen, I think we both need some rest. I am completely spent and I know you must be exhausted too, is she going to stay there tonight? I really don't want her on the roads this late." Dean said.

"She is sleeping in my room and I am on the sofa. I will feed her breakfast then send her on her way in the morning. I don't want to fight with you Dean, Ok?" He said getting emotional again.

"I know man, I'm sorry. I really am. Get some sleep. We can talk tomorrow." Dean said then hung up.

When Tim finally walked back in the house he saw Jesse standing in the middle of the room her eyes wide as saucers, with a horrified look on her face. He quickly surmised what had happened and rushed over to her wrapping his arms around her. She had heard the whole conversation through her ear piece, Dean must have forgotten to mute it on his end, plus he had Tim on speaker phone.

Then walked her back to where his room was and sat on the edge of the bed, bringing her alongside him. "Oh God Jesse, I am so sorry you heard all that...I just had to know you were ok." He stated apologetically.

"I do not want you and Dean fighting about me, I don't want to come in between you two..." She started.

"And you aren't. Honestly. Listen I was just very upset about the mission Friday night and about what went on while I was here tending to Wex. I just needed to see you Jesse and make sure you were ok honey. I would die if anything happened to you. My inner circle is very small Jesse, and it primarily consists of Wex, Dean, his family and now you. That's it. So I am very protective about those that I love and care about." He stated a single tear escaping down his cheek.

She reached up and hugged his neck tightly, "I love you too Tim. I know I haven't known you or Wex for long but I feel like you are family too. You look so tired, why don't you sleep in the bed and I will be fine in the chair or sofa. Please." She pleaded with him.

"No this house only has one bathroom in the hallway, if he needs help I need to be able to assist him and not embarrass him with you in the den...I will be fine honey. Honestly I'm so tired I could sleep standing up at this point." He stated yawning.

He stayed in the bedroom for a little while telling her stories about being at the hospital, and about the nurses flirting with him. Then he told a few stories about he and Dean over the years and they laughed and just relaxed it was good to just spend time with her, Tim felt like he could be himself and not have to be on guard. That was the same thing that Dean loved about her, she didn't have an agenda, and she was just loveable and so easy to talk to.

When he could tell she was really winding down he tucked her in and then sat there a couple more minutes until he felt like she was settled. Then he gave her a quick kiss then went back into the den to try and help get Wex into bed.

Wex had heard him through the paper thin walls laughing in there with Jesse, and it did him more good knowing his boy was happy than all the medication they were trying to give him. For the life of him he couldn't understand why Jesse wasn't the *one*. She certainly looked like the one and acted like the one, maybe Tim was getting his loyalties mixed up? At any rate, Jesse being in the house tonight made everyone happy and so he went to bed willingly and tried to focus on sleep and not the constant throb in his hand.

The sun streamed in through the thin curtains in Tim's room lighting up the room with a warm glow. Jesse slept like a rock and wondered how in the world Tim ever slept in this bed, he was so long that he had to hang off the end. The mattress was comfortable but the bed was only a full size and Tim definitely needed a king or a California king sized bed. She laid there just looking around at the small mementos in the room like ribbons Tim had won, and pictures of he and Wex when Tim was a teenager. The aroma of freshly brewed coffee wafted under the door into the room and started to draw her out from under the covers.

She slowly padded out of the bedroom in her bare feet into the kitchen to find Tim and Marie busy making breakfast for everyone. Marie handed Jesse a little makeup bag and in it was a small toothbrush, toothpaste, hand lotion and a comb. Jesse grinned and hugged her new friend then excused herself to use the restroom to freshen up. Tim crinkled his nose at Marie and smiled appreciatively. The house smelled wonderful, freshly baked biscuits, skillet sausage with gravy and coffee and juices. Tim was even attempting Wex's home fries, and was doing a pretty good job, but they weren't exactly right. The only ones of course that would know that would be Wex and Tim, and neither one of them were going to tell.

They all sat at the kitchen table holding hands and this time Tim returned thanks for the meal, for Wex's health, Jesse's visit, and Marie's selfless friendship and help this week. Jesse was moved to hear Tim's sweet honest prayer and she squeezed his hand as he lifted them up. They all dug in and the food was just what the doctor ordered. It was delicious, so much better than anything a restaurant could provide. Jesse helped clean up the kitchen and then made up the bed she had slept in last night. She lingered in the room once again looking at the pictures, and Tim meandered in there wondering where she was.

"Look at you, just as cute back then as you are now. I wish I had known you back then. So much missed time." She said softly. Then he whipped out a photo of him and his real parents. He had his mother's dark hair and dark brown eyes. He was somewhat built like his father, only a good six inches taller. Other than that he really didn't look like either one of them, and it could be because neither of them were smiling. It didn't look like they had smiled in years to look at that picture, and Tim was laughing and smiling all the time. No wonder he thought he was adopted.

"Hey I promised Dean I would get you back on the road this morning. How are you feeling?" He asked looking at her hard.

"Good actually, I feel much better today than I did yesterday. By tomorrow I should be my old self again." She said smiling.

"Thank you so much for coming out last night, really it means the world to me, and Wex was so happy to see you." He said holding her hand.

"Listen, I just hate I didn't know any of this was going on, or I would have come sooner. You guys are great and always spoil me, why wouldn't I come?" She said with a wink.

"Well come give this old goat a hug, he's back on the couch." Tim said. To which Wex replied hearing him through the walls, "I heard that Timmy." Tim made the 'oh no' face and they both grinned.

"I'm sorry I have to go so soon, maybe I can come back next weekend and check on you?" She offered.

"Any time you want to come here darling you are welcome. Whether Tim is here or not." He offered once again. She stepped over Diva who was laying at his feet to give him a hug and a kiss. She gave Marie a hug and whispered *thank you* for the toiletries. Marie just patted her arm and smiled.

Then Tim walked her back out to her car, and stood outside her window chatting for a few minutes. Wex had Marie spying on the two of them to see if they could see him make any moves or kiss the girl. Finally he reached in for her hand and kissed the back of it then let her drive off. *Boo hiss. Not what they had hoped for!*

CHAPTER 20

SPY GAMES

S he kept the sunroof closed this time as it looked like a storm was rolling in and it was already sprinkling. Her phone started ringing and it was a number she didn't recognize. It was Doc calling to check in on her and make sure she was doing ok. Jesse assured him she was much better and thanked him over and over again for his help. She said to please thank everyone on her behalf that she was privileged to know them. He assured her he would and said they would see her soon at Reed's.

Since she missed church she stopped by Sue's house on the way back home. She managed to score lunch by showing up at this time and they were having chicken pot pies. Susie was becoming quite the cook now that she was home with Samantha. She sat with Sue talking to her for a long time while Sami took her nap and Matt was watching baseball in the other room. She told her about her time with Tim and Wex and how much she cared about them. Then she told her how things were going with Carter, and her sister just beamed. Finally her baby sister had a shot of having real love in her life that would carry her the rest of the way in life's journey. Jerry would have always been a source of pain for Jesse even if he hadn't strayed. Sue was still waiting for her opportunity to punch Jerry right in the kisser for what he had put her sister through.

Jesse said her goodbye's then headed back to her apartment, and Carter's car was in his parking spot. She ran upstairs to get Casey and saw another note from Andy that he had taken her out this morning for her. *Wow, how does he know to do that?*

So she walked back downstairs and stood outside Carter's door debating as to whether or not to knock or not. If he was sleeping she didn't want to wake him, and if he was awake, she didn't want to go up and not see him. While she was trying to decide what to do, the door opened.

"Can I help you miss?" He said looking completely disheveled and gorgeous. His blonde hair all over his head like he just woke up, he stood there in black shorts and no shirt. *Have mercy!*

"I'm terribly lost and need help finding my apartment. Is there a big strong handsome man in there that can help me?" She said with a wink.

He snatched her out of the hallway and brought her into his apartment. He then twirled her around to the music he had playing on his stereo and then bent down to kiss her. She brought her arms up and encircled his neck, then he scooped her up and carried her back to his bedroom and laid her on the bed. Then he laid down beside her and began kissing her passionately.

She pulled away momentarily to adjust and then snuggle with him. He laid there with his arm around her for several minutes, then bent down sweetly kissing her again. He made no attempt to do anything else, he was just seeking her company and her simple tender touch. Nothing more, he just wanted to be close to her.

"I got home and you were gone, where did you go?" He asked quietly.

"Tim's step father had emergency surgery the other day and Tim has been with him non-stop. He called me and asked me to bring him something from his apartment, so I did then went to see my sister Sue." She answered.

"I hope his dad is going to be ok. Was it serious?" He inquired.

"Yeah, I mean he is a fisherman and a giant hook nearly severed his thumb. So they had to do hand surgery to reattach and make sure he will have full use of it again. It cut right through his palm."

He pulled her in closer and inhaled deeply, then kissed her forehead. She looked around his bedroom never having been here before, it was laid out similarly to hers but was a little bigger. She noticed that everything matched and was well coordinated but very manly. There were no personal pictures of him or family in there, which she found a little odd. He had mentioned having a mom and a sister, but then again in her new apartment there were no pictures of her family. Just a selfie of her and the Reed's crew on her refrigerator door.

"Did you get to finish your project?" She asked yawning.

"Well most of it, it's going to be ongoing, but a large part of it was finished this weekend. With technology it's always something." He said rubbing her arm.

"I love how your skin feels, so soft and tender." He whispered to her.

"I love being held by you, I feel safe when I am here in your arms, safe and treasured."

Once again he bent down and began kissing her, they were getting a little revved up when they heard a commotion on the steps and Casey began barking. Immediately he was on his feet, grabbed his gun and told her to *STAY!* She obeyed and sat there wide eyed trying to listen to what was going on. She could definitely hear voices on the stairwell and it sounded like someone was shouting. Carter stepped out of his apartment with his gun tucked in the back of his shorts.

There were two men at Andy's door wanting inside but Andy was blocking their entrance.

"Andy, is everything ok up there?" Carter called up. The men instantly stopped talking and stood very still, and Andy looked very relieved to see his neighbor.

"Ah yeah, thanks man, they were just *leaving*. Sorry we got loud, we were just um, cutting up and it got out of hand. Won't happen again, ok?" He said nervously.

Carter could see the imprint of a gun on the guy to the left's jacket and suspected that the guy on the right was also carrying. What in the world was Andy doing that brought armed men to his door? He continued to stand out there until the men turned to leave. They hurried down the steps and one of them looked Carter right in the eye, the other turned his head in the opposite direction. Andy nodded to Carter then shut and locked his door. Carter moved to the window and got a description of the car that pulled away. It was a Lincoln MKz black with Maryland plates.

He texted it to himself so he would have it in case of an emergency. He locked his door and walked back to his bedroom and found Jesse sitting frozen in the middle of the bed. "Hey baby, sorry. False alarm, just some old friends of Andy's who got a little carried away. It's all good now they are gone." He said stowing his gun. She thought he handled himself pretty deftly, and she attributed it to his military training.

Well now that the moment was absolutely killed, he walked over to her and took her hand and helped her off the bed, he grabbed a tee shirt and put it on then walked into the kitchen.

"Hey are you hungry?" He asked looking through his refrigerator.

"No not really, I ate at Sue's and she made chicken pot pies and well I ate quite a bit…" She said apologetically.

She stood at his bar and he leaned in on his elbows and smiled at her. She reached over and attempted to tame his wild hair, and he let her. He found it incredibly sexy the way she touched him and he was beginning to crave it, and her more with every passing day. She decided to call the evening short, she could tell he was still tired and she was beginning to fade, so he walked her upstairs.

"I've missed you this week, but you are so tired, I can see it in your eyes Carter. Please go to bed early and get some rest. It worries me to see you running on so little." She said sweetly touching his face.

"I'll be fine, are you feeling better now?" He asked looking into her baby blue eyes.

"I am feeling better. All the way around." She smiled. He leaned down and gave her a quick kiss. Then touched the tip of her nose with his finger. "I'll talk to you tomorrow, Ok?"

"Yes please." She responded then went back inside.

She undressed and took a quick shower then went straight to bed. She texted Andy a Thank you for looking after Casey. Once she was in bed she pulled Casey up onto her blanket at her feet, then cuddled with her and she laid back and they both exhaled and closed their eyes.

Jesse's phone started buzzing. She looked down and it was a text from Tim. *You are killing me sis, would it kill you to let me know you made it home safely????*

I am so sorry. Yes home safe. Stopped by Sue's, begged off more food then finally came home, ran into Carter and just got in. Safe and sound. Miss you and how is our patient? ~Jess

Forgiven. How is Sue? Miss you too, patient is the same, and better. –Tim

She's good. Please get some sleep. Your country needs you. :--) ~Jesse

Off to bed with you, we will talk later. –Tim.

She remembered that she needed to change her ear piece and got back up to take it out, when Dean came online. "Jess? Are you there?"

"Hi, yes I am here, was just getting ready to shut down for the night. Are you ok?"

"I want to apologize for last night, Tim told me you over heard the entire conversation. I guess I am just tired, I never make mistakes like this and well, I'm sorry." He stated contritely.

"Dean, please, we are fine, as long as you and Tim are ok. I just don't want to come in between you too. I love and care for you both in different ways. Mistakes happen. It's all good. I am home and I'm feeling better. Actually I don't think I properly thanked you for helping me Friday night. Thank you." She said sincerely.

"No thanks needed, it never should have happened, and I will be re-running that in my head for a long time to come I think. Listen, get some rest, we can talk more tomorrow." He stated.

"Ok, please get some rest yourself." She replied.

Finally she crawled back into bed and fell fast asleep and did not stir until the alarm went off Monday morning.

Dean was back in the office for the early morning meeting at 5:00 a.m. and everyone on the team was there except for Tim who was still out with Wex for one more day. Adam was going to run his monthly sweep on the units at the S.E.A apartments where several of the CIA staff lived, including Tim, and would advise if any unknown devices or bugs were found. This was done monthly as a precaution, all team members were to turn in a list of all devices used as a matter of routine, so they could be screened out. They were continuing the investigation of the sex traffic ring and more surveillance was ordered, they were getting a step closer to knocking a chunk out of this operation on the East coast and there was even more pressure on Dean to perform and get it right the first time.

In a meeting with the director, Dean was told to assign another Handler to Charge 25 so that he could devote his time to this investigation fully. As much as he wanted to protest, given what had happened this weekend it was probably for the best. He was so tired, that he made two mistakes which for him was unheard of in his job. He was always so meticulous. He decided to assign Craig to Jesse temporarily and then he would still review all her reports and communications but the day to day interaction would be handled by Craig for a few weeks.

He had just informed Craig of the change which was to begin tomorrow and he did not relish having to explain this to Jesse. He needed to find just the right words as to not send her into a panic. They were just starting to get their rhythm back and now it was going to be interrupted again. Since this was for the greater good and ultimately her safety it had to be done.

"Dean. We have a bug in the house." Adam came on the line.

"Go. Which unit." He commanded.

"1-A. Sir. Camera. Is this yours sir? If so I can record it on your sheet for you." Adam stated trying to cover for his boss.

"Negative. News to me. Find the source." Dean stood up now and was pacing, *who in the world would be spying on Jesse? This makes no sense.*

"Adam. 1-A was swept before she moved in correct."

"Affirmative. Did it myself. Clean bill of health."

"Permission to enter her premises and deep search?" Adam requested.

"Affirmative. Report back please." Dean requested. He sat on the edge of his desk and thought about this and Tim was the only one that made sense. *He had access and cares about her, but would he really do this and not tell me?*

"Tim, check in please. Code 3." Dean called out.

"Tim here, what's up?"

"I don't know how to say this so I am just going to say it. Jesse used your code the other night to get into the safe house after her drugging incident. Did you give it to her? It's ok if you did, I just need to know Tim."

"No. Dean I swear, I have never given my code out, not even to her. Could she have seen me do it when she was there and remembered it? Or tried one similar to hers and lucked up? On my honor I did not." Tim said. Codes were huge business and you could be fired immediately if yours had become compromised. Tim started to pace himself, now becoming nervous.

"Ok. One more question. Did you place any surveillance equipment in Jesse's apartment in an attempt to monitor her and keep her safe?" Dean asked levelly.

"Are you telling me someone has that apartment under surveillance? And it's *not* us." He said shouting into the phone, giving Dean his answer.

"Affirmative, Adam is checking now. I didn't think it was you but after the code incident I had to ask Tim. I will let you know once we have answers." Dean stated and closed the call.

"Uh Dean. What do we know about 2-A? I'm tapped into his video feed and he's got a couple weeks' worth of data. Proceed?" Adam called back in.

Dean swore under his breath. That little sneak has been spying on Jesse and well, anyone else who has been in her apartment like Carter or Tim or Sue. *Is he a spook? Or is he a stalker?* Either way this was getting settled today.

"Adam, kill the feed and wipe what he has, then bring me the evidence." Dean said trying to calm his tone because now he was pissed.

"Understood." Adam replied.

Great, a lonely tech is about to undermine an entire operation. What else can go wrong here?? Dean continued to pace then finally shot out of his office and ended up in the gym, he changed into his work out gear and started running on the treadmill. He had to focus and get this thing back under control. He had a good five miles in when Adam checked back in on line.

"Dean? You there?"

"Go."

"Camera has been removed, and I left a note for him in case he tries to replace the feed. I have wiped everything in that directory on his pc that was named Jesse. Now if he has backed this up anywhere else like a thumb drive, it's in the wind. I did not see anything else on his system with the naming configuration or size wise that matched what I wiped. I'm headed in now. Do you want me to take the camera to your office?"

"Affirmative. Thank you Adam."

Dean grabbed a towel then wiped his face off and wrapped it around his neck. He walked over to the mini fridge and took a bottled water out and downed it in a couple of gulps. Then he started back for the showers when Tim called in.

"Dean?"

"Yeah, go."

"Well what the heck did you find out? I want to know who has been spying on us. Dean you are on that tape, me, Carter...That could be used against us and it could get nasty." He stated concerned.

"The camera has been removed and the data wiped. Adam is on his way back in now with the equipment. Stated he left a note for the perp. That should prove interesting. Sad thing is I have seen this guy, I think he's lonely and infatuated with our girl, and is just going about it all the wrong way. Either way, he's nice but misguided or he's a slimy perp it has to stop and immediately. I'm on it and Jesse is not to know about this Tim. Do you understand me?" Dean demanded from his friend.

"Affirmative."

Jesse was working as usual, and since they were a little slower this morning she took a walk outside and down to the garden area of the office park. She just felt compelled to be outside for a few minutes and feel the sun on her face. She found an area near a tree that afforded her a bit of a shade then sat down and closed her eyes for a few minutes. She began lifting up Dean, Tim, Carter, Wex and others in prayer, and praising God for his mighty provision this weekend in sparing her what could have been a life changing horrible ordeal. Even amidst the turmoil He was there watching over her and shielding her, and she praised him for his favor.

When she opened her eyes again, she sat there so quietly it was as though she just blended right into the garden scenery invisible to the passerby's so engrossed in their own little worlds. Two men appeared to her right, she could see them in her peripheral vision, one was in a suit, and the other man was in skinny jeans a black tee shirt with a print on it, a black rumpled cotton jacket and Doc Martin's. The suit was a thirty something, hair short and neat with sunglasses on. The other man was twenty something with hair so black it had to be dyed, it looked unnatural with wispy spikes and pale skin. He reminded her of the character Johnny Depp played in Edward Scissor hands. Their striking contrast is what caught her attention.

"Report." She whispered.

"Charge 25 go." Dean replied as he walked back to his office from the gym.

"I'm in the garden in the park. Interesting meeting going on in broad daylight. A suit and Edward Scissor hands having a meaningful conversation." She stated.

"Ok, what is your assessment?"

"Still going down....ok here we go. An envelope is being passed, I'm thinking cash. And Edward is handing him a box. Smallish 6 x 6 inches. Suit is opening the box and ok, there are pills. Lots and lots of pills. Edward is away and Suit is heading towards the USA Bank tower." She said trying to keep her voice very low.

"What color are the pills Jesse can you see them?"

"Bluish from what I can tell, they were in a clear plastic bags, but had to be at least five hundred of them or more. I can't believe I just witnessed a drug deal." She said incredulously.

"Why are you outside? Shouldn't you be working?"

"I needed a moment and felt compelled to come outside for a moment, since we were slow. Is that a problem?" She asked almost offended.

"No honey. I'm sorry Jess, lots going on. Awesome call. Any pictures?" He said trying to recover.

"No I didn't want to move for fear of being seen. I didn't want to spook them." She replied.

"Good call. If you saw a photo of Edward Scissor hands do you think you could pick him out?" He asked smirking at her choice of description.

"I believe so yes."

"Ok I am going to run this information through a few channels and see what pops up. Thanks Jess. Great job."

"Okay, I guess I'll head back to Reed's." She started.

"Wait Jess. I need to talk to you. I found out this morning but was holding off until you got off work, but I might as well explain this to you now." He said trying to make sure his voice remained calm and unemotional.

"You are scaring me. What is it?"

"No don't be, it's going to be fine. Just a slight temporary change ok? Temporary being the key word, ok Jess."

"Ok..."

"The Alpha mission has taken a turn for the worst/ best I am not sure, but its exploding in regards to size and it is now requiring my full attention. So the Director informed me this morning I am to put 110% of my time and energy in to this and the Beta program will be secondary. I had to assign you another Handler, for a few weeks, and his name is Craig. I will still review all your video or pictures and tapes, so I will still be involved, but just not able to take your daily reports. Craig will do that for a short time. However if you need me you can still call or text me. Ok?" He said awaiting her response. It seemed like an eternity before she responded at all.

"I understand." She said softly.

"Jesse, I am so sorry. But again it's just temporary until we get this investigation under better control. This thing is big, really big and I for one don't want this kind of trash in my back yard. Even if we only put a dent in it, it's a start." He said trying to convince her.

"When does it start?" She asked calmly.

"Tomorrow." He stated. His heart ached when he heard her gasp.

"Ok. I better go, I'm sure they are getting busy at Reed's." She stated levelly trying not to cry.

"Sure, ok. We can talk some more, later this afternoon, ok?" He said not wanting to let her go.

She didn't answer him back, but stood and quickly walked back to Reed's jumping right into the thick of the pre-lunch crowd. The rest of her day was a blur as she kicked into autopilot and stuffed all her feelings and emotions to just get through so she could go home and process all of this information.

Carter was home when she pulled up, but she bypassed his door, and went straight up to get Casey and the leash. She grabbed a juice bottle out of the refrigerator and then headed back downstairs carrying Casey to put her into the car. She put the sunroof back and set Casey in the floor board of the car and took off for the beach.

Carter stood watching out his window and wondered what was going through her mind, it was not like her not to come by when she saw that he was home. She looked upset or determined, he wasn't sure which, and figured she must need some space. He would just touch base with her later and see how she was doing.

Dean tried to raise her on the ear bud, but the beach was so windy it was hard for her to hear him so she ignored him. She wasn't quite ready to talk to him, she wanted to be composed not emotionally wrecked. Two minutes later her phone started beeping. *He is persistent.*

Dean at the beach with Casey, too windy can't talk and hear you. ~Jesse

Fine. Are you ok?-Dean

I will be fine, just walking and processing. Please let me do this. ~Jesse

Ok, Jess…please call me before you go to bed. –Dean

She stayed on the beach until dark and then she took Casey back to the car. Her sweet puppy face and big brown eyes searching her masters to understand what was going on. She cocked her head when Jesse spoke, and nuzzled her with her nose as if she understood every word Jesse was saying. *What would I do without you my sweet baby girl? You always listen and know just how to make me smile. Silly puppy.*

Jesse walked her one last time before they came up for the night. Carter's apartment was dim, but his car was out front. She didn't stop, thinking he may have gone to bed early still trying to catch up from this weekend. She fumbled around trying to get her keys out to open her door and suddenly Andy's door cracked open and he peeked out at her.

"Hi Andy, it's just me trying to find my keys." She said with a smile. He just looked at her with a blank stare then shut his door. *Yeah I know how you feel buddy, that's the kind of day I have had too.*

Finally unlocking the door they entered the apartment and she put some kibbe's in the bowl for Casey who was famished after all that beach exercise. She washed her hands at the sink then took her shoes off and rinsed them as well in the sink then let them sit on the edge to dry. Plopping down on the couch she reached for the remote and flipped through 54 channels of nothing interesting tonight. Finally she knew she could not put off the inevitable any longer, she had to call Dean.

"Report." She said solemnly.

"Hey you, I was wondering if you were actually going to call me back or not." He said smiling, happy that she had called in.

She couldn't actually speak in that moment and there was an awkward silence that wrenched Dean's heart and so he spoke back up again.

"Jess, baby, this is all going to be fine. Craig is a junior handler, and has been working with a Charge that was just released. And it's Temporary, I promise. We can still talk at night if you want to or need to, I just have to have my day hours freed up for this investigation." He said calmly.

"I understand Dean. I will be fine, so don't worry about me. It just caught me off guard." She replied.

"How is Carter? How are things there?" He said trying to change the subject and lighten things up.

"Fine. When is Tim coming back?" She asked quietly.

Ok that backfired. "He's coming back sometime tonight. He might actually be back already, I haven't spoken to him since this morning." He said quietly.

"Ok, well I think I'm going to go to bed, I'm kind of tired tonight." She said.

"Ok, Jess. I'll let you go." He said his chest tightening. He knew she was struggling and yet wouldn't just say what she was afraid of so he could help her. They ended the call, both sitting in the dark hurting and searching for answers.

Jesse prepared for bed and brushed her teeth then put Casey on the bed. She read in her bible for a few minutes then turned her light off and went to sleep. She slept fitfully and around 3:00 a.m. reached for her phone and texted Dean.

I realize that I am acting completely ridiculous, and I want to say I am sorry Dean. I know you have a very hard, very important job, and I am being so selfish. I know this is not the case, but I feel like we are breaking up. I know RIDICULOUS. Just ignore me, I will be fine. ~Jess

Dean also was not sleeping well, so many things moving around in his mind, he was trying to manage and make sense of all the information he was juggling. When his phone buzzed, he immediately grabbed it, and when he read her text, he smiled then pressed the phone to his forehead. Then he texted her back, *I completely understand. You are fine, no worries here. Thank you for understanding. I am here for you. Always. –Dean*

CHAPTER 21

MISS-STARTS

J esse read Dean's text when she woke up the next morning and smiled. She had to get a grip and be a part of the team and not such a Diva. She arrived at Reed's a little earlier than usual so she gathered some Danishes and prepared a breakfast box to go and took it to the CIA office for Dean and his team. She even wrapped up one for the receptionist.

She arrived on the second floor lobby of the CIA office and stated she had a special delivery for H25Dean. Miss Lane looked blankly at her then pressed a button. Then a few seconds later Tim came bounding out the door with a huge grin on his face. He picked her up and swung her around with Miss Lane continuing to look blankly on at the jubilant display of affection going on right before her.

"What are you doing here sis?" He said with a more serious face, his hands resting on his hips.

"Peace offering. I hear the way to a spy's heart is through pastries." She said grinning.

"Well I don't know about a spook's heart, but a driver's heart is completely won over by pastries." He said laughing.

"Ok, well ya'll enjoy." She said smiling.

"Hey wait, no juice or coffee?" He stated with his hand on his hip, giving her the *eye*.

"I'm just a mere delivery girl, not a pack mule." She said with her hands on her hips giving him the *eye* right back.

He snatched up the box laughing and said "Loooooove youuuuu" as he swiped his badge then disappeared behind a solid steel door. She turned to look at the receptionist who just looked at her with lifeless looking eyes. So

Jesse extended her hand and gave her the special homemade orange marmalade Danish she had saved for her. Miss Lane's eyes softened slightly and Jesse thought for a moment that she saw the corners of her mouth faintly turn up as though she were going to smile.

"Even receptionists need love too. Enjoy." Jesse said as she walked back to the elevator. Just as the door opened she heard her say, 'Thank you' and it made Jesse's heart happy. *I'm breaking them down one at a time* she thought smiling to herself.

During her mid-morning break she decided to go into the office and check in with her new Handler.

"Report." She stated.

"Go ahead Charge 25." He stated gruffly.

"Just wanted to introduce myself, I'm Jesse" She said.

"Not necessary I know who you are, do you have a report or not?"

"Wow. Um no." She said stunned.

"Handler out." He replied and the line went dead.

Holy cow, what was that all about? No wonder she and Dean had the most productive leads in the Beta unit. With handlers like Craig, no doubt details and nuances were going to be dropped as unimportant. Thank goodness this was temporary, she didn't know how long she could tolerate Craig. The next few days were an adjustment and she only checked in when she started her day then when she signed off at six in the evening.

She was beginning to think he and Miss Lane were related. Tough to read and even harder to talk to about anything. Dean had managed to check in once or twice in the weeks that followed but she could tell he was distracted and just trying to keep his promise to stay in touch with her. Which was sweet and she appreciated it, but everything was definitely different and she had to keep reminding herself that it was only temporary.

Carter was home today when she pulled up, so after she let Casey out, she walked back down to get her mail, and tapped on his door. She had only seen him a handful of times in the last couple of weeks due to his schedule or hers and she was missing him terribly. He answered looking kind of somber or deep in thought she was not sure which.

"May I come in for a minute please?" She asked.

"Sure, of course." He stated moving out of the way so she could enter.

"Carter, I owe you a huge apology. Please, please forgive me for being selfish and distant lately. I have just been processing a lot of things and I have been horrible company. I don't even want to be around me." She said trying to smile.

He walked over to her and took her face into his hands and just deeply looked into her big blue eyes lined with a black curtain of lashes. Then he placed his mouth over hers and the heat he exuded slammed straight to the pleasure center of her brain and she responded in kind. She dropped the mail that was in her hand on the floor and then it was on. Both of them no longer able to hold back on the sexual tension that had been surrounding them for weeks on end now. The yearning and desire they had for one another had reached its peak. He lifted her onto the countertop in his kitchen so that she was more in line level with him and she wrapped her legs around his waist in an attempt to pull him closer to her.

He slid his hand under her shirt, his hand running over the smoothness of her back and feeling his hand on her skin caused her to arch towards him again, seeking to get him even closer to her. She wanted him like she had never wanted anyone or anything before in her life. This was pure carnal lust at its base form and she was caught up in the emotion of it all, she wanted him to fill in all the voids in her soul and claim her as his. He also could not get enough of her, he longed to make love to her for hours on end and then start all over again. His desire to touch, taste and discover every inch of her took over, and reason was out the window. They both breathlessly kissed touching each other, this energy driving them closer and closer to the bedroom.

Suddenly his phone started screeching with an alert. He was still kissing her but hesitated and when the phone continued with its alert he abruptly pulled back to look at it so he could turn it off but stopped. She sat there breathing heavily awaiting his return to her lips. She watched as his face crumbled and he looked back up at her desperately wanting to continue where they left off but he did not.

"Oh My God, baby I have to go, *right* now. I am so sorry." He stated lifting her off the countertop then looking for his shoes.

"What? Wait, what's going on?" She said in complete disbelief.

"Main server is off line and I only have 30 minutes from the time it goes down to get it back up or it starts a chain reaction of server shut downs that will impact things at the company globally. It will take me weeks to get it restored if it totally shuts down. My time is ticking. I am so sorry. I have to go literally right now." He stated grabbing his keys and pulling her out the door.

"Carter...?" She pleaded.

"I'll call you later if I get it back up. I'm sorry." He said bolting out the door not looking back. She watched as he pealed out of the parking lot toward the highway. She stood there outside his door, looking a little disheveled at the bottom of his steps when it hit her. The emotional tsunami of stored rejection and pain that threatened to crush her right there in the middle of the foyer.

Her breathing became labored and she struggled to move at all, she desperately wanted to get back upstairs to the safety of her apartment and her dog. Eventually she willed her legs to start moving and made it inside her home.

The anguish that engulfed her was so severe that she couldn't even cry. There were no tears only a heaviness at the realization of abuse she had suffered under Jerry that was so immense that she prayed she could endure it. She laid there in bed trying to shut it back out of her mind, trying to stuff it back down but it kept rolling over her like the waves and the beach that relentlessly pounded the sand below it.

Night fell over her and she still laid right where she had collapsed on the bed. Hours had passed and she still had not moved from that spot. She heard her phone buzz several times and she could not be bothered with looking at it. Since Dean was no longer on line for her she started taking her ear buds out at 6:00 p.m. No need to keep them in, she felt like if he needed her he would call or text.

Carter arrived back home around 1:15 p.m. emotionally spent. Finally she had come back to him, and they were clicking then the alert happened. *Really??* To say he was frustrated was putting it mildly. He raced up the steps hoping she was still up. He tapped lightly on her door, but no answer. Casey didn't even bark which was unusual. He tried one more time and still no answer from her. He had texted her and she didn't respond to that either. As Carter knocked one last time, Andy's door cracked open.

"I don't think she is going to answer. She looked wrecked when she got home. I think she has had a bad day." He offered hoping he would quit knocking and throwing off the rhythm of his game.

"Oh ok. Thanks Andy." Carter replied then slowly walked back down to his apartment.

Jesse woke up around 5:30 a.m. and texted Libby that she was horribly sick and could not get out of bed, to call Reed if they got stuck. Why did life have to be like this? High highs, and low lows. Maybe she needed some medication, because this roller coaster she was on was making her physically ill. She wanted off and to leave this horrific theme park and never return.

She tried to take a shower, and get dressed but when she passed her mirror the image that it returned looked like that of a homeless person. Hollow looking eyes and pale skin. Maybe she wasn't meant to be in love or have that someone special in her life. Jerry turned out to be a nasty disappointment, Dean was a spy therefore completely unavailable, Tim was gorgeous and they had perfect chemistry just the wrong kind of chemistry, and with Carter the chemistry was there in spades but they could not seem to get in sync. Maybe she needed to abandon the idea of having a man in her life and just go it alone? Her and Casey.

She had missed texts from Carter and Dean today. She did not have the energy to respond to either. Finally around lunch time she read her texts, the first being from Carter.

Jesse, I am so sorry I had to leave like that, please forgive me. It could not be helped. –Carter.

Jesse please call me so we can talk. –Carter

Jesse please text or call me when you get this, I need to speak to you. –Dean

Jesse please, I know you are upset or angry. Let's talk. -Carter.

Tim has been in an accident. I need you. –Dean. The last one caused her to sit straight up and gasp. She immediately dialed Dean's number.

"Hello?" He stated his voice heavy and low.

"What happened to Tim, where is he?" She demanded.

"He was in a car accident last night, really bad one, he had to be cut out of the car with the Jaws of Life." He stated flatly.

"Where is he? What hospital." She asked in a full blown panic.

"He is at General, but they are releasing him today to go home. He was very lucky. No broken bones, but he is really banged up and has a concussion. Cuts from the glass and bruises. Scared the crap out of all of us. I saw the car, he shouldn't be alive." He stated in disbelief.

"Praise God he was spared. Is he going back to his apartment?" She asked.

"Yeah I think so, why?" He asked curiously.

"I will go and make sure he has food, drinks, Advil or anything else he might need. I took off work today and I'll go do that now." She stated.

"Jess, you don't have to..." he started.

"Dean I am not arguing with you, I am doing this for him and I will not be told differently. You two have moved heaven and earth for me lately, I can certainly buy the man some groceries and fix him some food. Understood?" She stated emphatically.

"Do you know how to get into his apartment?"

"Yes, I've got this. Please text me when you guys are on the way." And with that she hung up.

She ran a brush through her hair and slipped her sandals on then flew out the door. She went to the grocery store first and filled the carts with fruit and some already cut veggies. She bought some stock to make soup, bread, tortillas and a rotisserie chicken. She could make several meals out of that alone. She also bought some yogurts and jello in case he had trouble chewing things. She purchased a couple of ice packs, drinks, bottled water and some Advil then headed back over to his apartment.

She started by cleaning out his refrigerator then loaded the new groceries in and started making a pot of chicken tortilla soup. While that was simmering, she went and cleaned his bathroom and threw in a load of laundry. His place wasn't horrible for a bachelor pad, but messy since he had been back and forth at Wex's and not home long enough to really do much. She folded some towels he had in the dryer and put them away. Soon she heard a commotion at the front door and it was Tim, and someone from the Agency assisting him inside.

His face lit up when he saw her and he asked to be taken over to the couch. He had a red leather sectional sofa much like the black one Carter had in his apartment. Must be a guy thing she thought.

"He is still pretty drugged up right now, don't try and move him alone. He's a big guy and could crush you." The agent said.

"No worries, I'll make him a pallet on the sofa for now, that way he can at least listen to the stereo or television while he is infirmed. I'm Jesse by the way, a neighbor." She said smiling.

"Hi, I'm Derek. Nice to meet you." He said shaking her hand. He was tall, blonde hair, blue eyes and he sounded a little like Dean. Once Tim was on the couch, Derek handed her his bag of hospital goodies and snuck out the door.

Tim laid on the sofa so she went to fetch him two of his pillows out of his room with the fresh linens on them to prop him up. He smiled as she came back into the den and started telling him everything she had done so far today. He grabbed her hand and kissed the back of it.

"I had a bad day yesterday." He said with a loopy grin. Finally laying back on the pillows she had brought him. She sat on the edge of the couch and gently touched every single place on his face that was cut, scratched or swollen. Then she kissed each one of them and got him an ice pack.

"I heard sweetie. I am so sorry. Were you driving?" She asked.

"Well no, if I had been driving there would not have been an accident. Silly girl." He said smiling, closing his eyes.

"Ah of course, what was I thinking? I have Captain America living below me and I'm tending to Superman right now...I am a silly girl." She said kissing the tip of his nose as she laid an ice pack on his forehead near his right eye.

"That's about the only place that doesn't hurt." He said solemnly.

She went to the closet and got a blanket out and laid it across him then she removed his shoes. She was in the middle of tucking him in, when he opened his eyes and took her hand again.

"Why couldn't it be you? I love you, you are so sweet, so pretty, and nice and yet...it's not you. I wish it was you." He said sleepily.

"I don't know buddy, God has that special person for you already picked out, and I'm not sure I'm meant for anyone at this point. I love you too, but I need you to rest." She said lightly kissing his forehead. She went back into the kitchen and checked on the soup. He fell asleep and she sat nearby watching him and said a quick prayer over him. The dryer buzzed and so she went to finish the laundry she had started.

Dean had tried to text her and she did not immediately respond. After she put his clothes away, and checked on the soup, she checked her phone.

Hi Dean, was tending to the patient. He is pitiful, but he is sleeping now. I am playing housekeeper. ~Jess

Ok, just checking in on you two. Are you staying there all day? –Dean

Why does it matter? I'm sure Craig doesn't miss me at all. He is a horrific handler in my humble opinion. But I am sure you will just take it as, he is not you and that is why I am finding fault. Which he is not. ~Jess

It matters because I care. And wow please tell me how you really feel. Is it that bad? Seriously? –Dean.

Yeah it is, but I am muddling through doing what I can, praying your big project ends soon. ~Jess

I noticed your numbers for Reports are way down, I thought it was just transition. This has me concerned. Let's talk more about this later. Have Tim call me when he wakes up, I need to speak to him. It's important, ok? -Dean

Will do, TTYL ~ Jesse

The smell of the soup simmering on the stove wafted its way and he began to stir. Jesse was sitting at the foot of the sofa reading a book she found on the shelf. She saw him stirring and gently placed her hand on his foot. His eyes fluttered and he tried to sit up a bit, she moved to help him and readjust his pillows so that he was supported.

"You're still here?" He said with a weak smile once again reaching for her hand.

"Of course I am, are you hungry? I made some fresh tortilla chicken soup." She said smiling.

"Yeah that sounds good, it must be what I am smelling. It smells wonderful. Thank you Jesse."

She started for the kitchen when she realized he was trying to stand. She rushed back and had him hold onto her. He looked down at her and winked, then mouthed *Bathroom*. She helped him get to the door, then pulled it to so that he would have privacy. She went back into the kitchen and scooped him some soup in a bowl and let it cool while she crisped up the tortillas in a skillet. She heard the door crack and then rushed back to his side.

Tim was finally settled at his breakfast bar and she placed a bowl before him, along with some tortilla strips. He smiled at her and thanked her again for being there, he devoured his soup then asked for another bowl. He was starving. After a third bowl he finally started to slow down, and then drank some juice and took a couple of the pills the doctor had prescribed. This time he wanted to go to his bed to lie down and asked if she would walk him. She managed to get him into his room and to the edge of the bed and then helped him remove his pants so that he could be comfortable. He started to protest but before he could get the words out she informed him she had seen a man undressed before, and that she wasn't looking anyway. He quickly withdrew his protest and let her help him since every muscle in his body was screaming out in pain. He slowly laid back and she went back to the couch to bring him his pillows.

As she was putting them under his head, he reached up and kissed her, it was sweet, so tender and very nice, but there was no spark there. Realizing what he had done, he then began apologizing profusely.

"It's ok buddy. I understand, just get some rest. I'll be here for you." She smiled. She knew he was just making sure she was *not* the one. The kiss was nice, but nothing like she felt when she kissed Carter. She relaxed on the sofa and dozed off at one point. It was close to 7:00 p.m. when he woke up again. She took him some yogurt and a ginger ale this time for a snack. She told him she needed to go check on Casey, and he told her he would be fine for the rest of the night if she wanted to stay home. He was just going to go back to sleep.

"If you are sure honey, I don't mind coming back. I will come back in the morning to check on you, ok?" She said looking at him hard to make sure she wasn't missing anything. She checked his medicines one more time and then she put the soup away in a container. She walked back in his room, and told him his phone was on the bedside and that Dean needed to speak to him, that it was important. That if he needed anything he was to call her immediately she was just around the corner. Even if it was in the middle of the night. He assured her he would be fine, and appreciated everything she had done for him.

"I love you Tim, sleep well and call me in the morning." She said kissing his cheek.

"I love you too sis." He said his eyes filling with tears, overwhelmed with emotions over the tender sweet care she had provided for him today. She patted his hand then left his apartment.

She drove back to her building and parked. Quickly before she went inside she called Reed to say that she needed one more day off and apologized for the inconvenience but it was necessary, Tim needed her. She gathered her things and walked in the building only to find Carter sitting on the steps waiting for her.

"Carter... please now is not a good time" She stated with a heavy sigh trying to walk past him. He gently caught her arm and begged her to please sit and speak to him for a couple of minutes. She stopped and then turned to sit down next to him.

"Please Jesse, I am so sorry I had to bail last night, you have got to know that I did not want to leave you like that." He started.

"Carter I am not angry with you. I am not upset with you, I completely understand that you had to go." She said looking straight ahead and not at him.

"Then what is it? Please talk to me." He pleaded. She let out a sigh then began.

"Carter, when you took off last night I found myself looking tousled left standing outside your door at the bottom of the steps and it triggered an avalanche of painful memories so excruciating that I could hardly move. You see, anytime Jerry had a *need*, he would find me, play nice until his need was met, then he would immediately withdraw and rush to go take a shower, like I was some sort of filthy creature. Then he would go back to whatever he was doing before, leaving me all alone and unfulfilled. He never once considered that I had needs that needed to be met, and believe me they never were. I kept hoping in time it would come, but during our whole marriage, eight long years he used me and then would just as quickly abandon me, causing me to feel worthless. You are different Carter. You make me feel special and cared for, so when I came to you last night I was prepared for once to go wherever our desire or passion took us, and for the first time in my adult life I felt *alive* Carter. *Completely* alive and I sought you with my whole being... then the alarm came and *you* left me." She stated wrapping her arms around herself.

"Again I understand and I'm not angry at you, but watching you walk away from me caused all those feelings, eight years of abandonment, humiliation and pain to hit me like a brick wall. It's not your fault Carter, you are a wonderful man, but I've been doing a lot of thinking. I think that maybe it's not meant for me to be in a relationship, at least not one right now. I never in a million years would have thought I would have reacted like I did, or have all those feelings that I had stuffed away for all those years cut my legs out from underneath me like it has. You deserve so much more than someone like me who is more damaged than I ever realized." She stated unemotionally still looking straight ahead.

She shifted and started to stand, "I love you Carter, and I won't do this to you. I'm not fit to date or be in a relationship. Please understand, I am so

202

very sorry, but I can't do this anymore." She said now tears falling down her cheeks one by one. She took off up the stairs to her apartment leaving Carter sitting there all alone. A single tear escaped his steely blue eyes and rolled down his cheek, and his chest felt so tight that he could barely breathe. He sat there for a minute then stood shaking his head. *No… it's not ok, I don't want to be without you Jesse.*

Carter went to her apartment and started to knock on her door but noticed that when she went in that the door did not shut to. He could hear her sobbing and it felt like a knife was tearing through his heart. He cracked open the door and saw her laying on the couch with her back to him, her small body racked with sobs. He could not bear it another minute so he went to her and just laid behind her, spooning her and putting his arms around her holding her tightly against him.

"You may be ready to walk away but I am not! Jesse I *love* you and I want to be here for you in every way. All this that you are dealing with, you do not have to go through it alone. You have been alone for far too long as it is, and I am not afraid of your tears or your fears. I want to be here for you, holding you during the tough times and laughing with you during the good ones. There has to be balance sweetheart, and even though times right now are heavy and hurtful, it will balance back out and become less painful with time. Jess it's been a very long time since I have had feelings for someone like this, and I can't let you walk out of my life. If you can look me in the eye and tell me you *don't* love me…then I will leave you alone. I will walk away." He whispered in her ear as he held onto her. She was crying so hard that her whole body jerked and shook as she tried to catch her breath.

"Tell me, can you say it? That you don't love me?" He pressed her.

"N-no." She finally managed, shaking her head still crying uncontrollably.

"There then. It's settled. I'm not going anywhere, and anything you face, *we* will face together. I love you Jesse with my whole heart…I *love* you." He said sweetly holding her tight.

CHAPTER 22

SUNRISE

This time Carter did not let the clock chase him away, he was not about to leave his sweet Jesse, not after this hurdle they had finally cleared. They slept together on the couch all night, at one point he went and found a blanket to cover them. She awoke to find his warm body enveloping hers and she finally exhaled and relaxed sinking into him. He nuzzled her hair and neck and then pulled her on top of him then readjusted the blanket. She laid there with her head on his chest, infinitely content.

"You stayed?" She asked sleepily.

"I'm not going anywhere baby." He said softly.

"I love you for staying." She whispered. He kissed her forehead tenderly and slowly stroked her arm as he held her. Her head was pounding and her voice was hoarse. She laid in his arms for a bit then she slowly sat up to see about getting some water and an aspirin. He sat up with her and reached for his phone to text that he was going to be late today, if he came in at all. She walked to the bathroom to find a washcloth and ran cool water over the rag and placed it over her swollen eyes.

Carter leashed up Casey and took her outside while Jesse was in the bathroom. *Girl you have got to quit crying! You look like Quasimodo.* She attempted to apply more of her eye cream, and swiped the chapstick across her lips. She picked up her phone and quickly texted Tim to see if he was ok.

He buddy are you awake this morning? ~Jesse

Surprise visitor, Ninja! She brought breakfast which was great but YIKES, she is missing your bedside manner. –Tim

LOL. Happy she came by to see you, are you feeling any better? ~Jesse

No. She is going to drive me to the Chiropractor at 9:00 a.m. After that I am back to bed. You have no idea how much I appreciated you being here for me yesterday. I love you sis.

I didn't want to be anywhere else. Happy I could be there for you. Let me know how the chiro visit goes. I'm home all day, ok? ~ Jesse

Sounds good, thanks baby girl. –Tim

Jesse heard Carter come back in and she walked back out into the living room and placed her arms around his waist, he encircled her with his tender embrace. They just stood there slightly swaying to the inaudible sounds of their newfound soundtrack. Finally they were in sync.

"Why don't you take a long hot shower and I'll fix you some breakfast?" He said sweetly.

"Oh I can make breakfast." She quickly offered.

"No I want you to rest today, just let your body heal. If you want to sleep- -then sleep. If you want to go for a walk on the beach, I will take you there. Anything you need to help you quiet your mind and find peace, I want to see that you get it. OK?" He said earnestly.

"I do not deserve you Carter." She said still clinging to him.

"Jess you deserve way better than me." He said.

She looked up at him and he gave her a sweet tender kiss on her lips then kissed her forehead. She slowly moved away from him and in the direction of the shower. Jesse sat in the tub allowing the shower spray to flow over her aching body. She determined that being that emotional too many days in a row just takes a toll on your body. However, today for the first time in a long time she had a feeling she was over the hump now and things were going to be better. Knowing that Carter was by her side gave her a new found sense of belonging. Carter made a few phone calls then headed into the kitchen to see what was available to fix for breakfast.

He found some eggs, bacon, and some veggies. He started the bacon in the skillet and soon the whole apartment smelled heavenly. He was convinced the smell of bacon could fix just about any ill in the world, and wondered if they made an air freshener that was bacon scented. He was calm and relaxed, being there with her, making breakfast, it was nice and he felt very much at home like this. He allowed himself to day dream as to what life would be like if he were married to Jesse. Coming home to her every night, and waking up to her every morning. *Yes I could get very used to this…*

Tim finally got to speak to Dean and was updated on the accident, as it turns out it was just an accident and not something sinister as they suspected at one point. Tim was grieved to hear that the driver of the other vehicle did not make it. They were texting and driving, ran a red light and T-boned Tim and the other agent.

The other agent was bruised but nothing like Tim and he knew he was lucky to be alive. It was amazing right before the accident, there was something that just told Tim to relax. He knew God was in this and had spared him for some reason. The fact the he was still alive, and nothing was broken and he was not maimed, was testimony that God was holding him in the palm of his protection. *Thank you heavenly Father, I am not ready to go just yet.*

Ninja got him loaded into the Suburban and took him to the staff Chiropractor Dr. Luciano. He was slow moving and looked forward to the massage and adjustment that had his name on it. Once he was checked in, Ninja was busy on her phone reading and replying to emails. He for once was content to sit there and just be still which was normally not in his nature. Ninja looked over at him a couple of times curiously, then put her head back into her business on her phone.

How is our patient today N? -Dean

Quiet, very quiet. Not like Tim quiet. –N

Just keep an eye on him, ok? I don't think it's fully hit him yet. –Dean

Roger that. –N

Jesse came out of the shower actually feeling refreshed. She was still congested a bit from all the crying but over all felt so much better like a weight had been lifted off of her. She walked into the kitchen smiling.

"Wow it smells so good in here. Can I help you?" She offered.

"Nah, I've got this, you certainly look better. Do you feel any better?" He asked eyeing her.

"I actually do, the heaviness I have been feeling in my chest is gone." She said walking up behind him and placing her arms around his waist. He turned back towards her and kissed her lightly on the lips.

"How do you like your eggs? Over medium? Scrambled?"

"Oh scrambled, definitely scrambled." She said laughing.

"Okay then--scrambled it is my sweet lady." He said smiling. A tingling sensation rushed over his body, he was experiencing a completely blissful moment right here with her, being all domesticated and husbandly. He longed for this kind of intimate connection, he was ready to settle down and think about his forever, which was with her.

They sat at the bar together, their legs and elbows touching as they ate, he craved her company and her touch. She was drawn to him like a moth to a flame, and now felt safe to be herself with him, whether she was happy, sad, mad, irrational, he proved to her that he was not of the faint of heart. Seeing her relaxed and smiling this morning made his heart soar. Perhaps for this wave, they were through the worst of it, there were always going to be moments in life that undermined the spirit, but for now she seemed to be coming out of the darkness and back out into the sun light.

Carter's phone started buzzing and he looked down at it and for once wanted to throw it off the balcony. He swiped through to see what was clamoring for his attention this time, while she chatted to him about Susie and baby Samantha.

"Would it be ok if we checked in on Tim? I promised I would today, he doesn't have family here in town. You could come of course, he wouldn't mind at all." She stated biting the corner of her lip.

"Baby why don't you go and check on him? I was wanting to skip work today, but I don't think that is going to be possible. I have a couple of small things screaming for my attention. Maybe I could scoot into work while you are visiting with him, then we can hook up in a couple of hours? How does that sound?"

"Ok if you are sure, thank you. I just hate for him to be all alone." She said reaching for Carter's hand.

"Then it's a plan, you go see Tim for a bit, and I'll run into work and take care of a few things and we will come back together after lunch? Say 2:00 p.m.?" He said checking his phone again.

"Yep. It's a date." She said grinning.

"Ok, then I am going to run home and take a quick shower, then head out." He stood then lifted her up and kissed her goodbye.

Jesse gathered her purse and keys then walked out behind Carter to walk over to Tim's place. As she was walking up the sidewalk to his unit, she saw Ninja coming out of his apartment.

"Hi Ninja" She smiled and waved.

"Hey girl, what's up?" Ninja said with a sly smile.

"How did the doctor's visit go? Is he ok?" She asked.

"It went really well, but he is going to be sore for a while. He's been really quiet today, so I think he is percolating. Just so you know." She said hopping up into the SUV.

"Gotcha. See ya soon!" She said waving goodbye. Ninja just smiled. She had to admit Jesse was a likeable gal and not like other women Ninja was used to dealing with, she could actually imagine them being friends. Ninja threw up her hand too as she pulled out of the parking.

Jesse tapped on the door then let herself inside the door. She called out to him in case he was not dressed.

"Tim, honey it's me. Are you ok? More importantly are you dressed?" She called out.

"Back here Jess." He replied, but did not sound like his chipper self.

She walked back to his bedroom and he was lying on his side facing the door. His face relaxed a bit when he saw her and he stretched out his hand reaching for hers. She walked over and sat on the edge of the bed, holding onto his hand placing it in her lap. She very gently began to examine his scratches and bruises again along his face, neck and chest area. He closed his eyes and allowed her to examine him, he was longing for her touch and attention. She made him feel peaceful and calm inside. She brought some homeopathic salve with her today and planned to apply it to his wounds if he would let her.

"Hold still ok, I am going to apply a light coating of some special salve that will help those areas heal quickly and it should help with any scarring. I don't think it will sting." She placed a small bit on her fingertip and gently applied some to his largest cut near his right eye. Then lightly blew on it in case it stung. He just laid there letting her do whatever she wanted, he didn't care as long as she was caring for him. He missed this so much, not that he thought of her as a mother figure, but she was treating him and tending to him much like he wished his mother had treated him when he was growing up. Jesse was warm, inviting and loving, and he was definitely void of this type of dynamic in his life.

Once she had applied all the ointment, she lightly kissed his lips. "There you go, it will absorb quickly and has antibacterial properties. You look so tired honey. Did you rest last night?" She asked concerned.

"Yeah I slept I guess. I'm just very sad. There was a fatality in my accident. The woman who hit us died." He said his eyes fluttering open and tears filling them up.

"I know honey, I am so sorry. It was a senseless accident and yet I am so thankful that God spared you. I would be beyond consolation if anything worse than this had happened to you." She said running her fingers through his hair, instinctively knowing what he needed. A woman's tender touch to console him. He pulled her in tight and hung onto her as he allowed his tears to freely flow. All the pent up anxiety of the accident and near death experience, the empathy for a family who did lose a loved one, the physical pain he was in, and the emotional realization that he was truly alone in this world except for a few close friends and Wex. Tim could have any woman he wanted, he was that good looking, kind hearted, and intelligent, but he didn't want any woman. He was seeking his true soulmate and as much as he loved Dean, he truly hated Jesse was not it. She was perfect in so many ways, he just didn't understand God's plan or timing in this one. His heart hurt so much and he just wanted to be held.

Jesse held onto Tim allowing him to work through his emotions, she sat there patiently holding him and stroking his hair and rubbing his back. He was trying to keep it in and be manly at first, but soon the accumulation of pent up feelings caught up with him and he had no other choice but to succumb to the flood of emotions that over took him. In the safety of Jesse's arms he let go. When he started nearing the end he let out a long cleansing sigh and closed his eyes. She reached over and handed him some tissues, then slowly stood to get him a damp wash cloth.

She walked back into his room and he had rolled over and turned his back to her now, she made him scoot over in the bed and she sat up in the bed with him, and placed the cool cloth over his eyes. She just let him rest there and she stayed close lightly rubbing his back. His breathing regulated and she realized he had dozed off. She continued to sit there and took this opportunity to pray over him and for his crushed spirit.

Her phone started vibrating, and it was Dean checking in on her.

I'm here with Tim. He is struggling, but resting now. Happy I was here with him, I know how overwhelming emotions can be. ~Jess

I am happy you are there, I was worried about him. I know he is fine as long as you are with him. Are we ok Jesse? —Dean

Sure I guess so, I miss you. It's hard working with Craig. He is crass and harsh which is such a stark contrast to you. I can't even imagine that he is a good junior agent. Just please catch the bad guys and get back to Beta. ~Jess

I wish I had someone else available to switch you off with but at the moment I don't, I am so sorry. —Dean

I just keep praying I survive him. We are good. It's just weird and hard knowing that you are not there to have my back. You have spoiled me by being a fantastic safety net and now that has been ripped away. Like I said, hurry back. ~Jess

Trying my best, I promise. —Dean

Jesse slowly got out of the bed and meandered into the kitchen to see what she could fix him for lunch. She looked in his freezer and found some ground chuck, and then rummaged through his kitchen and found enough tomatoes and onions to make spaghetti sauce. That would be easy to eat and would last him a couple of days. So she set out to make him a big pot, she found some garlic powder which would have to do, and even found a small can of tomato paste that was still in date. She put it all together and after simmering for about thirty minutes the hearty aroma filled the apartment, she turned it low and allowed it to keep simmering.

She walked back in to check on him and he was awake now, just lying there quietly. She crawled back onto the bed next to him and laid down behind him and threw her arm over his and he reached up with his left hand and held hers.

"I love you sis. Thank you for spending time with me." He said quietly.

"Tim I love you so much, and I am so sorry your heart is hurting right now. I wish I could take it all away for you. God has a plan for your life, and it's going to be fabulous. Be patient and watch it unfold for you my friend. It will be worth the wait, I just know it." She said softly.

"How do you always know just the right thing to say? It's like this special gift you have." He said kissing the palm of her hand. "Hmmm, Garlic, you smell good enough to eat. What have you been doing sis?" He said with a grin.

"I made you a big pot of spaghetti and you can have it for lunch or dinner, or both. Up to you, there is plenty. Well, on second thought I have seen you eat, it might last you a meal." She said teasing him.

"My head is pounding. This emotional stuff is for the birds, it makes you feel like crap." He stated with a huff. She stood to go get the Advil and brought him back two along with a glass of apple juice. He obediently took them and proceeded to drink half the glass of juice.

"Do you want to rest some more?" She asked.

"Nah, I think I'm gonna move to the couch, watch the romance channel until I am compelled to get ahold of myself, get my man card back and then get back to my cars and work." He said with a grin.

"That's the spirit!" She said smiling. She left his room so he could throw on some sweat pants and come out into the den.

He came walking slowly into the den carrying his two pillows, he looked like a little kid who was home sick from school. He laid down on the couch and Jesse was right there with a blanket to cover his legs since he was barefoot, and she didn't want him getting chilled. He just smiled and let her dote on him. She sat next to him and they watched the end of a movie that had them both laughing. It felt good to see him coming out of his funk and getting back to himself. Overall he was still quiet, but his smiles were coming back and that made Jesse feel so much better.

Jesse stayed to fix him a bowl of spaghetti and made sure he was settled in good on the couch. He had a couple of yogurts left and plenty to drink. She kissed him on the forehead as she got ready to leave and told him to text her later and let her know how he was feeling and if he needed anything. Dean had texted that he would swing by for a few minutes if he got the chance to this afternoon. Tim waved and thanked her again for coming to spend time with him.

She quickly walked home to see if Carter was back yet and he was not, so she went upstairs to get Casey and take her for a walk. She ran into Andy at the mailbox and he was acting very odd. He barely made eye contact when she spoke and then rushed to get back to his apartment. *How bizarre. I wonder what's up with him.*

She was walking Casey back up the stairs when Carter called. He stated he had one more thing to do and would be there shortly. She went inside and decided to freshen up a bit, she noticed that the swelling in her eyes were finally starting to go down and she was starting to look like herself.

CHAPTER 23

BETWEEN YOU AND ME

Dean arrived at Tim's apartment for a quick visit on his way to another appointment. He let himself in and found Tim still propped up on the sofa. He walked over and sat next to his friend and winked at him.

"So how long are you going to milk this invalid thing buddy? Just so I know what to tell the Director." Dean said smiling at his best friend.

"Well after the tearful episode I had while Jesse was here today, I told her I need to buck up and get my man card back and get back to work pronto." He said with a grin. "Just having a hard time Dean. You know? She has truly been a God send. Always knows the right thing to do and say, she is amazing." He confided seriously.

"Yeah I know." Dean said nodding his head.

"I have to tell you something, because it's killing me." Tim said eyeing Dean carefully.

"Okay. Shoot." Dean braced himself for what was about to come.

"Ok, I um, kissed Jesse yesterday while I was medicated, but honestly I probably would have done it even if I hadn't been doped up. I'm sorry it just happened and well, there was no spark. She's a good little kisser, but she's not mine, her heart belongs to another. I'm sorry Dean. I just had to make triple sure I wasn't missing anything. Will you forgive me?" He said his eyes cast downward.

Dean sat there quietly for a long time, and was not surprised by Tim's confession. He understood that Jesse and Tim had chemistry in spades but it wasn't romantic. He also knew Tim was soul searching and seeking his special forever lady, and why couldn't it be Jesse? Tim shifted uncomfortably waiting for Dean to respond, and was starting to sweat.

"Timmy, its fine. Honestly I've been expecting it. What did she say when you kissed her?" Dean asked curious to see what he would say.

"Nothing really, I told her how sorry I was and she was really sweet about it. She said again that God had a special someone just for me and I needed to be patient, but that it wasn't her." He said humbly.

"Listen man, I am not tossing you off the boat for something like this, you have been through a major trauma, and Jess is fantastic, I know you love and care about her. It's fine. Just don't let it happen again." He said cutting his eyes over at Tim, then grinned.

"Thanks man, as soon as I did it I felt so guilty and remorseful." Tim said.

"Seriously no worries. At least you had the guts to tell me to my face and not lie about it. That I respect more than you will ever know. Look I need to head out, I'll try and swing by in the morning, when is your next Chiropractor appointment?" He asked.

"Tomorrow afternoon, and I have a massage scheduled with Linda. I am looking forward to that for sure. I can't believe how sore I am." He stated honestly.

"Ok, I'll make sure you have a ride for that, seriously get a lot of rest, we need you healthy. Text me later ok? Let me know you are not flinging yourself off the roof or anything." Dean said standing and shaking his hand.

"Roger that." Tim said smiling.

Dean left and went back to his car and called Jesse.

"Hi Dean." She answered sounding chipper.

"Just left Tim, he told me he kissed you yesterday." He just blurted out at her.

"Yes he did. I felt so bad for him. I mean I understood what he was doing, and I think he was just making sure that our relationship was familial, not romantic. He was vulnerable and so sweet. Apologized like crazy. Please don't be angry with him." She said taking up for Tim.

"I'm not mad at him, we go way back and I understand how his mind works. So were you going to tell me?" He asked pointedly.

"No, it was not mine to tell. It went no further than the one kiss, and he apologized so we moved on. I'm not going to betray a weak moment that he had after nearly losing his life. It's not that I want to lie to you, or that I want to keep secrets from you, but it was born out of need Dean, not sneakiness or in an effort to betray you. So are you angry with me now?" She asked her voice feeling shaky.

"Jess one of the things I love about you is your loyalty. To me, to Tim, to people you care about in general. I appreciate your honesty. No I could not be angry with you. I understand." He said calmly.

"Did you mean it when you said that you would be ok if Carter and I dated?" She asked.

"Jesse if he makes you happy then yes. I told you, Jesse and Dean can't be, it's just not in the cards for us." He stated.

"I think I am falling for him. He is very kind and I think he loves me. It's kind of terrifying, but he is so different than Jerry and that is wonderful." She stated tentatively.

"How could he not? Above all I want your happiness. Hey I need to scoot, we will chat later ok, and thank you for taking such good care of my best friend. It was a close call with him the other night and it nearly killed me when I got the call." He said, the honesty etched in his voice.

"I know, I'm sorry Dean. Thank God he was spared. Love you." She said, before he hung up.

She sat on her couch with her phone pressed to her head. She needed to start getting stuff together since she had to go back to work tomorrow. All her adult life she had worked non-stop, and here lately since she had taken a few days off here and there she was starting to realize there was more to just existing here on planet earth, and that she needed to engage and live her life. Approximately fifteen minutes later, Carter tapped on her door. When she opened the door he swooped in and picked her up then spun her around. He set her down gently and then began kissing her. She threw her arms around his neck and responded in kind.

"I want to take you out, let's go get something to eat. An early supper since we both have to get up and work tomorrow." Carter asked unleashing his dazzling smile at her. Seriously, as if she could say no to that.

"Ok what did you have in mind?" She said smiling.

"There's a place on the beach that I love called the Wave Runner, its seafood. But local not for tourists, I think you would love it. Dress comfortable, jeans and flip flops or tennis shoes. I'm going to go downstairs and throw on a pair of shorts and get comfortable." He said turning to trot down the steps. She put Casey away and then locked up her apartment waiting for Carter at the bottom of the step. Mrs. Smith was coming in and stopped to get her mail and smiled sweetly at Jesse, asking after her and Casey. Carter stepped out of his apartment and upon seeing Mrs. Smith reached over and hugged her.

"Son you smell amazing, trying to woo our Jesse here?" She teased him.

"Yes Ma'am, pulling out all the stops." He said grinning.

"Well it's working, you look like you just stepped out of an episode of Bay Watch. Fit, tan amazing body *and* you smell wonderful. I think I am sufficiently wooed." Jesse said laughing.

"You kids get going and have fun." She said waving them off.

They drove for a few minutes just listening to the radio when she finally spoke up. "I got my court date today. It's in a couple weeks. June 20th at 11:00 a.m." She said unemotionally.

"Are you ok with that baby?" He asked eyeing her for her response.

"I know I am completely ready to be rid of him and the memory of him, it brings nothing but pain and humiliation. But I would be lying if I said I wasn't nervous. I just don't know what to expect, I've never been to court before for anything." She said.

"Who is going with you, do you have an attorney?" He asked concerned.

"Susie is going with me, and no I don't have an attorney. He filed all the paperwork and I just had to sign stuff and send it in, since I was not contesting anything. I just hope he doesn't bring the new fling. That would just be like rubbing salt in the wound."

"Well I don't care how much of a jerk he is, I can't imagine him bringing her, talk about bad form. Will you call me when it's over? I won't be able to concentrate until I know you are ok."

"Yes of course. I have a favor to ask."

"Anything." He said smiling.

"My cousin Peter is getting married July 6th and I was wondering if you would be my plus one?" She asked biting at the corner of her lip. "I think you just need a suit, or a sport coat but I can find out from Pete for sure."

"I would be honored. Thank you for asking. I have a suit, a tux, a sport coat, and ties. So you just let me know what would be best and I'll be ready." He stated with a smirk.

"I'll text him right now. I'm so excited you said '*Yes*'." She said grinning from ear to ear while she texted Peter. Carter could not contain the smile that spread across his face seeing her reaction to something so simple. He had not been anyone's plus one in years.

"Peter said a suit and tie would be fine and that the reception is at the Wave Crest Country Club and will begin directly after the ceremony, and it's a sit down dinner. Fish, chicken or steak?" She asked.

"Steak is fine. I hear the Wave Crest is really nice." He stated taking her hand in his.

"Ok I'll let them know."

"I haven't been anyone's plus one in a very long time. Thanks for asking me, this should be fun."

"They are having a DJ after dinner, so we can dance too. I am so happy you are coming. You will get to meet my whole family. I hope that won't seem daunting. I know they will love you. Susie already thinks you are the cat's meow." She said laughing. He lifted up her hand and kissed the back of it.

Jesse leaned back in the seat and just gazed up at him, amazed that she was here with him, and trying to soak in every minute they had together. She didn't want to waste any of their time together, since Tim's accident she began really thinking and reevaluating her life. She felt like she wasted her twenties on Jerry, and wanted to experience her thirties to full capacity.

He pulled into the parking lot of a rundown looking Beach Shack that had surfboards all over the side of it. There were about ten other cars in the parking area, but it was still early in the day. Carter got out and came around to open her car door. They walked in the side entrance, and found a booth near the far end of the patio area. A cute dark haired waitress made her way to the table and handed Carter the menus. She stared and flirted openly with him even though Jesse sat right there, apparently invisible. Carter just ignored the waitress and kept his attention focused on Jesse. They ordered crab legs and their custom shrimp boil which was shrimp in a tangy boil with corn and onions.

The meal was messy but fun and so delicious. They laughed and ate until they were both stuffed. It was so much fun just spending time with him, and people watching on the beach while they ate. He really seemed relaxed and she loved seeing his face soften when he smiled at her, his eyes were bright and happy. He truly was criminally handsome. It was funny, Tim was amazing looking with this dark brown hair, big dimples and big brown eyes. Carter was blonde and blue eyed, but they were both tall with Tim edging out by an inch or so and both were very physically fit, tan and gorgeous. Carter's demeanor was definitely a little more intense than Tim's, he was unquestionably the class clown, heart of gold type, and Carter was the strong silent type. She was grateful to have them both in her life, both showing her examples of how a real man should act and treat a woman. Dean was not to be left out either, he was a big protective teddy bear. Sweet and tender, yet fierce when he needed to be, she was blessed to have these men be an example of how she should be treated, given the deplorable way Jerry had treated her.

They finished eating and the waitress brought them each a wet towel to wipe off with, and then Carter went to pay. After that they took a stroll along the beach holding hands just enjoying each other's company. Jesse's phone started buzzing, when she looked down it was Sue.

"Hi Sue" Jesse answered.

"I just heard you have a plus one!" She screamed into the phone causing Jesse to pull it back and of course Carter heard her and began laughing.

"Wow word gets out fast. Yes I asked Carter and he accepted." She said smiling.

"Ok, well I just wanted to hear it from you, is he ready to meet mom and dad?" Susie asked snickering.

"Sue you are so bad, you know they will love him. I guess he's ready, he's a big boy. I'm sure he's met parents before." Jesse stated giving him the 'I'm sorry my sister is crazy' face.

"Ha-ha, just warn him, mom may try and do a double ceremony once she sees him. He is *gorgeous!*" Sue teased. Very excited that her sister had caught the eye of a Greek god like Carter.

"Ok Sue, I am going now. Love you." She said hanging up as Susie continued laughing.

"Sorry about that my sister tends to get a little over zealous at times." She said apologetically.

"It's ok, it's kind of funny." He said with a wink.

They walked back to his car and she kicked the sand off her shoes before swinging her legs in, once she was secure he shut the door. *Such a gentleman.* They drove listening to the radio while he put the sunroof back, she loved the way the wind blew in, and would never get over the fact that she had lived her whole life up until now not ever experiencing the joy of a sunroof until she got her new car. *Shame.* He held her hand all the way home.

He desperately wanted to come inside her apartment but knew it would be a late night if he did, and he had to be at work early and so did she, so he walked her to her door and said goodnight there. Back inside her apartment, she called to check on Tim and they chatted for a few minutes, then she checked in with Dean. He seemed distracted so she did not keep him on the line long, and started getting ready for bed. She dreaded having to put the ear piece back in knowing that Craig was going to be on the other end.

She fell into bed closing her eyes and dreamed of Carter, still feeling the softness of his lips on hers. It was unbelievable how he made her feel, never in a million years she ever imagined that a man could make her feel this incredible it was almost as though she were starring in a movie and had landed the perfect leading man.

Jesse floated off into dream land, and slept soundly all night for a change. Carter lay in his bed beneath her room and wondered what she was doing, longing to be up there with her, but knowing for now he need to stay the course with her. He let out a long sigh and rolled over pleading for sleep to come.

CHAPTER 24

BAG OF CATS

A fter a week at home on bed rest, chiropractor visits, and massages, Tim was finally well enough to go back to work, but was on restricted light duty for another week or so per the doctor and the Director. Director Johnson knew what an asset Tim was and did not want him unduly stressed out or working while injured. Tim was a once in a lifetime find, and he did not want to jeopardize him in any way shape or form. The Alpha team was meeting back in Dean's office discussing new leads in the investigation from the warehouse bust.

Jesse entered the CIA offices to drop off an ear piece and pick up a new one. The repair center near Reed's wanted her to turn it in and get a new one right away. One of the frequency channels appeared to be compromised. She walked off the elevator to an empty reception area and it piqued her curiosity. It was odd not to see the stoic Miss Lane sitting there monitoring Lord knows what behind the desk. Jesse stood there for a minute or so and still no one came. In a moment of folly she walked behind the desk and sat down as though she were the secretary and pretended to be in charge of the front office.

Just as she was getting ready to get up and go back to the other side of the desk the elevator doors opened and a thirty something man wearing a jumpsuit coveralls brandishing a weapon came in demanding to know where Kara Lane was hiding. Jesse immediately hit the button she had seen Miss Lane press when she brought in deliveries for Dean. She prayed it buzzed him and not someone else.

"Whoa, hold up there buddy." She stated trying to calm him down. "How do you know our Miss Lane?" she inquired.

"She is my *wife* and she is *not* leaving me… ever!" He shouted looking wildly around for her.

"Well I don't know anything about any of that, I just know she went on break and they asked me to fill in for a few minutes." She stated calmly praying that Dean or someone was watching this spectacle. Then she heard Dean in her ear piece say "Jesse we see you and him, stay calm, we have you surrounded but we don't' want to spook him and get you shot in the process, but we are here."

"So Wayne, what makes you think that she is leaving you?" Jesse asked.

"How do you know my name? Who are you?" He shouted at her.

"Well for one thing, it's stitched on your uniform, so it's not a big secret and my name is Jesse. I am a secretary here too, and honestly man, I hope you aren't planning on shooting me, cause this $22,500 a year job is *not* worth it." She stated trying to feel him out.

"Kara makes 25k a year." He stated distractedly, still wildly pacing about with the gun in his hand.

"Great. Well thanks for rubbing salt in that wound mister. Ok, so here you are to fight for the love of your life I'm guessing, what are you offering her besides violence?" She asked trying to engage him in conversation.

"What you do mean, what am I offering her? I am her husband! That's enough." He spat at her.

"Oh I beg to differ, if you please. So are you gainfully employed? Or did you quit your job today to come here and harass her? Or are you merely on break and hope to have this resolved in ten to fifteen minutes?"

"I have a job. I work." He stated indignantly.

"Ok but clearly you have anger management issues and a personality impulse control issue, so from where I am sitting you are plus one on the job, but negative two on the wholesome personality evaluation." She stated looking him straight in the eye. Causing him to stop dead in his tracks as he just looked at her. Obviously confused.

"So who are you now? Dr. Phil?" He asked mockingly.

"No, but I *am* taking a psychology class during night school at the community college and I'm just telling you if you want to keep a girl, wife, whatever you have to bring your "A" game. You can't be some guy that works a minimum wage job, then comes home and plays Call to War video games for hours on end, eats take out and never helps around the house. Seriously? What is appealing about that? *Nothing* from where I am sitting. I'm just saying." She said grabbing a nail file off the counter and pretending to file a nail looking bored.

The look on his face was telling, it was as though she had been spying on them and knew their family dynamic and he was stunned. Her words stung more than he wanted to admit but she had him intrigued and now he was fully engaged. Dean and Tim stood by ready as they listened to her handle him and Ninja and Derek had gone out and around the building. Ninja was in the elevator and had it locked down so no one could go up and accidently walk in on this standoff.

"Shut up, what do you know? You aren't married are you? I work hard every day driving this truck and doing displays, I deserve to come home and relax." He said pacing again. She was undaunted.

"I know, I have a boyfriend. Ok so she works hard every day too, and comes home to what? You playing video games? Do you ever take her out, or ask about her day or are you just selfish and sucked into your own little world? You can't always have it *your* way, when you are in a relationship you have to at least *try* and make her happy or meet her needs. Do you even know what her needs are? I bet you don't." She said looking him right in the eye.

"You need to find her so I can talk to her or I will shoot you!" He said now waving the gun in her face. She remained eerily calm and stood up to look him in the eye. Dean and Tim were about to give the word to take him down with force when Jesse started speaking again.

"Sure you can shoot me if you want but let me tell you something, they had eyes on you the minute you hit the floor. Eighteen cameras trained on you gathering all your stats, and by the time you crossed that midway point they knew you had a gun, and can probably even tell you how much pocket change you have and what you ate for breakfast and how much you weigh with all the scans they do remotely. So getting away with shooting me isn't an option, because I guarantee you will be dead before you get to the elevator. Taking me hostage isn't going to work either because as you so kindly pointed out earlier, I only make 22k a year or therefore I am a dime a dozen in the workforce workplace. So ain't nobody gonna risk their lives to save me. So you just need to get a grip and *STOP* acting crazy." She said emphatically.

He slowed his pace and just kept looking at her trying to figure her out. She stood there not backing down and praying Dean was getting all of this. *Feel free to jump in any time guys... seriously!*

"Ok Miss Smarty pants, what should I do to show her I love her?" He asked exasperated.

"Ok, well the fact that you are asking is a good start, you need to show her you love her, help out around the house, take her for walks on the beach, make her dinner sometimes, try doing some things *she* likes to do and treat her like she matters. You coming in here acting all large and in charge and saying she ain't going *nowhere* is crap. She is your wife, not a piece of furniture or a dog that you own, and you need to adjust your attitude accordingly." Jesse said firmly.

"Ok. Well when can I talk to her?" He said taking a breath and letting out a heavy sigh.

"Well you are not allowed to talk to her with a gun in your hand, I will tell you that right now. So if you want to have a conversation, you need to check your piece with me and I will put it in this drawer down here. Then I can try and find her and see if she wants to talk to you now that you are calmer and not acting bag of cats crazy." She said smiling and extending her hand to see if he would turn over the gun.

Much to her and everyone else monitoring this situation's amazement he placed it in the palm of her hand and then took a seat in one of the brown pleather chairs.

"Thank you Mr. Lane. I am placing your gun in this drawer down here and I will write you a receipt for it." She stated calmly. Once the drawer was shut, the elevator door opened and Ninja walked thru and in one fell swoop she had him on the floor, cuffed and then the rest of the team stormed into the lobby. Dean could not believe she had done it, she talked him down, and got the gun away from him, no shots fired, no punches thrown, and no lives lost today.

Tim made a bee line for her and immediately whisked her away to the first interrogation room to check her over. He was trembling by the time he got her back there and he just held onto her as though his life depended on it.

"Oh My God sis, I cannot believe what I just witnessed. What the heck were you doing here today? You scared the ever loving fool out of me and you nearly gave Dean a heart attack. But watching you in action made him so dang proud of you he's about to bust. More importantly the director saw it all and he was definitely impressed. Weren't you scared?" Tim asked breathlessly.

"I came to get a new ear piece, and the lobby was empty so I was just curious and fooling around by sitting in her chair. But then when he came in I just tried to be calm, and if he had shot me, I know I'm going to heaven, so it's all good. I knew you guys would catch him. Man that Ninja is fast..." She said in awe.

Tim could not seem to let go of her and he sat on the edge of the desk and pulled her close to his chest. He knew Dean was dying to speak to her and would through the ear piece, the only person who was not engaged in this rescue was Craig and that certainly did not go unnoticed. Dean got to his office after Derek and Ninja took Wayne into custody and he shut the door. He collapsed into his chair and held his head in his hands. This was the second time in less than a month that two people he loved had near death experiences that he was powerless to prevent. It was becoming abundantly clear that he was not in control like he once thought he was and it was frustrating and humbling on so many levels.

When he got the 'man down' alert with Tim's accident he literally almost lost it thinking his best friend had been killed. Then here in his place of business, a place that he has wired and full reign over, his Charge comes face to face with an emotional domestic violence offender. *What the heck??* He felt sick to his stomach and all he wanted to do was run to her, console her and himself. Of course he realized he was going to have to out run Tim to get to her. Dean was grieved as he watched his best friend envelope her in his protection, while he once again had to lurk in the shadows.

He felt like screaming out at the ocean like she did at the safe house. He needed to go run or punch something to settle this agitated nervous energy that was consuming him at the moment. He tapped into her ear piece and spoke softly to her.

"Jess?"

She looked up at Tim and mouthed *Dean,* and he gave her a little space, but continued to hold her hand, he did not want to break contact with her.

"I'm sorry if I scared you, I was trying *not* to get shot. Did I do ok?" She asked.

"Baby, you are killing me. Between you and Tim, I am completely strung out. Are you ok, he didn't hurt you did he?"

"No, but wow was he a trip or what? I'd hate to be married to that, I hope he gets some help. No wonder she looks completely miserable every time I see her." Jesse said honestly.

"Are you ok to go back to work? You seem really calm, are you sure you are ok?" He asked.

"Yeah, I mean I'm a little rattled but I knew you guys would come, I was just hoping I could distract him long enough for you guys to come in and rescue me. By the way, what the *heck* took you so long? I had to do all the work." She said with mock exasperation. Dean couldn't help but laugh at her, she was right, this time she did do all the work.

"Well why don't you get back to work so I can take comfort in the fact that you are safe at Reed's? I think I am going to have to go to the doctor and get some nerve pills, since you and Tim are bent on giving me gray hairs." He said trying to joke.

"I love you Dean." She said sweetly.

"And I you."

Tim walked back over and gave her another bear hug, then said he needed to walk her out of the building. He escorted her back to Reed's making up a story as to why she was gone for over an hour, when she was only supposed to walk up the park and back. She stepped back into her waitressing shoes and dove back into serving.

Tim walked slowly back reflecting on everything that just happened and wanted answers from Craig as to why he wasn't on top of where Jesse was and why he wasn't present when she was being held at gun point. If Dean didn't manage this situation soon, he was going to step in and do it for him and Craig was not going to be a happy camper.

When he came back through the second floor entrance, Miss Lane was back at her desk, looking a little more wide-eyed than usual but still didn't speak or really acknowledge what had just taken place here. He found Dean sequestered in his office trying to sort through his dictionary of emotions he was going through at the moment. Tim walked in and shut the door and sat across from his friend.

"Dean we need to talk. Where was Craig while all this was going on is what I want to know? It is ridiculous, that he had not even checked with Jesse at all today. Are you going to address it with him, or can I just go ahead and kick his butt right now?" Tim asked, speaking very seriously.

"I know Tim, I'm watching him. I have to build a case first, please let me. He knows too much to just turn him out, but I swear if he puts her in danger or fails to keep her out of it again, he will be scrubbing toilets in Antarctica." Dean promised.

"Are you ok buddy? I know you were dying to go to her this morning." Tim asked concerned.

"Tim your accident shook me up really badly, and now this. I know it turned out ok, but the 'what ifs' are killing me. There was the warehouse incident, now this, what else can go wrong? I'm frustrated that I can't fully protect her short of locking her up somewhere. Am I slipping? Is it me?" He asked seriously.

"Dean you are one of the best handlers I have ever seen, and when it comes to planning a mission, there is no one better. You have got to know that, but honestly we are not in control, God is. I'm really seeing that more and more lately and I'm trying to get back to my roots. You can trust God Dean, I know your family was shaken to its core when Camden was taken. God is here and he cares for you and your family so much. You can rely on Him, and not have to take on the full burden yourself. I love you man." Tim said standing and patting Dean on the shoulder.

"I'm going back down to the basement where I can boss some kids around and take out my frustrations on an engine. Call me if you need me, bro." Tim said as he left the office. Dean sat there for a few more minutes until his phone rang and it was the director.

Jesse finished out her day, and then took the deposit over to the bank, the new guy was working out great, and everyone seemed to be getting along great. Reed had apparently told the staff he was considering selling and it was all on their minds. Jesse just tried to steer clear of the conversations, since she was still on the fence as to what she wanted to do. Today she found herself scared yet invigorated by the experience at the CIA office, perhaps she could take some psychology classes for real or go into criminal justice or something along those lines. She walked back toward the park and was going to sit under the Cherry tree again and just enjoy the day for a few minutes. She had only been there a few minutes when she saw Edward Scissor hands again.

"Report." She said waiting for Craig to answer.

"Charge 25 go ahead." He stated gruffly.

"I'm back in the park, and I'm seeing Edward Scissor hands again. He's waiting on someone again." She stated.

"Come again, who? Describe in detail please." He stated.

"Dean knows, we've been through this. Repeat report. Male 29-ish, jet black dyed hair, super pale face, approximately 5'10 and 160 pounds. Skinny jeans, Doc Martins, frumpy black cotton jacket." She stated exasperated.

"What is this, a fashion show? What is your point Charge?" He stated impatiently.

"Seriously? Last time I saw him he was selling drugs. I am waiting to see what he's doing today, he appears to be waiting for someone."

"Call back when you have something. Craig out."

"Are you flipping kidding me?" She said to apparently no one. Where did he go and why could he not wait five minutes?

Sure enough two younger guys in their early twenties hooked up with him, both handing over brown paper bags she suspected had money in them, and once again he gave them each smaller bags of bluish pills. She pretended to be playing on her phone totally distracted and *not* paying any attention to them. She was able to record it on her phone but was afraid she might be too far away.

She texted Dean, *I have a report and a video. Can I send directly to you? ~Jesse*

Did you report it to Craig? –Dean

Tried. Do you want it or not? ~ Jesse

Yes. Of Course. Hey what is wrong? I can't talk right now but I will call you later. Please send. –Dean

Ok, it's coming your way. ~ Jesse

Jesse proceeded to send in the video with her brief assessment and told him she would speak to him later. She then got in her car and drove to the beach. Lately this was her go to place, she had lived here all her life and yet this was the most time she had spent at the shore in years and years. It just seemed to really calm her and bring her back to her center.

With everything going on today, she just remembered that it was Wednesday and so she headed over to the church for mid-week services barely making it in time. It was after 7:00 p.m. when she arrived home, and rushed upstairs to let poor Casey out. She hadn't heard from Carter all day and was a little worried about him. She brought Casey back upstairs and fed her then walked down to Carter's apartment. She lightly tapped on his door, and he opened it slowly his face looking completely haggard and wiped out.

"Oh Carter, are you ok honey?" She said reaching in to hug him. He wrapped his arms around her and just stood there motionless.

"Hey you." Was all he was able to manage.

"Are you up for any company, can I get you anything?" She asked looking him over.

"Just come sit with me, rough day." He mumbled. She placed her arm around his waist and walked with him over to the couch. He laid down on his side with his back against the pillows and held her close to his chest in front of him. She just held onto his hands and enjoyed being near him, he seemed to really need the connection tonight and was just very quiet, even for him.

"Carter are you sure you are ok? I'm worried about you." She said softly.

"I just need to hold on to you...is that ok?" He replied his voice but a whisper.

"Yeah, of course it is, I'm not going anywhere."

They laid there on the couch in the quiet of his apartment for close to an hour and a couple times she wondered if he had fallen asleep on her since he had gotten so very still. However, he was awake, just lost in this emotional abyss that had taken over his day. Laying there with her reminded him that he was not all alone and he just tried to concentrate on her breathing and the steady beat of her heart strangely synching up with his beat for beat.

"Some days I just cannot seem to get enough of you." He said softly.

"I love you Carter." She whispered.

"I am crazy about you Jess, I have never felt this way about a woman before. I want to be in every aspect of your life, I just need to be near you.

"I am here."

At some point they sat up and she sat in his lap facing him, then she kissed him gently while she ran her fingers through his hair. He had his arms wrapped around her, craving her affection even more. A thought popped into her head and she started telling him a funny story, she was so cute and animated, he slowly started smiling and focusing on the good in his life and not the painful moments he had no real control over. Before long he sat there just watching and listening to her and the heaviness in his heart slowly started to fill with joy. She was the healing salve that his heart needed tonight.

"I'm sorry I have been so morose tonight. It's been a brutal day, and I just was so over everything. Thank you for checking on me and helping me to refocus. You are truly an angel." He said his mouth seeking hers again. She leaned in and they joined once again both lost in each other trying to fill the voids their days held for them. They longed to be together, but the timing was not quite right yet so they once again had to depart and go to their separate bedrooms.

CHAPTER 25

COURT

J esse woke up ready for her court date, or so she thought. She kept vacillating between excitement and full blown panic. *Is this normal?* She called Dean to remind him, and then she called Carter who said he wanted to know the minute it was over. Then she called Susie, who said she would pick Jesse up because she didn't want her driving in an impaired mental state. *Impaired mental state? Thanks Sue!* Tim had texted her and stated that he wanted to be onsite for the event, and would meet her and Sue there at the family court building. Her mother had called to say she was praying for her and for Jerry as well, since he apparently needed it. By the time she put the last spritz on her hair, Susie was knocking on the door.

She opened the door to find Susie and baby Samantha there beaming with ear to ear smiles. Sue could see the worry on Jesse's face so she walked in and hugged her.

"It's going to be fine, precious. It really is, I know you are nervous, but I will be there, your friend Tim will be there too, and Carter will be there in spirit. You are so much better off without the louse, and I know you know that, but it's the death of a dream. One you believed in at one time, and I know that part hurts. Mom and I prayed for you this morning, I know it is all going to be okay. Let's get going so we aren't late." Sue said trying to help her gather her pocket book and keys. Baby Sami kept smiling and pulling at Sue's earrings that dangled in front of her in a teasing fashion.

Susie placed Samantha in her car seat in the back of the White Mercedes 250 that she drove, and Jesse got into the passenger's side and buckled up. Sue made it to the court house in record time, whipping in and out of traffic,

Jesse was thankful they did not get a ticket. *Someone is in a hurry to get this thing over with...*

Tim was there when they arrived, and he motioned for them to follow him through the courthouse check points. He went ahead and was cleared earlier before the girls got there, since he was conceal carrying as a government employee. They had to turn over their pocketbooks and diaper bag for inspection and once they were cleared with a wand, could pick up their things at the end of the conveyor. Tim informed them that Jerry had arrived about twenty minutes ago and was with his lawyer.

They all walked solemnly down to courtroom number three and entered in through the huge Oak doors and sat the right of the aisle. Jerry and his attorney sat to the left and did not look over at Jesse at all. She was relieved that the pregnant girlfriend was nowhere to be seen. Jesse sat on the front row and Susie, Samantha and Tim sat on the row directly behind her. The judge arrived about five minutes later and they all stood. Then the judge announced the case, had each one of them verify who they were and confirm that there was no new developments since the documents were submitted last week for her review. Jesse and Jerry both nodded and agreed that there was nothing new to submit or discuss.

The judge read the report and asked if there was any circumstance under which this marriage could be saved and they both said "No your Honor." After reading the notes again, she looked sympathetically over at Jesse, and declared them now officially divorced. She explained the papers would be filed and stamped today and copies would be mailed out within the next two weeks. Then she dismissed them and exited the court room.

Jesse looked a little astonished that eight years of marriage was dismissed in under fifteen minutes of court time, and didn't quite know how to react. Tim and Susie fist bumped behind Jesse's back and grinned at one another. Neither of them had any use for Jerry and were happy she was now officially unyoked from the likes of him.

They all stood to leave and reached the Oak doors at the same time. Jerry's attorney exited but Jerry made the mistake of cutting his eyes over at Susie then dissing Jesse by making a snide remark about what she was wearing, right in front of Sue. Tim was appalled and ready to jack him up but before he could say anything Susie piped up.

"You worthless piece of crap don't you *ever* speak to my sister like that ever again." She stated as daggers flew from her eyes.

"Thanks for bringing the *mouth* Jesse. Couldn't you have just come alone like I did?" He remarked snidely.

"Jesse honey can you please hold the baby for a moment?" She stated sweetly as she passed the cooing child to her sister. Tim was watching this whole thing unfold and he knew instinctively that Susie was getting ready to open up a can of *I'm gonna whip your tail*. Her comment 'Jesse please hold the baby' was the married version of '*Girlfriend you need to hold onto my earrings cause this is about to get real*' and so he positioned himself to intervene.

Once Susie had the baby safely passed off, she balled up her fist and took a wide round house swing at Jerry's face. Thankfully Tim was there to wrap his arms around her arms in bear hug fashion lifting her up and away from Jerry. Susie fought him kicking and squirming demanding to be let down so she could smash in Jerry's face.

"Hold up there slugger, I don't have enough cash on me today to bail you out of jail." He said smirking trying to hold on to a very determined angry older sister, and he continued to hold her up and off Jerry while her legs were kicking trying to get away from Tim, to go back at Jerry again. Jesse stood there speechless holding on tightly to the baby watching as Tim wrangled her sister.

He looked over his shoulder at an incredulous Jerry and said, "I suggest you high tail it out of here before I turn her loose on you, and I guarantee you one thing, you will *not* be the last man standing. She is Mike Tyson strong and I'm doing you a favor, you have about two seconds to get out of here before I set her back down." Tim said sternly. Jerry took off quickly and murmured something about the whole family being crazy.

Tim leaned down then whispered calmly into Susie's ear "Honey I need for you to calm down, you are in family court and if they see you fighting, you risk losing Sami to child services. Do you understand me? I need for you to calm way down before I turn you lose. Ok?" He said drinking in her scent and trying not to swoon at this amazing protective sibling display of love. He felt her go limp, her arms now by her side and her feet dangling a few inches from the floor.

"Ok." She said softly.

Slowly he set her down and loosened his grip on her but did not fully let go of her until he was sure she was on board. She stood there very still, and Jesse walked over to her and hugged her then handed Samantha back to her. Sue hugged the baby tightly then looked up at Tim, with gratitude.

"Um, sorry about all of that." She said sheepishly.

"Listen sister, I thought it was totally hot, and if we had been anywhere other than family court I would have sold tickets to this smack down event." He said unleashing his best flirty smile.

"Well in hindsight it was not prudent to go after him here, I see that now, he just makes me so angry; eight years of pent up anger." She said defensively. "I know honey, his time will come, and I just hope I am there to see it too." He said leaning in and kissing the top of her head as he gave her a side squeeze hug. "Let's go get some lunch, I'm buying." He said walking over to give Jesse a big hug.

Tim carried the diaper bag to Susie's car and made sure they were safely in the car before he went to his vehicle. He was in a Black Mustang fastback today, and led the way to the restaurant across town near the beach. He picked this place especially for Jesse since he knew the beach was her special place lately. Jesse texted Dean that it was over and done, and he missed a great showdown between Sue and Jerry but that Tim undoubtedly would fill him in on the whole thing. Then she texted Carter.

It is now official, I am a single person again. The whole thing lacked fanfare and seemed strangely sterile. ~Jesse

I am happy that it is past you now. How are you feeling sweetheart? –CJ

Good I think, I was nervous this morning, but it's done, and I feel ok. Tim is taking us to lunch at Davis Family Buffet. More than anything it now frees me up completely to be with you. There is nothing in the way now. ~Jess

Music to my ears love. I'll see you tonight.- CJ

They arrived at the restaurant and were seated at a large round table in the corner with double window views. Davis' was known for their seafood buffet or you could order meat and three veggies off the menu. Tim started salivating as he passed by the buffet, and she was happy he was paying, since that man could eat. He had the appetite of two teenage boys slammed together, and she was amazed he was as thin as he was at 6'3 and about 190 pounds of lean muscle.

Susie sat at the back of the table with Samantha, and Tim sat on her other side, and Jesse sat with her back to the buffet line. They were discussing what they wanted to get, when Susie stopped speaking and just started grinning from ear to ear which caused Jesse to pause. She looked over at Tim who winked at her and then she turned around to see Carter standing there with flowers for her. She immediately stood throwing her arms around his neck, and then he leaned in and kissed her. Tim and Susie once again smiled at each other, then fist bumped.

"Oh I hope you are staying for lunch. Can you?" She said excitedly.

"Absolutely." He said smiling at her.

The waitress came and took their drink order and then got a head count for who was doing the buffet verses ordering off the menu. They all decided on the buffet, Susie stated she needed to use the rest room and asked if Jesse would please hold Sami. Before she could get it out, Tim offered to hold the tyke and Sue tried to explain that Sami didn't do well with strangers or men right now, that it was a phase she was going thru but that she hoped she would outgrow it.

Tim paid her no mind, and took the child out of her arms and within seconds, Sami was belly laughing and playing with Tim. Sue stood there completely speechless. She spun around to look at Jesse and said, "I cannot believe this, even her own father can't get her to belly laugh like this and a total stranger has charmed her into a happy cooing baby. *Amazing*." Susie stated as she made her way around the table to use the facilities.

Tim continued to talk and entertain the baby while Jesse and Carter chatted. They shared crackers, had baby gibberish conversations and were totally engrossed in one another. Jesse could not help but watch the ease at which Tim handled her niece and thought what an amazing dad he would make one day. She snapped a picture of the two of them with her cell phone that was precious. Tim was making a face and Sami was facing him smiling. It was so cute.

Once Susie got back they started one by one filing out to the buffet line, when Tim went to hand Sami back to Sue, she stuck her little lip out and it started quivering, then big crocodile tears formed in her big blue eyes. She did not want to leave Tim, and it broke his heart. Tim immediately took her back and carried her through the buffet line while he filled his plate.

Susie was again speechless. She followed Tim through the line as she filled her plate too and then once they were back at the table he held Samantha on his lap while he ate, talking to her and feeding her tid- bits that Sue signaled were safe for her to eat. She was absolute putty in his big strong hands and he never looked more content. You would have thought it was his child seeing how calmly he handled her, he really seemed to be in his element.

After he had eaten two plates from the buffet and fed her some of his food she started getting sleepy then crawled up on his chest and laid her head on his shoulder. He reached up and was rubbing her back and within minutes she had dozed off. Again Jesse reached for her phone to photograph this amazing evidence to prove to her parents Sami could be charmed by a man. Sue for once got to eat an entire meal uninterrupted and was still flabbergasted at the way her daughter took to Tim.

Carter said he would pay the bill since Tim obviously had his hands full, and Tim nodded then said the next one was on him. Once the bill was paid, he carried Sami to Sue's car and gently placed her in the car seat as she slept and he kissed her gently on the forehead as he buckled her up.

"Ok, I know who I'm calling at 2:00 a.m. when she won't go back to sleep. That was amazing. Seriously. I mean she will go to Matt of course, and my dad after some coaxing, but screams if Matt's brother comes near her and usually reacts the same way if other men try to speak to her or hold her." She said earnestly.

"Yeah… I'm a babe magnet." He said laughing. He handed her one of his business cars for the maintenance shop like he gave Jesse when the Escort broke down and told her if she ever needed anything to please call him day or night.

Susie placed it in her pocket book and then got into the driver's seat and started the car. "Thank you again for everything today. I truly owe you one." She said smiling at him. He winked back at her and told her it was his pleasure.

Carter walked Jesse to his car and asked if he could please take her home. She was still holding her pink and red roses and took a seat in his vehicle. Carter waved Sue off and said he was taking Jesse home so that she could put Sami to bed. Sue waved back and mouthed 'Thank you' and then drove towards her house. Tim walked back over to where Jesse was sitting and kissed her cheek, "I'll talk to you later sis, I'm happy for you that all this is over with for now. Love ya." He said then stood up and shook Carter's hand.

Carter drove back to their complex slowly not wanting his time with her to end. He had to go back to the office now and hoped to see her once he got off work tonight, since she was going to stay home for the remainder of the afternoon. He pulled into his spot and then walked around to open the door for her. She was still smiling and sniffing the roses and wanted to get them in a vase with some water. He walked her to her door and helped her get inside. She rummaged around and found a glass that was large enough to act as a vase for now and placed the flowers on her coffee table.

"Thank you Carter for the flowers they are lovely, and I am so happy we were able to eat lunch together. Thank you for paying for everyone's meal, that was so sweet of you, since Tim was supposed to be treating. I think it is amazing how he handled baby Sami. She *loved* him, and he seemed so comfortable with her." She said smiling.

"I know she really took to him and he seems like a natural. Susie was really surprised that's for sure." He said smiling.

"I hate you have to go, can't you call in sick or something?" She said pouting.

"I don't want to go believe me, I would much rather stay here holding you and take a nap." He said with a wink.

"Well go if you must, so you can hurry up and come back home to me." She said reaching up for a kiss.

He leaned down and began passionately kissing her, reminiscent of the one that got them fired up a couple of weeks ago that almost got them into trouble. This time it was her phone ringing that broke the spell, it was her mother calling for a courthouse update. He leaned his forehead against hers and had to smile in spite of how he was really feeling. He kissed the tip of her nose then headed back downstairs to his car and back to work.

She filled her mother in on the court scene, lunch and baby Samantha with Tim. Her mom listened intently and laughed at the stories Jesse was sharing. Jesse hung up with her mom, then took Casey for her walk, it was nice out today, the temperature was hot, but there was a cool breeze coming in due to a storm front that was coming through. She and Casey headed back inside, she took the leash off and lifted Casey up on the bed since she was planning on taking a nap. All of a sudden the events of the day made her feel wiped out and lethargic. She took off her clothes, and put on an over-sized tee shirt, then laid under the lightweight covers stress left her body as she relaxed and focused on Carter. Soon she drifted off to sleep with Casey curled up by her side.

CHAPTER 26

WHY WHY WHY?

W hen Jesse woke up it was pouring down rain and thundering in the distance. She reached for her phone and saw that it was close to five o'clock. She sat up in bed and rubbed Casey's belly then went into the bathroom and washed her face. She didn't realize how tired she was and couldn't believe that she had slept that long. Pulling on her shorts, and grabbing the leash and an umbrella she walked Casey outside. The rain was still coming down but not as hard and Casey didn't seem to mind the rain pelting her coat at all as she sniffed the grassy area and investigated all kinds of things in the rain shower. *Great...Hurry Casey, really??*

Finally the drops slowed to a drizzle and Casey was ready to move on to a new area of the grounds to investigate. Jesse slowly walked her around to the front of the building. People were coming home from work and the parking lot was busy with activity. Jesse noticed one vehicle that kept circling around like it was looking for something. It was a Black Lincoln MKz, and it was just creeping along up near her unit then it would drive down near Tim's unit in a loop. She tapped into her earpiece "Report."

"Go ahead Charge 25" Craig said in his normal uninterested tone.

"I am at home at S.E.A. and there is a suspicious Black Lincoln MKz circling the parking lot this is like the fifth time it's come around. It appears there are three men in the vehicle." She stated as Casey started to bark when the vehicle came close to where they were walking.

"Ok, and why is that suspicious?" He asked off handedly.

"Ok Craig I don't have to quantify my reports to you, I have to tell you what I see and it's up for you guys to determine if it's anything or not. Do you understand how this program works?" She said sarcastically, frustrated with his constant negativity and disinterest.

"Is that it? And can you get away from the barking dog?" He said agitated.

"Are you ready for the plates? Maryland 897-GKP. Do I need to repeat?" She asked.

"Ah no, it's being taped, so it's recorded. Is that it?" He stated back sarcastically.

"Get me Dean. I want to speak to Dean right now. Go find him please." She requested as Casey was flipping out when the car would pass by, pulling on the leash, jumping and barking. Jesse had never seen her respond to a vehicle that way before and she was trying to hush her as she kept trying to reason with Craig.

"He is not available. Craig out." He stated.

"Wait!! Don't you dare hang up on me..." She started shouting at him when the Lincoln passed again and this time Casey was being so protective of Jesse that she shimmied out of her collar and took off after the car, with Jesse trying to raise Craig again and chasing after her dog at the same time. She was calling Casey when the unthinkable happened the car window cracked and she saw the man from the Chinese Bistro and Reed's in the back seat, he motioned for the driver to speed up and when he did he jumped the curb hitting Casey. The shrieks that escaped Jesse got the attention of a tenants arriving home from work who immediately stopped to see if they could help her as the Black Lincoln sped off out of the complex.

Jesse ran over to pick up her sweet limp Casey and wailed out in grief. Mr. Smith was just arriving home and Mrs. Smith heard the commotion and came running out of the house to see what she could do. Mr. Smith assessed Casey and gave Mrs. Smith the look that she was *gone...* Jesse was inconsolable. Mrs. Smith bent down to help Jesse stand and was going to take her inside so that Mr. Smith could do something with the limp lifeless body of her beloved pet.

As Mrs. Smith was walking her into the foyer, Carter pulled up to the chaos and parked sideways seeing that something dreadful had happened. He ran up to where Mr. Smith was and saw Casey lying there and Jesse being escorted upstairs. She was crying so hard and just kept murmuring, *"Get Dean, I just need Dean, where is Dean?"*

Carter ran inside to check on Jesse, he tried to touch her arm and she pulled away and buried her head in Mrs. Smith's bosom. Mrs. Smith whispered to a crushed looking Carter that she was hysterical and in no shape to talk right now, that she had seen the whole thing happen and couldn't stop it. Carter's heart was breaking for her, and he nodded knowingly at Mrs. Smith, who encouraged him to go out and help Mr. Smith take care of the animal so that Jesse wouldn't have to worry about it.

Once she had Jesse upstairs in her apartment resting, she went back downstairs to get an old pillowcase for them to place Casey in so she could be buried somewhere. Carter found a box in his apartment and they placed Casey's body in the box and he put it in his trunk and he knew just where to take her to bury her.

An hour had passed and Jesse tried desperately to wrap her mind around what had just happened when Dean tapped into her earpiece.

"Jesse? What in the world is going on honey? I just heard the tapes and I am furious. Are you ok?" He asked concerned.

"No I am not ok. I just lost my best friend!" She screamed then started crying again.

"Oh baby, I am so sorry. I don't know what to say. Did you recognize the car that was driving around your unit?" He stated calmly.

"No, but after it circled around half a dozen times the guy in the back seat rolled down the window and it was him Dean. The gunman from the Chinese Bistro, and the one who ordered sandwiches at Reed's. Why is he following me Dean? Did he recognize me? I'm scared, what do I do now?" She said starting to cry again.

"I am not sure that he is after you sweetheart. But we are running plates now, it could still be coincidental. Either way I am on it and it will be resolved." He stated trying to reassure her but his radar was going off like crazy.

"Where is Carter honey, is he there tonight?" Dean asked.

"No I haven't seen Carter tonight, not since lunch today." She answered in between sobs.

"I am putting extra surveillance on you and your place for a bit until we know what this Lincoln is up to, ok baby?"

"Dean make Craig go away, I hate him. He is horrible. I can't work with him anymore. Please, please make him go away." She pleaded.

"I'm working on it baby, he will definitely be pulled temporarily. I'm sorry Jesse, this hurts my heart for you honey." He said sincerely.

"Thank you." She said softly.

"I have to go, call me later if you need me, I am getting some hits and need to go look at data and get people in place." Dean stated ending the call.

Dean had notified Adam and Tim of the recent events at Jesse's and both were immediately placed on surveillance. Another sweep of Jesse's apartment was ordered and Tim was going to see if he could locate the vehicle and get close enough to put a tracker on it.

Carter arrived back at his apartment several hours later, filthy from digging a hole to bury Casey on his parent's property in the rain. They lived on a twenty acre compound where each one of the kids were given an acre or two to build their homes on. His brother and his family lived out there alongside his parents and Carter had three acres of land but it was not developed. He decided to take a quick shower before going up to check on Jesse.

She was laying on the couch staring at a television that was not turned on. Carter arrived at her door and noticed that the door was not shut well, so he tapped on the door and then let himself in. She started to sit up then threw the covers back and ran into his arms burying her head in his chest. He placed his arms around her and just held her, slowly moving her towards the couch.

She sat there leaning against his chest with his arm around her and him stroking her face. While they sat there quietly he asked her, "Jesse who is Dean to you?"

She sat up and looked closely at him tears filling her eyes. "What did you say?" She asked softly.

"I came up to you when Mrs. Smith was walking you upstairs and you kept saying *I want Dean, I need Dean*. Not I want Carter or I need Carter." He said his eyes searching hers.

"I never saw you..." She said quietly.

"Jesse please I need to know why you would cry out for another man and not me." He said his face reflecting a pained expression.

"What? No Carter it's not like that at all. Dean is someone I kind of work with, he works for the government. I mean I don't even know what he looks like, we just talk on the phone and he has helped me a lot at Reed's with regulations and stuff. He was very sweet when I first left Jerry, and I guess we are sort of friends. But I was talking, no arguing with a guy filling in for Dean at their office, he is an idiot. I was telling him I wanted to speak to Dean, because Dean and I had worked on this issue before, but he kept arguing with me. All that was going on when Casey got hit, and so I don't know. I didn't even realize I was saying anything." She said pleading with him taking his hands into hers as tears threatened to spill onto her cheeks once again.

"Okay, I just wanted to make sure, I thought we were good, ya know? But when I heard that I just didn't know what to think." He said trying to smile.

Jesse crawled into his lap facing him wrapping her legs around his waist then laid her head on his shoulder. He wrapped his arms tightly around her holding her as she continued to nuzzle his neck.

"Carter, I love you. My heart desires *you*. Please believe me." She confessed looking into his steely blue eyes that looked blood shot like he had been crying or had terrible allergies.

"I love you too Jess." He said placing his warm mouth over hers and kissing her deeply as he ran his hands through her hair.

"I'm so sorry if I hurt you, I would never do that on purpose. I'm sorry Carter." She said in a whisper.

"I know baby, I'm fine. I believe you. I just needed to know if I am the one for you." He said his forehead pressed to hers.

"If you saw me in the stairwell, where did you go? Did you go back to your apartment?" She asked.

"No baby, I took Casey and buried her in a special place for you. I own some land and I placed her there. I hope that is ok?" He said searching her face for a reaction.

"Oh Carter, that is so kind. Thank you for caring enough about me to do something so thoughtful. I'm overwhelmed." She stated tearing up again, taking his hands into hers then kissing them.

"Listen, it was the very least I could do, and that way you can visit if you ever want to later on down the road." He said softly. "Listen it's late, have you eaten anything?" He asked her.

"No, I'm not hungry." She replied.

"Why don't we split something like Chinese? Do you like Kung Po or the Triple Delight?" He asked. Her face lit up.

"I *love* Triple Delight, I could probably share some with you but I like white rice, is that ok?" She asked.

"Of course. I am not particular about rice, I can go either way. I'll order us some of that and a couple of egg or spring rolls, ok?"

"Yes please." She smiled. She heard her phone buzzing with a text and stood to find where it was laying. It was Tim checking in on her. *Hey sis, I am crushed to hear about Casey and plan to annihilate the person responsible for this travesty. Can I do anything for you baby girl? –Tim*

Thank you Timmy. Very hard and painful. I keep seeing it all over again when I close my eyes. Punch Craig please, that is something you can do for me. ~Jess

Done. Heard how the punk spoke to you and I told Dean to handle it or I would rip his head off. –Tim

Thank you, Can we talk tomorrow? I am wiped. Love you for checking in on me. ~Jess

Absolutely. I am on patrol and we have eyes on you… You are safe. Promise. –Tim

Carter indicated that dinner had been ordered and he turned on the television and sat back down on the couch waiting for her. She plopped down next to him and cozied up, placing her arms around his waist. He leaned over and kissed the top of her head and then asked if she had any headache medicine. He stood to get it out of her bathroom, bringing her two and himself two. Approximately fifteen minutes later their food arrived. Carter dished it up for the both of them, she just wanted a spoon full or so of rice and a little of the triple delight. Her appetite was just not there, however his was full steam ahead. He ate both egg rolls and the rest of the rice, meat, and veggies.

He stood to clean up the dishes and throw the trash away when she asked if he would please stay with her overnight. She just didn't think that she could be alone tonight after what had happened. He told her that he had some work to do but that he would definitely stay with her. She took a warm shower then got ready for bed, he tucked her in, then went downstairs to retrieve his laptop so that he could work for a bit and keep an eye on her.

He set up in her den with the laptop so that he could monitor her as she slept. He smiled at the gentle wheezing sound she made as she slept since she was still so congested from all the crying. Why couldn't she seem to catch a break? Today started off so good with the finalization of the divorce from Jerry, and then lunch was great, but now this heartbreaking turn of events. He continued to work until around 11:30 p.m. then decided to turn into bed himself. He grabbed her blanket off the couch and then he laid on top of the covers in the bedroom throwing the blanket over him. He laid there watching her as she slept and smiled as he mentally traced the outline of her petite features with her straight perfect nose, luscious bow shaped lips and high cheek bones. Her skin was flawless with or without makeup. He drifted off to sleep as he lay keeping watch over his love.

As they slept, Adam was busy tracking down the boogieman dog killer and feeding Tim leads as he drove through the streets of town trying to locate the vehicle. Finally finding it at a night club at the far end of town, Tim pulled in and searched the lot for a place to park. The club was a new one that was currently getting a lot of hype as the new trendy "it" place to hang out. Tim was able to park a few places down from where it was, pull into a make shift parking spot, and after doing surveillance for thirty minutes or so was able to approach the vehicle and place a tracking device onto it, the minute the unit was in place it went active. Adam confirmed it was live and told Tim to get the heck out of dodge, to which Tim complied.

Andrew sat in his den surrounded by the whirring of his laptop and his rack of servers. The dim light his monitor emanated gave his surroundings an eerie glow as he sat there mesmerized staring at the screen. A pop up alerted him to an email, and when he opened it he shuddered at what he read.

Sorry about your dog, But that will be your fate too if you don't get us what we need.

Andrew immediately felt ashamed for the mess he had gotten himself involved in, and grief for the sweet dog he enjoyed so much. He could only imagine how Jesse must feel, he overheard her crying out and it pierced his heart. He vowed to somehow make it up to her, but he wasn't sure how he could. Someone had removed his surveillance and had threatened him but he didn't know who. He thought he could protect her if he could keep an eye on her. Now he was relegated to just the bug he placed in there so he could hear when she left for the day and came home. He was still taking Casey out while she was at work but didn't really tell Jesse. He was afraid that she had found the camera she would press charges against him, so he had been avoiding her lately. *I will make up for what they did to Casey, I promise. If I survive that is.* He thought to himself.

He responded to the email that he understood, and then hung his head in shame. Desperately trying to hack the code he had before him, he kept searching the code and de-bugging as he went along. He was so stressed out that it made it hard to concentrate and hearing her off and on next door didn't help. He was unsure how he had exactly gotten to this place of desperation, but knew after this job some things in his life were going to have to change. There were going to have to if he wanted to live past the ripe age of thirty five.

CHAPTER 27

LULL

The next couple of weeks proved to be difficult for Jesse as she tried to adjust to a routine that did not involve or revolve around Casey. On most days she was ok, but occasionally out of the blue she would tear up and cry, her heart aching for her furry friend and constant companion. Carter was completely sympathetic and supportive, just letting her work through her emotions with him close by ready to step in with a hug or cuddle as she needed it. The crew at Reed's sent her a nice card and bought her a charm bracelet with a little dog on it, along with a cross, a heart and a sandwich charm. She was touched by their sweet gesture and made a point to wear it daily to honor them.

Dean was back on duty with Jesse since Craig had been suspended. They settled easily back into their routine and all seemed to be well in their faux spy world. Based on the events surrounding Casey's untimely demise, and the warehouse busts they were getting specific data feeds and information on a daily basis now. Still no arrests other than the bartender and cronies, but they were building a strong case and trying to see how far up the food chain they could go in this operation to bring down the criminals orchestrating this heinous enterprise. He was working closely with other operative teams in New York, New Jersey and Virginia Beach running down leads on perpetrators operating under the same M.O.

Tim and Jesse had made another weekend trip down to see Wex and she couldn't wait to show him the pictures of Tim and baby Samantha. Wex teared up upon seeing the pictures and exclaimed that he had hope for that tall lanky boy yet. He was still struggling with his hand since he didn't have full strength in it yet, but overall was able to do the majority of what he needed to do. He had trouble casting and reeling in the bigger nets, but other than that was managing. Tim tried to keep an eye on him to make sure that he did his exercises, he would come down when he could to help do stuff around the house, and restaurant as needed. Occasionally Jesse would come with him and fuss over Wex who adored the attention another female would bring.

Overall life for Jesse had finally hit a nice rhythmic flow and things were good. Really good. Things with Carter were going very well, and she finally told Reed that she wanted to go back to school and would not be pursuing keeping the restaurant on her own as much as she appreciated the opportunity. She wanted to dare to dream her life could be really different and that she could pursue something she was passionate about.

Peter's wedding was this upcoming holiday weekend and her parents had come in a couple days early to spend time with Susie and Matt. Sue was having them all over for supper on Thursday night for Lasagna and salad. Jesse and Carter were all set to go when he got an urgent work call and had to divert. He sent her along ahead of him, and said if he finished early he would still stop by Susie's to meet her parents. She arrived at Sue's with a chocolate cake and no date. Everyone was gracious and stated they understood and hoped he would still make it. Dinner was delicious and they were just sitting down for dessert when the doorbell rang. Matt got up to answer and it was Carter, he had made it after all. Sue immediately made him a plate and he sat and ate supper while they had dessert.

Of course Jesse's mother was completely charmed by Carter, and her father who was watching him very closely seemed to be relaxing as the evening wore on. Carter was respectful and very attentive to Jesse, which went a long way with her parents. He was even good with Samantha, but not as charming as Tim, and in light of that revelation, he was convinced that Tim was indeed the child whisperer.

"Mr. and Mrs. Whitmore, it was a pleasure to finally meet you both." Carter stated as he shook their hands as they got ready to go home for the night and stated he would see them tomorrow night at the rehearsal dinner.

Jesse was just beaming and her parents were delighted to see their baby girl so happy. Susie had already filled them in, but she made him seem too good to be true, however after seeing him for themselves they concurred with her assessment. *He was a catch.*

He followed Jesse home then walked her to her apartment and stayed for about thirty minutes or so before tearing himself away to go back to his place. These evenings were getting harder and harder to deal with and he longed for the day when he wouldn't have to leave her at night. When he could claim her rightfully as his and wake up beside her the next morning. *It will come. One day it will happen and we will be joined.*

The rehearsal dinner was light and fun, with family in town from all over the south east. It was like a mini family reunion and Carter was doing his best to keep up. The women there were flabbergasted at the hunk who was Jesse's date. One jealous cousin made the mistake of jokingly stating that Jesse must have spent her life savings to pay for him to escort her to this event since she was now divorced from Jerry. Carter overheard the comment, then stepped up and replied that he would have gladly given *his* life savings to pay Jesse to bring him. That seemed to shut them up, and he was thankful that she did not hear their snide remarks. He leaned down and sweetly kissed Jesse then slid his hand into hers and walked outside to enjoy the light breeze.

They decided to duck out of the party a little early to head home and have some alone time. Since her day was pretty much planned out for her tomorrow and he wouldn't get to see her until he picked her up for the wedding, they made haste getting back to her apartment. They ended up on the sofa making out like a couple of teenagers. He craved her scent, her touch, and her lips. He just wanted to feel her next to him. She laid there with her head on his chest just listening to the strong beat of his heart and it lulled her to sleep.

Soon after he too drifted off to sleep. He woke early the next morning to some muffled noised next door. Carter had just began to stir, when the loud crash came thundering through the unit. He immediately jumped up and shot out the door, and met Mr. Smith on the landing both of them looking at Andy's door. Mr. Smith stepped up to knock on the door first. Andy finally answered and they could see past him and inside his apartment which appeared to be in shambles.

Andy looked like he hadn't slept in days and seemed more strung out than usual.

"I um, am sorry. I tripped and knocked some stuff over. I'll try and keep it down. Sorry if I woke you up." He managed.

"Andrew you don't look well, are you sure you are ok? Can we help you with anything?" Mr. Smith offered.

"I wish you could help Mr. S. I will be fine." He said softly, looking very guilty. Mr. Smith and Carter looked at each other knowingly and then told Andrew to take care. Carter tip toed back into Jesse's apartment and was stunned that through all the commotion she didn't wake up. He covered her back up then went into her bathroom to wash his face and rinse his mouth out.

He knelt down by the sofa and gently traced her forehead with his forefinger, then lightly ran his finger down her cheek to her chin then he leaned in and kissed her like sleeping beauty. Her eyes fluttered and she slowly began to smile.

"Now that's an alarm clock." She said sleepily. "Love waking up to you Carter."

"I need to head out baby, I have some things to do today before I pick you up at three for the wedding, and you need to get ready for your day of beauty or whatever it is you ladies are embarking on today." He said smiling.

"Ooooh, do you have to go?" She said poking her lip out to pout.

"Keep doing that and I will have to stay here all morning kissing you until you get up." He said playfully.

"Ah so very tempting, but I know you need to go. See you later?" She asked as though she weren't sure.

"You know it baby. I'll be here at three sharp." He said unleashing a dazzling smile as he kissed the tip of her nose. She managed to get up off the couch and saw him to the door.

Dean sat in front of his monitors and tried to disseminate the data that was coming in waves, Adam walked in and wanted to update him on the bug sweep in Unit 1A.

"The sweep produced a bug, a listening device, but no video feed this time. It's new because I swept that place twice when I found the video feed. So I tried to make a point by making it look like I wiped his data and I left him yet another warning. But from what I can tell he is flipping out, so I started digging into what he was working on. It's hinky boss." Adam said sitting on the edge of the desk.

Dean leaned back in his chair and rubbed his stubble as he thought. Then he pulled up some surveillance he had Adam put in the man's apartment while he was in the shower. He looked like he was trashing his own place, either that or someone else had. Yes something has definitely upset his balance and he was not reacting well.

"So what do you think he's involved in Adam?" Dean asked curious for his assessment.

"Hacking, definitely trying to hack something and to me it looks like a bank or financial institution. Why I don't know. It really doesn't fit his profile. other than he is in some debt right now, and who knows maybe he's doing it for someone else. I mean honestly if he needed to pay off his debts he could hack a single account and steal their identity, which is easier than taking on the whole bank. That's what makes me think he is working for someone else. In my humble but astute opinion." He stated grinning from ear to ear.

"I agree, I mean I have been looking over his profile and he's not really a criminal. He's a free-lance programmer, but his history shows no prior brushes with the law and previous employers were pleased with his work. He also doesn't flag as perp. So I am not sure why he was bugging Jesse's place unless he has just become paranoid?" Dean pondered out loud.

"I don't know boss but I think I have majorly stressed him out. I would hate to see him snap and take it out on Jesse. Should I give him back his stuff and just monitor him from afar?" He asked.

"Keep copies of it here and yes definitely keep a close eye on him, if he is trying to hack a bank we need to be on top of that before he succeeds." Dean stated levelly.

"From what I am seeing he is nowhere close to hacking it. I mean I ran it here and had it hacked in like an hour. So I'm thinking hacking isn't his forte. But I will definitely keep an eye on him. I'll advise as things progress." Adam said as he slid off the desk and headed back to his watchful perch.

Dean went back to his data and continued working on the next stake out that was scheduled for mid-week. Tim was now setting up a new Audi S7 and seemed to be in mechanic hog heaven. He took it on a test drive this morning and made it to Charleston in an hour and five minutes. That trip normally takes a little over two hours one way. He was on his way back, so he called Dean to report in on the trip.

"Report." Tim stated.

"Go." Dean replied.

"Oh my my…I think I want one of these." He stated laughing.

"I hear ya buddy. You are gonna have to get a second job at a convenience store working second shift if you get another vehicle." Dean teased.

"True that. Trip was smooth, SC Highway Patrol was on board and gave me space. Car handles very smoothly. Heading home now, but taking it at a relatively normal pace. I should be home in about an hour or so wanna grab some lunch?"

"Yeah hit me up when you are ten minutes out and I'll come on down." Dean replied.

"Roger that." Tim said disconnecting.

Jesse was at the Salon getting another trim and splurging on a facial for the wedding. Susie and her mother were next door at the nail salon getting a mani-pedi. After that they were all heading out for a quick snack since all of them had skipped breakfast to get an early start. When she finished the facial, her skin felt new, like baby Samantha's, so very soft and supple. She almost hated to put any makeup on, not that she wore a lot, but she decide to put on a light layer, mostly playing up her eyes and lips.

They finished lunch and then sat near the beach at a cabana type bar sipping juice smoothies. The beach once again calmed her nerves as her mother grilled her on the prospects of Carter's intentions. Sue sat back laughing and enjoying every minute of this conversation spurring her mother onward. Jesse remained optimistic, but did not give anything away. She knew Carter loved her but he had made no mention of making an honest woman out of her. Then again her divorce was still so recent, she wasn't expecting anything this soon, and pretty much told her mother that.

The ladies finally pulled themselves away from the hypnotic lull of the ocean and back to reality and the wedding ceremony which awaited them.

CHAPTER 28

WEDDING BELLS

C arter arrived right on time to pick Jesse up and was blown away when she opened the door. She was a vision with her naturally high-lighted blonde hair and the Indigo dress making her eyes completely stand out. He was actually speechless for a few moments as he took in the vision that was his girlfriend.

"Jess you look so beautiful. I doubt the bride will want you anywhere near her, because I assure you all eyes will be on you my love." He bent down and kissed her ever so lightly on the lips.

"Carter, you look amazing in a suit. I mean you pretty much look amazing all the time, but you look like you stepped out of a magazine. I am going to have to beat my cousin, Larisa off you. She talked non-stop about you last night to Sue and mom." She said with a nervous laugh.

"Angel, I assure you that even in a sea of women, you are the only woman for me. I'm not letting you out of my sight." He said winking at her. He held his hand out to take hers and walk her down the steps and out to his car. He made sure he had it detailed before tonight's venture. Nothing better looking than a Black vehicle that has been freshly washed and detailed.

They arrived at the church and she had to go back to the Bride's dressing area since she and Sue were honorary bride's maids. Carter ended up sitting with her parents and Matt. As the music started she and Sue were the first two to be escorted down the aisle, Carter beamed with pride that he was there with Jesse. He realized that he was partial but Susie and Jesse were definitely the two prettiest girls in that wedding party except for the bride, who was a cute girl.

There was one point in the service where they were reciting their vows and Jesse looked over at Carter grinning and his heart absolutely melted. It was in that moment that he knew she was going to be his happily ever after and was not about to let her get away from him. Jesse's father watched the whole exchange and couldn't help but smile, he longed to see his baby girl happy and content, if this strapping young man was the one, who was he to interfere? If he had already managed to win over Susie that was half the battle, there is no way on this earth that Sue would allow another Jerry into Jesse's life.

The happy couple was presented as husband and wife and everyone stood as they exited the church, then the guests followed them out and left to head over to the reception area. The bridal party stayed to have pictures taken so Jesse had to lag behind and Carter sat patiently as they posed and took various bridal party shots. The photographer even took a picture of Jesse and Carter as a favor for Susie. Once the photographer was finished with them he released them to go since he only had the bride and groom shots left to take. Carter took Jesse's hand and escorted her to his car.

"Jesse, this may seem wildly inappropriate, but I want you to know that I have every intention of marrying you. I don't know when, a lot of that will depend on you, but I want you as my wife. I have never been surer of anything in my life." He stated seriously as his beautiful eyes teared up.

"Me?" She whispered. "You want me?"

"More than I can adequately express. Yes." He said smiling. He helped her get into the car then stooped down ardently kissing her. "God how I love you." He stated breathlessly.

"I love you too, you have shown me what true love is Carter and I treasure every moment I get to spend with you." She said casting her big blue eyes up at him causing his stomach to flip flop.

They arrived at the country club and were seated at a table with her sister and brother in law, and her cousin Courtney and her husband Jackson. The reception was classy, the food was delicious, and they had a wonderful time mingling and dancing. The bride and groom exited the festivities around 9:30 p.m. to catch a flight, but the rest of the crowd stayed until a little after eleven. Jesse and Carter took one last turn on the dance floor lost in each other as they swayed back and forth to the soft music that flowed out of the speakers. All eyes were on them as they moved ever so slightly across the floor, as though they were the only two people on the planet. Most of Jesse's family understood her marriage had been a difficult one, and were thrilled to see her with such a handsome man who seemed to be crazy about her.

He took her hand and led her off the floor as the DJ began to shut down the show. They hugged her parents and Sue and Matt as they all started filing out of the country club and back to their vehicles. His phone started going off the minute he got into the car. He took one look and let out a heavy sigh.

"Hey baby, I am going to have to drop you off and head into the office to check on a server that is overheating. I am so sorry. Tonight has been one of the best nights I have had, maybe ever." He said forlornly.

"Oh Carter, I'm sorry, you must be exhausted. There is no one else who can go in for you?"

"I am afraid not, I will walk you up, but then I have to head out. I'll call you in the morning, ok?"

"Sure. I'll be waiting for you." She offered.

He got her secured upstairs then ran into his apartment to quickly change out of his suit, then he headed into the office. Jesse hung up her party dress, washed her face and then collapsed into her bed. It had been a terrific day, and the wedding was so beautiful, she knew Peter was going to be very happy and was elated for them. They flew to St. Thomas for their honeymoon, a place that Jesse longed to visit. She was asleep within minutes barely stirring during the night, dreaming of Carter.

CHAPTER 29

REALITY CHECK

S unday proved to be a disappointment after such a wonderful Saturday
since Carter had to work all day. He did touch base with her and texted,
but she did not get to see him again which was hard on both of them.
Monday morning rolled around a little too early for Jesse's liking and she
struggled to get moving and down to Reed's on time. Today's specialty was
the Tuna Melt, not one of her personal favorites, but seemed to be a patron
favorite. Hannah was there bright and early and Libby showed up about
twenty minutes later, and then they started wiping down the tables and prepping the meats and veggies for the sandwiches and Jesse set out the Danishes
and started the coffee brewing.

The morning rush was a little busier than usual, it was as though no one
had eaten breakfast at home this morning and were all filing into Reed's for
their pre-crush of the day nourishment. Jesse was thankful since it caused
the morning to go by quickly. She was setting up the fans outside when her
table of eight came romping across the street whooping at her. Jesse put her
hands on her hips and then waived her hand over their table as if to say, *just
for you, it's all ready.*

Doc, and Mack gave her a big hug before sitting down and Yoshi held
up his hand for a high five. The rest of the crew took their seats and started
rattling off their drink orders at her. She smiled and left for the kitchen to
fill their order. Doc and Mack took turns calling and checking on her after
the warehouse incident, but as a group it was never spoken of again. She was
grateful for that show of kindness. Even Yoshi was quiet about it and she
felt like Mack must have threatened his life for him to remain this silent. Or

perhaps it was that they all felt the gravity of the unfortunate situation and realized what could have happened was no laughing matter.

Today they each ordered something different and no one got the daily special. To be honest it was so hot outside today that the thought of eating a hot tuna melt sandwich even made her stomach lurch. Perhaps this should be moved to the winter menu. After they had finished eating, she broke the news to them that Reed's might be changing hands or worse case closing, and another restaurant would take its place. Either way, she was going to be going back to school and finding another part-time job. They were saddened and yet happy for the opportunity that she might have for a career change. The table of eight was very fond of Jesse and wanted nothing but the best for her, she was more than their favorite waitress, she was their friend.

This time as they left to head back to the base, they all hugged her as they said their goodbyes. She cleared off their table then proceeded to finish working the tables inside. The crew made haste as they cleaned up today, all of them ready to get out of there on time. Jesse went into the office to make up the deposit and check in with Dean. She stopped to text Carter first.

This day feels like it is three days long, or that God added extra hours to it... Miss you. Had the most incredible weekend, wishing it was last Friday all over again. ~Jess

You read my mind sweetheart. I'm afraid I'm going to have a late night, lots of issues going on here. If it's not too late I will pop up and say goodnight. Miss you so much I ache. –Carter

If you are working late, then I might go to Susie's for dinner. Please come up regardless of how late. ~Jess

Give them my best and I will see you later tonight. Love you. –Carter.

Love you. ~Jesse

"Report." She stated feeling tired all of a sudden.

"Hey Jesse, go." Dean replied.

"Hey buddy, nothing much going on here. I'm exhausted. Question." She said.

"Go." He replied.

"I'm thinking about school, what should I do? Am I too old for criminal justice? I'm kind of liking the spy stuff but, I'm sure I can't just show up on the second floor and say *Hi I want a job*. Ya know?"

"True, but you do have an excellent reference in me and of course Tim. There are a couple of positons here like unit admin, or secretary. Pay isn't bad, and if you were to get assigned to my team, well then you would get the awe-some perk of getting to work with me and Tim and Ninja." He said laughing.

"You mean I would actually get to see what you look like? For real?" She said laughing.

"Yes. I just hope you won't be disappointed with my looks. We make a great team Jess. Perhaps if you did come on board here, it might help you decide what your passion is, if you are unsure." He said earnestly.

"I will definitely keep that in mind. Thanks Dean. I'm heading to Sue's for dinner, so I will chat with you tomorrow, ok?"

"Be safe."

"I will. Night."

Jesse took the deposit over to the bank and before heading to her car, once again left cold cut sandwiches out in the box with four bottles of water since it was so hot outside. Part of her felt odd doing this, yet she just couldn't rest at night thinking about these youths out there with no food rummaging through trash cans. Regardless of how they got into their situation, she felt like she needed to do something to minister to them.

Susie threw open the door, looking ragged and completely unprepared for company. Jesse immediately came in and took over with Samantha. She followed Sue into the kitchen and asked where their parents were.

"They are over at Aunt Linda's house right now but will be here any minute and nothing is ready. Samantha has been fussy all day and Matt actually had to go into the office today so it's been a little hectic." She said exasperated.

"What did you want to do for supper tonight and I can get it going?" Jesse offered.

'Honestly I bought crab legs which should be easy to do but I was going to make baked potatoes but it's too late to try and get that started."

"Ok I can get the crab legs washed and started. Do you have any red potatoes, mixed spices and an onion? I have a quick side recipe that is fabulous and super easy. It would complement your seafood perfectly." Jesse said smiling.

"Sis you are a Godsend. Thank you and yes all the potatoes are in the bin over there and the onions are right above it in the hanging basket. I am going to lay her down for a few minutes and attempt to take a shower. I feel gross." Susie said.

"Sure you go on, I've got this."

She was well into washing the fifth pound of crab legs when her parents arrived. She explained that Susie had a rough day and was just now getting a shower. Her mom came in and helped her cut up the potatoes and onions for the side dish. Sue had a spinach salad already made so that was their green for the meal. It was nice all of them milling around in the kitchen, and the only one missing in her mind was Carter.

Matt arrived home right before they set dinner on the table, and he immediately checked in on Susie. Matt was six years older than Sue and had turned the big four zero last December. He was a financial genius and spoiled her older sister with affection as well as worldly possessions. They had a nice rhythm she was high strung and high maintenance, and he was very laid back and easy going, to a point. Sue knew exactly how far she could go, before he would put his foot down. Which thankfully wasn't often, Susie could be a handful, but she loved and respected Matt so there was balance in their relationship. Jesse often envied her sister and the charmed life she led.

Before Susie had Samantha she was a powerful buyer for a national retail chain store at the mall. She had gone to work for them right after college and had built quite a career for herself in a short amount of time, but the stress she put on herself was ridiculous. She had been making nearly six figures herself for the last couple of years, traveling all over the world for her job. Her early pregnancy was fraught with problems so Matt insisted she go to half days then stay home for at least the first year Sami was here. By the time Sami arrived, Sue was more than happy to quit her high profile job and stay home with the baby. The shine of the high profile job was losing its luster in her eyes, and she longed to get out of it and leave behind the fourteen hour days and work place drama. Matt made more than enough money to cover all their needs and wants, so Sue never had to work another day in her life if she didn't want to, and that was an awesome position to be in.

Jesse and her mom had the table set and food placed when Sue emerged from the upstairs bedroom looking a little fresher, and Matt was holding Sami who was finally smiling. They dove into the crab legs and the conversation was lively. Their parents were heading back to Florida in the morning, so Jesse was thankful to have this last bit of family time with them. The men cleaned up the kitchen so the gals could go relax in the den before Sami went down for the night.

Sue mentioned that she had seen in the paper where Jerry had already remarried almost immediately after the divorce, literally days after. Jesse, didn't even really react which caught her mom and sister off guard. She was completely over Jerry and the joke that their marriage was in retrospect. Jesse was moving on and with Carter, she felt like she had the love and balance in a relationship she had always desired. Cindy or whatever her name was can have him lock stock and barrel. *Good Riddance.*

The entire month of July went by so quickly, and they were into August before Jesse could blink. Things were going smoothly at Reed's and she began looking into the local college for career and curriculum ideas for the fall semester. Carter was becoming a permanent fixture around her place whenever they had a spare moment and they were still tearing themselves away to their separate homes with the late night stroke of the clock. Never in her life did she ever imagine she could be this happy and satisfied in a relationship. Dean was still acting as her handler and they continue to be a great lead team, surpassing the other Charges in credible reports. He was still pulling double duty handling her and leading the Alpha team on recon missions for this human trafficking ring.

August was also her six month mark and she needed to decide if she was going to re-enlist in the program, or move on. Leaving the program meant leaving Dean forever, and she just wasn't sure she was ready to let go of him and Tim and the friendships she had developed there. Part of her felt selfish about staying on, but she really did like the work she was doing; helping to make a difference in her community even if her community didn't know she existed.

Dean looked down at his phone at the 'all call' alert his father put out signaling to all the kids they were needed at the house immediately. He quickly responded he was on the way. His chest seized up and he felt like he had been punched in the stomach. For his dad to signal like that, it had to be something very serious. He ran down to the parking garage and took the first vehicle he could find at his disposal since his was being serviced. He tried to tap into Derek's ear piece to see where he was and he was already on the way by, approximately ten miles ahead of Dean.

His father devised this system in subsequent years after Camden was taken, and the children were much older. This was his way of getting to them immediately when he needed to impart information to them that impacted them as family. It had been several years since it had been used, and Dean could only imagine what was going on at his parents' home.

He pulled into the circular driveway, apparently the last to arrive. He saw his older sister Leah's car, Derek's and even Lily's. *How did she get here so quickly? She lives in another state.* He walked through the front door and his father met him in the foyer with Derek right behind him. His father looked weary and drawn, he looked over his shoulder and told Derek to go back and see his mother. Then he reached over and hugged Dean tightly.

"Son, we have found Camden, and he is dead." He whispered hoarsely into Dean's ear.

"No...no dad." He stammered starting to reel backwards. His father held him tightly and reassured him it was going to be ok.

"It's a very long story, your mother will fill you in, but he died shortly after he was taken from us son, about two to three days later. It was an accident of sorts, I guess if you can call it that. I love you son, so much. Please know that in your heart. Tell me you know that I love you." He pleaded.

"Yes sir, always. I know you love us all. I know it was hard to look at me sometimes and also see what you were missing, but I know you love me." Dean said softly.

"I am so sorry my son if I ever made you feel less important due to what happened to Camden. You are right, it was hard at times seeing you and knowing that he was missing that is true, but I never ever stopped loving you nor did I love him more." He said breaking down.

"No dad, we are good, I know you love me too. I do. I can't even imagine what you and mom had to deal with, having three little kids and then his kidnapping to deal with too. I love you dad." He said patting his dad on the back.

Derek came back out to the foyer, and gently put his hand on his father's back. He looked at Dean, and said, "Momma wants you now." Dean kissed his father's cheek and he and Derek traded places. He walked slowly to his parent's bedroom passing the kitchen where Leah, and Lily were huddled around the kitchen table softly crying and clinging to one another.

He lightly tapped on the door, and then entered. She was sitting in an oversized contemporary reading chair, he knelt down before her and laid his head in her lap tears streaming down his cheeks. She tenderly ran her fingers through his hair and stroked his face.

"Hello my sweet angel. I suppose your father told you our news? I need for you to listen to me, honey ok? It's important my love. I want you to know I made peace with God a long time ago over Camden, I had to or I would not have survived it and I had a family to raise. If he was dead then I had to release him back to God who gave me you two to begin with, and if he was alive, I prayed that one day we would be reunited. I need for you my sweet son to please make peace with God over this, otherwise I fear you will never be able to move on. Can you promise me you will try?" She asked.

He attempted to nod that he would try and reached for her hand.

"Precious, there was a death bed confession that led us to Camden. The troubled young woman who took him was seriously ill, and confessed everything to her younger sister and their pastor. Apparently as a young woman she had suffered three miscarriages all in her second term, and back to back. She was depressed and desperate for a child, her husband had left her after the third miscarriage, causing her to spiral out of control. She had observed

255

us at the park, and saw that I had two babies, and so she took Camden as he slept. Then she apparently traveled back to New Mexico to see her family, showing him off as her new baby son. What she didn't count on was that he was asthmatic and without knowing how to do CPR on a baby or without his medication, it proved to be fatal for him. He had an attack and she panicked, and was not able to get him the help he needed in time and he died. Her family helped her bury him there in New Mexico, and afterward she lived aimlessly moving from town to town drinking herself into a stupor most days. The gravity of her actions and her situation haunted her and eventually killed her." She said pausing. He looked up into her eyes and she reassuringly smiled at him.

"I take no pleasure in her demise. I ache to hear that she was in such pain, and that her desire to have a child pushed her beyond reasonable measures. Her younger sister started researching her confession and was able to confirm it all was as she had relayed. So then her sister contacted the detective in charge of our case, who was still with the San Diego police department and he called us on Monday two weeks ago. They got a court order expedited to exhume his little body and inside the casket was a picture of him taken the day he went missing and a note saying she was eternally sorry for taking him, and she asked God to forgive her. Of course the DNA test that was done, was a match and so they transported him home to us. We have made arrangements to have him buried here at The Gardens, perpetual cemetery. I know you have been searching for him all these years too, in an attempt to bring closure and healing to our family. Sweetheart, I love you so much for doing that, but it's time to stand down. We need to let him go, and I need for you to try and forgive her, and move on with your life my love. Forgiveness is freeing." She said lightly tracing his face.

"Mom, I can try, it just hurts so much. I'm trying to take it all in, are you sure *you* are ok?" He asked searching her eyes.

"My love, I had to start focusing on what good things God had brought into my life, and not focus on what had been taken away. It was a choice to focus on the good, and some days it was a very hard choice to make because all I wanted was my baby back in my arms. But I had your brother and sister who were so young, and you were still so tiny and you all needed me so much. God has richly blessed us as a family honey, and I cannot discount that because of what happened to Camden. Do I fully understand it all? No I have a lot of unanswered questions, but I trust God and I know he loves me and you more than words can express." She said smiling sweetly at him

"Mom..." He started but tears kept him from speaking.

"Oh my love, I know it's a lot to take in right now. I need to know you are going to be ok, because I could not bear to lose you too." She leaned down and kissed his cheek. He raised up clinging to her, and she held him. She took his face into her hands, kissed him then looked into his eyes.

"I need to see my gypsy son. Can you find him for me please?" She requested.

"Yes ma'am. Of course." He stood and reached for his phone and texted Tim.

Momma is requesting to see her gypsy son, can you come? It's urgent. –Dean

Tell her I'm on my way. Be there in 30. –Tim

Dean's whole family was blond haired and blue eyed. The first time Dean brought Tim home with him from the academy, his mother fell in love with this happy go lucky kid with the big brown eyes and dark wispy wavy dark brown hair. She used to tease him and say that he was her long lost gypsy son who had finally come home to roost. They had an incredible bond and he dearly loved her. She did for him on birthdays, holidays and throughout the year just like she did for her other kids. She instinctively sensed that he needed extra motherly love, and she intended to see he got it when he spent time with them as a family. They would have long meaningful talks at night, or over the phone, and he could always make her laugh.

Tim put the Audi through its paces once again, making it all the way from Wex's dock to the front door of their house in just under thirty minutes. Dean was sitting outside on the steps leaning against one of the pillars when he pulled up. Tim got out of the car, and Dean stood to meet him on the walkway. Tim grabbed him in a bear hug and held onto him.

"What's up man, you look wrecked. Tell me brother what happened." Tim encouraged.

"They found Camden, and he's dead Tim. He's been dead for a long while. Long story but his body is here now, and we are burying him tomorrow. Momma wants to see you." He said letting out a long heavy sigh.

"Oh God, I am so sorry brother. Why don't you go lay down for a few minutes while I speak to mom, ok? You look like you are going to drop. Come on I'll walk with you." He said turning him back in the direction of the house. Leah walked up and gave Tim a kiss, and then led Dean towards the guest room. Derek and his father were in the living room talking quietly, so Tim walked over and shook his hand and nodded at Derek.

"I knew she would ask for you, thank you for coming son." The elder stated.

"Sir, yes sir, of course. I am so very sorry for...everything. May I go see her now?" Tim asked.

"Yes she is in the bedroom. Go on in." He said reaching up to hug his adopted son.

Tim slowly walked down the hall to her room and tapped on the door.

"Momma, it's me? May I come in?" He said softly.

"Come in precious."

He walked over to where she was sitting, and he too knelt down near her taking her hands into his and kissed them.

"He met me in the yard and told me briefly that Camden has been recovered, I am so sorry for your loss. Truly. I am not really sure what to say." He said his big brown eyes searching her tear filled eyes.

"Oh my Timothy. I love you my gypsy son. You are a joy to me. I need some help with your brother, he is taking this especially hard; as I anticipated he would. He is still so angry with God, and confused. Please pray for him, pray that he would be able to let go of this and get on with his life and learn to walk with the Lord again. His still waters run so very deep, and I need to know he is going to be ok Tim, do you understand?" She asked as she moved a wisp of hair out of his eyes.

"Yes ma'am. Can we pray for him now?"

"Lets." She closed her eyes and bowed her head, and he did the same.

"Dear Father, I beseech you on behalf of my brother Dean. You know his heart Lord and how his mind works since you so wondrously made him. But we are troubled with this last turn of events Lord and we need to know that he is going to be ok. Please comfort this family as only you can Lord and soothe their wounds and heal their hearts." He paused momentarily because now the entire family including Dean had made their way into the room and were kneeling around the chair, eyes closed and holding hands.

"Jesus, I know you hear our prayers and I want to praise you and give you the glory for returning this lost son back to his family so that they might have closure. Father please be with them as they lay him to a final rest, but encourage them that they will see him again in heaven. Emotions are high here and I pray that we will seek you out in the still quiet moments that are to come Lord. I know you are faithful to meet us where we are, as we are, we don't have to clean up to come to you. Thank you for that father. I know my brother Dean is especially troubled and has a lot on his heart right now, please make yourself real to him and bathe him in your love. I lift all these prayers, and the silent ones up to you in Jesus name…." He finished, but stayed in a praying positon for some time.

Dean was the first to stand and hug his father once again, then went into the guest room to lay down. The girls hugged Tim and thanked him for praying and then kissed their mom. The doorbell alerted them that company had arrived. Leah's in-laws had brought over a feast for the family in light of the tragic news.

Tim walked outside, then texted Jesse and Wex.

Can't elaborate at the moment, but I need you praying for Dean right now! Don't cease. Spiritual warfare going on. -Tim

Wex responded first. *On it son, count on me. Praying now. –Wex*

Praying right now for Dean and for you. I love you both, please convey. –Jesse

Jesse started praying, but she heard her phone and thought it might be Tim again, so she stopped to look. It was Carter.

I had to leave for an unexpected business trip to Atlanta. I will be gone a few days, will try and call later. No time to come by unfortunately. Not alone. I love and miss you.-Carter.

Please be safe! Call me when you can. I love you Carter. ~Jess

Jesse went back to praying and now added Carter to her line up. She was suddenly feeling quite small and alone. Matt had taken Sue to Maine to visit some friends up there for a week, Tim and Dean were now apparently out of pocket and enduring something serious, Carter was being whisked away on a last minute business trip and Casey was not here to keep her company.

CHAPTER 30

MAKE IT GO AWAY

S o once again Jesse grabbed her keys and headed to the safe house. She prayed all the way there, and hoped it was not occupied. She crept down the driveway slowly and did not see any cars or lights on inside. The auto sensor on the outdoor flood lights lit up the driveway as she pulled in and parked. She wasn't interested in going inside, she just wanted to sit on the back deck and listen to the waves, or go sit on the beach.

Adam had her in sight the minute she turned down the driveway and monitored her remotely turning on outside lights around the perimeter so that she could see to the beach if that is where she wanted to go. He alerted Tim that she was there, and would leave it up to him as to whether he informed Dean or not. The director had given strict instructions that Dean was not to be bothered, that there had been a death in his family. The news rippled through the team and they were equally sad and concerned for Dean and Derek.

Tim had walked back to the guest room and lightly tapped on the door, then let himself in. Dean laid there on his back with his arm laid over his eyes. Tim sat on the edge of the bed and Dean didn't move.

"Hey buddy, can I get you anything to eat?" Tim asked.

"Nah, I'm not really hungry. I'm not sure how I feel. Partially nauseous and so very emotionally wiped out." He said softly.

"I don't want to push my luck here brother, but I want to read Isaiah 40 vs 31 KJV to you. *But those who hope in the LORD will renew their strength. They will soar on wings like eagles; they will run and not grow weary, they will walk and not be faint.* Dean you have carried the burden for so many things for so long, let God have this one. Listen I may not be worthy of your trust, your family may not be worthy of your trust, but you can Trust God.

I guarantee it Dean. Do you know what held Jesus to the cross that day? It wasn't the nails Dean, it was his love for you and for me that held him there. He suffered and endured that on *our* behalf. If he loved you enough to do that, can't you love him enough to try and trust him? I love you man. I'm here for you, always." Tim said as he started to get up then paused.

"Oh and give me your piece for now, I'll keep it for ya." He stated with his hand out.

"What? I'm fine." He said completely indignant.

"Give it. Please Dean. I told your mother I would put it in my car." He stated looking him right in the eye.

Dean reached back and handed it to Tim with the grip towards Tim, then let out a long sigh.

"Get some rest, I am on the couch tonight, since you are in here and Lily is home." Tim said.

"I'm now convinced you are mother's favorite child." Dean stated with a smirk.

"Her favorite child? Nah...her *best* looking child, definitely." He said laughing, as Dean tossed a decorative pillow at him as he walked out of the room.

Tim locked Dean's weapon in his car, then looked at his phone seeing he missed a text from Adam. So he called him up while he was outside.

"Adam, what's up man?"

"Goldilocks is back at the safe house. Still outside, and just sitting or praying or something I am not sure. I have lit up the back yard and I have eyes on her. What is it with her and that house? I swear Dean is going to have to buy it and give it to her. Either that or eventually she will get arrested for squatting." He stated with a laugh.

"That's my fault, I sent her a cryptic message about Dean, and she is worried. I kind of hoped she would go see Wex. Just keep an eye on her, I'm sure she is just there thinking and getting back to her center. How is her next door neighbor, any news there? We still have eyes on him don't we?" Tim asked concerned.

"Affirmative. He has had some interesting company lately. But I need Dean to eval first before I can do anything. She is walking down to the beach now in the pitch darkness, it's making me nervous. Should I send someone in to get her?" Adam said, dialing in the video so he could track her.

"No I'll text her and see if I can shoo her home. Thanks for the eyes man."

"Hey please send my condolences to Dean and Derek. I'm sure they are devastated." Adam said sincerely.

"I will man, thanks."

Jesse, hey sis. I just wanted to check in with you and let you know Dean is resting. Thank you for praying and please continue, not out of the woods yet. –Tim

I am at the beach...so worried about him. Feeling very alone at the moment and worried about my fellas. ~ Jesse

Please tell me you are not at the safe house in the dark by yourself? Baby girl, please if you are-- go home. That worries me and I can't get to you right now, if something should happen. –Tim

Ok I'll leave now, it's just a calming place for me and I was worried. I'll head home. I love you guys. ~Jesse

Please sis, text me once you are home safe and sound. –Tim

Jesse got back into her vehicle and headed back to her apartment. She was driving slowly, enjoying the sun roof back and the wind blowing her hair when the phone rang through the car. It was Carter. He sounded odd but she was so happy to hear from him.

"Hello?"

"Hey baby, I miss you so much right now." He said.

"Are you ok, you sound different?" She asked concerned.

"Ridiculously long day. Dread tomorrow. I just want to be in your arms right now." He said sounding exhausted.

"Oh honey, I know same here. It's been an intense night, a good friend of mine is struggling and I'm missing you and I've just been praying and seeking God's wisdom and comfort. I hope you get some rest, you sound so tired Carter."

"I'll be ok, I'm heading to bed shortly since tomorrow will be another long day. I love you so much Jesse, you have become my world."

"I love you too, Carter you mean everything to me. I hope you know that...? Call me tomorrow if you can."

"I will, goodnight baby."

She pulled into the complex and parked, then texted Tim she was home safely. Slowly she walked inside and unlocked her apartment then got a bottled water out of the refrigerator. She turned on the television and tried to distract herself as she rolled through the different channels. Finally she knew she would not be able to rest until she heard from Dean herself.

Hi Dean, I wanted to let you know I am not ready to let you go, so I am signing back up for another six months. Is that ok? –Jesse

Hey you, boy am I happy to hear from you tonight. Your decision is music to my ears. I'll make sure the paperwork gets renewed. –Dean

That was just an excuse to text you, I hear you have had a terrible, no good, horrible, awful, bad, bad, bad day. So I wanted you to know I am praying for you and that I love and care about you. Please take care of your-self, you are important to so many. ~Jesse

I know it was an excuse, and I love you for doing it. –Dean

Well it's completely selfish too on my part. I need for you to be ok because I don't want to be stuck with Craig again. It could be the death of me. ~Jesse

Ha-ha. Would never let you die, wish you were here, I could use a hug. –Dean

What's the address, I have GPS. ~Jesse

I love you Jesse. I wish you were mine. I know I shouldn't say things like that, but it's the truth. –Dean

I am so sorry you are hurting, and I wish I could take it away from you. Please check in tomorrow, but rest tonight. XXOO ~ Jess

He rolled over and threw the covers over his head. He could hear Tim in the dining room telling stories about his time with Wex at the hospital and all the crazy antics that took place that weekend. He could hear everyone laughing as he no doubt told them in his animated style, then he smiled himself. He was so happy to have a best friend and brother like Tim, someone who yearned to take away people's pain and make them smile. It was a gift, and he counted himself fortunate to have him in his life. Lord knows he tended to be too serious, and often needed the levity that Tim brought to their relationship. He often wondered what kind of brother Camden would have been, would he have been intense too? Or would he have been the total opposite?

He longed to quiet his racing mind, and so he just tried to focus on his family's laughter as he slowly drifted off to sleep.

Dean slept in until around 6:30 a.m. the next morning, and then laid there quietly as he listened to his mom or sister milling around in the kitchen making coffee. He had a splitting headache, and figured it was from all the crying, lack of food and water yesterday. He rolled over and thought about Jesse. How he longed to hold her once again, and drink in her scent. He was elated to hear she was going to re-enlist into the program, and knew that the director would approve it. A light knock on the door redirected his attention.

"Come in."

"Sweetheart, I hope you'll eat something this morning. I can make you anything you like." His mother offered extending her hand with two Advil, and a glass of water.

"Thank you momma. I was just thinking I needed something for this horrific headache." He said trying to smile.

She sat on the edge of the bed, and ran her fingers through his hair, and he closed his eyes and let her. He was so tired, tired of always being so responsible, tired of always having to be so careful, of having to take care of everyone around him and tired of having to hide in the shadows from the woman he loved.

"Timothy went to get you a change of clothes for the funeral. It's at noon today, and then we are coming back here to eat, and rest. I hope you will stay and spend some more time with us. Will you?" She asked her eyes pleading for a 'yes' answer.

"Yes ma'am, of course I'll stay." He said with a sweet smile, easing the tension in her chest.

"I'll let you wake up good, then come into the kitchen and I will fix you something." She said kissing his forehead.

He nodded then took the Advil and downed the entire glass of water. Closing his eyes once more, he dreamed of Jesse. *I must come clean, I am tired of holding back, I want my life back. But what will it do to her?*

Tim arrived back at the house with Dean's clothes and ditty bag. He also brought his swimming trunks since his parents pool was open and begging to be used. He knew Dean loved to swim and hoped that it would raise his spirits. He found him up and seated at the breakfast bar with a large glass of juice in front of him.

"Hey buddy, I'll put your things in your room. How are you feeling today?" Tim asked.

"Ok, thanks for coming and staying, it means a lot."

"You know I would do anything for you, I mean you saved my life Dean. At least once that I know of and I'm sure a hundred times that I don't know about. You are my brother, my family, where else would I be?" Tim said tearing up.

"Still, I feel better knowing you are here. I love ya man." He said standing and hugging his friend.

His mother walked in and joined in on the hug. Then got their request for breakfast, and pancakes won out. She whipped up the batter and brought out the large griddle and before the guys could blink she had made a mess of silver dollars. She put the I-HOP to shame. Both boys dug in and ate like it was their last meal, which made her heart happy. She called the rest of the clan in and they ate the rest of the short stacks.

Dean hugged her neck then retreated back to the bedroom to take a shower and get ready for the funeral. Tim used the other guest room while

Lily ate breakfast and even shaved today out of respect for mom, and Camden. Tim knew the day ahead of them was going to be a tough one, and once again he cried out to God on Dean's behalf. He dressed then walked outside beside the pool and watched as the clear water seemed to dance in the sunlight as the pump slowly pushed the water through its filter.

He called Wex to fill him in on what was happening and of course if anyone could identify with the loss of a child it would be him. His heart went out to the family and also to Tim who once again was caught in a family dynamic that had tragic roots. Wex determined that Tim was often the balm that helped heal hurting people, and praised God for allowing this extraordinary fella in his life. He knew that his life was forever changed for the better because of Tim, and knew that theirs had to be too.

Tim drove Dean to the funeral service and they arrived at the church a little before noon, seeing there were already a few cars in the parking lot caught Dean off guard. He thought this was a family only event. He didn't realize extended family had come in, and some very dear old friends of his parents were there too. It wasn't that he minded, he just thought private meant private. Tim stuck very closely to his best friend's side, Dean had lost people close to him before; he had lost men under his command and within his unit. However this was so very different, this was his twin and so much of Dean's life revolved around his brothers kidnapping and the chaos that ensued afterward.

His mother had seemed fine this morning, much better than the day before, yet Dean and Tim saw her knees buckle when she walked into the back of the church and saw the new small white casket placed at the altar. Thankfully his father and Derek caught her at the elbows and steadied her. Dean let out an unrecognizable sound that concerned Tim as they watched his mother's reaction to the tiny casket that held her other son. So Tim reached around and held onto him as they followed his parents down the aisle.

His sister Leah and her husband along with his parents came in behind Dean, and then Lily and her boyfriend came in and sat next to Tim and Dean. His parent's pastor arrived and spoke to family then made his way to the pulpit to begin the service. There were two huge sprays of flowers one from the San Diego Detective who never quit searching on their behalf, and one from the family of the woman who took Camden that simply said, *Please Forgive her, and we pray you will have peace. We are so sorry.*

Dean sat there staring at the small coffin as though he were in a trance. The words of the pastor fell short of his ears and all he could hear was the whirring swishing sound like the ocean in his ears. His eyes stung but no tears fell. Tim sat there quietly with his arm firmly around his best friend, just praying silently as the service took place. It seemed to him like everyone was taking their cue from Dean's mother, who for the moment sat there stoically, but with every breath she took she teetered on a full on break down. It was as though the other guests were also holding their breath to see how the family was going to do. The next thing Dean heard was the pastor say Amen, as though he were dismissing them, and thought how odd to have so short of a service. Little did he realize that approximately forty minutes had passed by while he sat there transfixed. His father, Tim, Derek and Leah's husband John acted as pall bearers while Dean escorted his mother to the family vehicle that would follow the Hearst to the cemetery.

Tim drove him to the cemetery and he was very quiet and solemn staring out the window at the lifeless scrub brush scenery that led to the perpetual care facility with its beautifully manicured lawn with small plaques and floral bouquets that lined the neat rows that fanned out across the grass. His father had selected a plot near the fountain in the center of the facility under a River Birch tree.

The family circled around the small earthen trench that was created to encase the small coffin, and the pastor once again said a few words then hugged his parents and shook his hand and left the family to say a private final good bye to their small son who had been brought back home to them but not in the condition they had hoped and prayed for all these years. It was when his mother started to turn to leave the grave side that she could no longer hold in her emotions and flung herself over the casket and began sobbing.

Dean's face distorted in anguish at his mother's grief and he took off across the lawn running from the demon's that had haunted him his whole life. Lily looked at Tim as she burst into tears, and her boyfriend held her tightly. Tim then nodded in acknowledgement at Lily and took off after Dean. He had made it all the way to the far right corner of the cemetery, now hemmed in by a fence that blocked him from running any further and he was on his knees. Tim slowed his pace to a trot once he had him in sight, then eventually slowed it to a walk, and quietly came alongside his best friend. No words were necessary between the two of them and Tim just sat there with him in the grass. He had already decided he would sit there for as long as it took for Dean to feel like he could process his grief and emotions.

A light breeze had kicked up and Tim for one was grateful as they sat there in the grass during the mid-day sun in suits. Dean who was always so in control of his emotions and thought processes had finally been broken and it grieved Tim to see him so emotionally compromised and fragile. Dean was the epitome of a man's man. Strong, loyal to a fault, smart and resourceful, he was one of the best team leads the Agency had and was a much sought after analyst. So much so that Director Johnson had to constantly fight to keep other departments from trying to steal him away. Tim would do whatever necessary to shield Dean during this time, until he could get back on his feet and mentally get back into the game. He wished Jesse could be there and help comfort Dean, somehow he felt like she could make it all right and ease his pain.

Tim reached for his phone and texted Derek that he had Dean and would bring him back to the house when he was ready, that they need not wait on them. Derek replied he understood, and that mother was finally calmer and that they were headed back to the house. Tim then texted Jesse.

Sis, please lift up Dean. He is in so much pain and oh how I wish you could be here to comfort him. -Tim

Praying for him. I too wish I knew what was going on, and that I could be there for him, like he has been so many times for me. Tell him I love him and I will continue to pray. ~Jesse

Pray for me, it's so painful to watch him like this, but it's necessary for him to process all of this. But God it is hard to see him suffer. -Tim

My heart goes out to you both. Please keep me in the loop-- I am here for you. ~Jesse

After an hour or so, Dean looked over at Tim and asked him "Why do you think it was Camden that was taken? I could have been the one sleeping and the one she picked instead. I guess that is what I think about sometimes. Why him, why not me? I never had asthma, I more than likely would have survived this woman, and could have been reunited with mom at some point, and Camden could have stayed with momma who knew how to care for him? Then we would both be alive."

"Buddy, I have no idea. God had different plans for you Dean, you have saved so many people, and been used as a mighty instrument for this country, so we can't really say. I thank God every day that it *wasn't* you who was taken, and I'm sorry if that sounds harsh. So many people love you and rely on you, and I am sure there are times that you feel crushed under that burden, but I also know you are so strong and capable. I admire you so much, you really have no idea of what you mean to people." Tim said blinking back tears.

"I have to let this go, and just accept what is…don't I?" He said quietly.

"Yeah buddy, you do. Take time to grieve, catch your breath and know you were created for a special purpose. Embrace that and live your life. Don't let the shadow of this tragedy beat you down anymore. It's finished." Tim said looking him in the eye.

"Will you take me home now?" Dean said softly.

"Yes."

CHAPTER 31

COMFORT

Tim stood first then extended his hand to help Dean up. They walked slowly side by side along the small structured pathways that led to and from the cemetery divisions, Dean turned looking one last time back at the place where his other half was laid to rest, which now was covered with damp earth and two grass sod squares. He paused for a moment, closed his eyes as if he was saying a mental goodbye, and then turned and walked back to Tim's car.

Jesse paced back and forth at Reed's and finally asked if the staff could cover her while she ducked out early. She got in her car and raced to the beach, kicked off her shoes and ran to the water's edge and just stood there as the waves gently lapped at her feet and she closed her eyes and prayed. It was if she was willing her spirit to envelop Dean to somehow let him know it was all going to be ok. *Please God comfort him. Please wrap your loving arms around him and let him see You Father.*

Dean sat back as Tim drove and took a deep breath, then exhaled slowly He closed his eyes, and remembered what it felt like when he held Jesse in his arms. He focused on that memory and it seemed to calm his spirit. They arrived at the house and both men changed into their swim suits and entered into the pool, finding that the water was soothing and relaxing. Tim needed the distraction and wanted to burn off some pent up energy, so he swam laps under water and Dean just needed the feel of the water surrounding his body in a virtual hug of sorts. They both were grateful for the refreshing water on this hot humid emotionally draining day. The pool was a 20x40 built in situated off the main living area, and had a lovely wooden Pergola covering half the pool offering much needed shade.

His parents retreated to their bedroom after extended family came by to bring food and visit for a few moments. Their friends went back to their hotel for now, but were going to come back later for dinner after everyone had rested. Derek and Leah went back to their respective homes and Lily and her boyfriend went for a drive.

Jesse was concerned since she had not heard from Carter all day and when she spoke to him last night he sounded strange like it wasn't even him. She had texted him a couple times today and he had not responded. She tried to rationalize that he was just busy, she knew he loved her, and so insecurity was not an issue, but it was out of character for him not to respond. Which caused an uneasy agitated feeling, so she decided to drive down to see Wex for the evening.

She arrived at the make shift restaurant and Godiva came bounding out to greet the favorite non-girlfriend. Wex had received her call earlier and so he was expecting her. He came out smiling, he had actually shaved and was dressed nicely in pressed khaki pants and a button down shirt.

"Hey sweet lady, I decided I wanted to take you to supper tonight if that is ok?" He said with a grin on his face.

"Oh my! I would be honored. Thank you." She said hugging his neck. Then she grabbed his hand to see how the thumb was healing.

"Oh now, it's much better. No need to fuss." He said laughing but appreciating her concern.

They got in his old truck and he drove several blocks to a local steak house that was a favorite among the home town crowd. He requested his favorite waitress, Edith and he waved at people as they walked to their table stopping a couple of times to shake hands and introduce Jesse as Tim's special friend. Everyone was very pleasant and all spoke speaking highly of Tim as though she needed to be convinced of his legendary greatness in that town. It was very sweet actually.

They were seated at his special "usual" table near the windows and she perused the menu with Wex pointing out the items of interest and the ones he felt like she could pass up. She opened up and shared how upset she was for Tim and Dean, especially not knowing what was going on. Wex explained that there had been a death in Dean's family and it was under very tragic circumstances. He actually teared up talking about it, and she knew he must be devastated knowing Tim was there dealing with his best friend's grief.

269

They had a very nice dinner and he told stories about Dean and Tim and how they had gotten in out of so many scrapes over the years, some serious and some funny. He focused on the funny ones, and they laughed together both enjoying the distraction and company. No wonder Tim loved him so, you couldn't help but love the gruff old man. Deep down he had a heart of gold and he was wicked smart without being obnoxious about it. He drove her back to her car, then stood and prayed with her before he let her head back to her apartment. She hugged his neck tightly, thanked him for his company and dinner then kissed his cheek.

He stood waving in the drive way until she was fully out of sight.

She arrived back at her apartment, parked and then headed upstairs. Her heart ached as she passed Carter's door knowing he was not home and she still had not heard from him. Once inside her apartment she locked up and then flopped on the couch. Her phone started ringing but she didn't recognize the number, but felt compelled to answer it anyway.

"Hello?" She said tentatively.

"Hey Baby!" Carter said.

"Oh-my- gosh, Carter, where have you been all day? I have *missed* you." She said half relieved and half irritated.

"God it is great to hear your voice, I miss you so badly. My phone is completely dead. I left so quickly I forgot my charger and I haven't had time to buy another one, but I am going out tomorrow and will get one then." He explained.

"Well don't be alarmed if you have fifty text messages from me." She said laughing.

"I'm just happy you miss me." He said smiling.

"Are you kidding me? Ridiculous." She scolded.

They talked for another twenty minutes or so, then he had to go and log into a site to install some software. He told her he would try and call her mid-morning tomorrow if he could get his phone charged up. She was so relieved all was well, and took a quick shower to wind down.

Jesse exited the bathroom, crawled into bed and reached for her phone. She texted Dean.

Getting ready to go to bed, thinking of you and hoping your heart is not as heavy tonight. I wish I could erase the pain you are feeling. Know you are loved. ~Jesse

I have thought about you all day today. I actually felt your presence at one point and I just focused on that. It truly got me through a rough patch. I long to see you. Maybe in a day or two I can call. –Dean

Take your time precious, I am not going anywhere. We can talk when you are ready. XO ~Jesse

I have so much I want to share with you...One day soon. –Dean

She laid her phone down, and rolled on her side thinking about Tim, Dean and Carter. Her life was so different now than it was six short months ago, and it was mostly all for the better. Even with the ups and downs she had experienced, she had never felt more alive in her life. She was grateful for every moment she got to spend with or near these extraordinary men. Now with her quitting her job at Reeds to pursue a career, it had her mind spinning. *Dare to dream...dare to dream.*

Lily had to head back home since she had been home for the last five days with her mother, but hated to leave knowing Dean was still grieving so hard. She disagreed that he should be the last to know about what was happening with Camden, but her mother felt like this was how she wanted it handled, so that is how it went. He was always so protective of her, and now she felt like it was her turn to shield him. She peeked in his room to see if he was awake, and then she walked in to hug him.

"Hey sweetie are you heading out?" He asked sleepily.

"Yeah I have to work tonight, so Mark is following me home." She said quietly.

"I hate I didn't get to spend much time with you, are you doing ok?" He asked.

"Oh yeah. I'm in a really good place, and Mark is amazing. So kind and attentive. Nothing like Nathan, thank goodness." She said with a slight laugh.

"Well he better treat you right, or he will have the whole CIA breathing down his neck." He said smirking.

"I know, right?" She said smiling. "I love you and I want you to call me when you can, ok?" She encouraged.

"I will try and do better, I know I have been really distracted lately. Maybe I'll come down and see you soon. How does that sound?"

"Perfect. Ok, *you* and Tim behave."

"I love you Lily-pad." He said holding her hand. She leaned in and kissed his cheek. She was the baby of the family but extremely independent and self-assured. Dean was thirty three and she was twenty five going on fifty. She was the female version of him, smart and intense, both of them were a lot like their father.

He laid back in the bed, thinking of his family and truly how lucky he was to have all of them in his life, and he cherished the closeness of his siblings. Of course he and Derek worked together, and Leah was a registered nurse at Grace Hospital across town, and then Lily was an event planner at a large hotel chain in Tallahassee. His father had retired from the military and now worked as a consultant for a firm that supplied the military with uniforms and lightweight equipment. His mother was a stay at home mother when the children were young and was a wife extraordinaire. Very active in military wives functions, entertaining as needed when her husband's job required it and she was a committed volunteer at various organizations in town and at church.

Another light tap on his door, made him feel like his room was grand central station on this early morning. This time it was Tim, who stated he had to run into the office, and did he want anything while he was there? Dean declined, and stated he would see him later. After Tim departed his mom stuck her head in to check in on him so at this point he threw up the white flag and surrendered. He threw on some shorts and came out into the kitchen to have coffee with his parents.

His father walked over and put his arm around Dean and gave him a side squeeze. Dean reached back around and hugged his father's waist. No words were spoken, but Dean appreciated the contact. His mom was busy cutting fresh fruit for breakfast and then started cooking bacon. She had already rolled the biscuits and they were baking in the oven, going all out for this early morning meal. They still had plenty of food left over from all the kind people who had heard about Camden and dropped off meals and snacks for the family.

Dean stood then walked over to where his mom was working away at the stove and kissed her neck then walked out to the pool area and sat down on the edge letting his feet and ankles dangle in the cool morning waters. It felt odd not to be at work, and he was at a loss as to what to do with himself, but was grateful that for the next couple of days anyway, that he didn't *have* to do anything or *be* anywhere.

He ate a hardy breakfast with his parents, then decided to lay back down for a while, and was asleep within minutes. He dreamed of Jesse, then dreamed of being on the beach, then nothing but darkness. His parents just let him rest, they were both worried about their youngest son, knowing that his job was a source of tremendous stress and responsibility, then with the news of Camden it was all a little too much. Director Johnson was a close associate of Dean's father, and he kept a close eye on the boys for him and he had relayed that Dean could take whatever time was needed. He had lured Dean away from Washington, D.C. and the grind of the CIA there. Dean was extraordinary at what he did, but the Director feared he would burn out and be no good to anyone. So he made Dean this sweet deal where he would manage a team, his hand-picked team, from a field office, near his parents and get to pursue his pet project of a civilian surveillance informants.

Tim arrived back after a couple of hours, with popcorn, movies and a full marathon line up. Something the guys hadn't done in years due to their work schedules, long overdue in his mind. Dean just grinned when he walked in with his arms full of movie paraphernalia and essentials. Dean's parents were happy to see them relaxing and enjoying some down time, between the pool and big screen television it was like it was when they were in college, and it made her heart happy to have her lifeguard and gypsy sons home.

Jesse put in another full day at work and then went to an orientation at the community college regarding some of the programs they were offering in the fall. She walked out feeling a little intimidated and very old. It had been a long time since she had been in school and although she was a decent student, she was never the scholar that Susie was in school. She drove through a drive thru and picked up a hamburger, then headed home to look over the literature she had picked up. She was just getting settled in when her phone started buzzing.

Hey Jess, how are you? I have been thinking about you today. –Dean
Ok, a little overwhelmed but ok. Looking at school stuff. ~Jess
Watching a Star Wars marathon with Tim and relaxing. Been a long time since we have gotten to do something like this, enjoying the break. –Dean
Sounds like fun! So happy you are getting some down time. You deserve it. I need to hit the hay, it's been a long day here. Poke Tim for me. LOL. ~Jesse

It had been almost twenty four hours again since she had heard from Carter and really didn't understand why. She texted him once after work, but never got a response. She was really missing Casey tonight too and laid there listening as a storm started rolling through the area. The thunder rumbled in the distance at first, and then it started to become more frequent, and intense as the minutes ticked by. She was getting ready for bed when her phone began ringing she nearly leaped off the bed it startled her so.

"Hello?"

"Hey you." He stated softly.

"Hi honey, are you ok you sound worn out?"

"Yeah, I'm just ready to be home, I'm not sleeping well, and I miss you terribly. Today was better, but my energy is waning again. How was your day, didn't you have a school thing to go to after work?"

"Yes, and wow was that intense. I guess it's just been a while since I have had to study or read all the material like the courses recommend and it's a little intimidating."

"Oh baby you are going to do great. I know you can do whatever you put your mind to, so don't psych yourself out. I am so proud of you." He said trying to encourage her.

The storm was in full swing now and she could hear the rain pelting her windows and the wind blew the rain in sideways, it was distracting as she tried to carry on a conversation with Carter. Now on top of the thunder which now bellowed, she had the lighting and howling winds buffeting her outer apartment walls.

"What is going on there, are you ok?" He asked since her participation in the conversation had slowly ebbed down to a few distracted sentences.

"I'm sorry Carter, we are having one heck of a storm here and it's a little disconcerting, and now the power is flickering. I'm starting to get a little concerned." She stated nervously.

"Wow, ok. Listen, why don't I let you go, and you hunker down and get some rest. I am hoping to come home tomorrow if things go well. I love you sweetheart."

"Oh I hope you can come home tomorrow. Please come see me the minute you get in, ok? I love you Carter. You know you are my forever, don't you?" She asked sweetly.

"I certainly hope so. I love you my Jess. Goodnight baby."

The storm continued to rage on for the next hour or more, and she was finally able to calm her spirit and was trying to fall asleep since five o'clock was going to come very early. She laid there and thought of Carter and how laying with his strong arms wrapped around her made her feel like she could handle anything with his love and support. She drifted off to sleep day dreaming about them getting married and getting to wake up to one another for the rest of their married lives.

CHAPTER 32

SPIRAL

D ean laid on the couch blankly staring at the television, his mother
came in and sat next to him reaching over and holding his hand.
"I've enjoyed getting to spend a little extra time with you these
past few days. I miss you. I had hoped when you moved down here from
Washington, D.C. that we would get to spend more time with you."

"Mom, I'm sorry..." He started.

"I am not trying to guilt you my love. I just want you to know you are
loved and missed. We will take whatever time we can get with you." She said
smiling as she rubbed the back of his hand.

"I love you mom. I have been involved in a high profile case and it's
beginning to suck the life out of me. Normally I just organize, plan and roll
with the punches, but there is a woman involved and it's so very complicated."
He stated looking over at her.

"Do you love her?"

"Yeah I do, but I can't in the position I am in, or I'm not supposed to.
Thus the complication."

"I will be praying for you my precious son. If she is the one, then it will
work out. You must have faith."

"She works for me and is a civilian, so I don't know mom. Anyway I will
try my best to come by more often, and not hunker down at the office. How
are you doing? Are you ok? Is dad ok? He seems really stressed out."

"You know your father. Stoic and brave. He was worried about me, and
once he knew that I was going to be ok, and that you were going to be ok, he
could relax. He tends to internalize so much of his own grief, it was important
for him to process this as well. He is doing better today. Having you here

so he can see you, has helped him. He does love you very much, I hope you know that honey."

"I do mom. I'm sorry you both have had to go through all of this for so very long. It's exhausting." He said taking in a deep breath then exhaling slowly.

She leaned over and laid her head on his shoulder. "I love you my lifeguard."

"I love you momma-best." He said softly.

He remained there again for one more night, then decided to head back to his place the next morning. He took one more day off from work and tried to get his head back in the game. Tim was back to work and so was Derek. The Director had called to speak to him and they talked for quite some time, and he was encouraged to come back when he was ready. Dean assured him that he was feeling much better and needed the job to keep his mind busy.

Jesse arrived home from work, and was saddened to see that Carter's car was still not home. She exited her car and started up the stairs after checking her mailbox. As she slowly ascended the stairway she noticed that Andy's door was ajar. She crept up trying to see if she could see anything since he had been acting so odd lately. She saw him lying in the floor, and feared the worst. She immediately called Dean, not thinking.

"Report. Dean are you there?"

"Jesse? What are you doing?"

"Oh-my-gosh, I'm so sorry, habit. I'll call Tim."

"No wait, go ahead what's wrong?"

"My neighbor is down. He looks hurt and he's not moving, I'm afraid to go in, but his door is ajar. It's Andy, the super geek." She relayed.

Dean quietly swore under his breath, and grabbed his other phone to call Adam to find out what had happened. He also called 911 and had an ambulance dispatched to her location. Then he came back to her and filled her in on what he had just done.

"The ambulance should be there shortly. Wait there and once they have him taken care of get inside your apartment. I will have Tim swing by to check on you ok?"

"I'm so sorry Dean, I wasn't thinking. I'm sorry I bothered you." She said apologetically.

"It's ok, Jesse, I'm glad you did. It's good to hear your voice even if it's for a report."

The wailing of the ambulance began to drown out their conversation and she stated she would check in later. The E.M.T's arrived and entered his apartment. It appeared as though he had gotten beaten up and although he was injured would be ok. She was frightened and wondered who in the world would want to hurt Andy. Tim came by about an hour later and tapped on her door.

After checking through the peep hole, she flung the door open and pulled him inside. He gave her a big hug then sat on the couch next to her.

"Hey sis, I can't believe your neighbor was hurt, that is awful. Have you heard anything going on over there?"

"No nothing. But he has been acting kind of distant and odd lately. Doesn't speak to me anymore, and just acts so withdrawn. He never even said anything about Casey when she died and I know he used to really enjoy her. I don't know, maybe I have made him angry?" She said casting her eyes downward.

"No, I'm sure you haven't done anything. Men can be moody too. I just hope it wasn't a robbery or anything. I am going to see we put some additional surveillance on you to make sure you are safe."

"Are you sure that is necessary?"

"Dean would insist on it if he hasn't done it already. Just keep your eyes and ears open." He said smiling.

"How is Dean? I'm worried about him. Wex told me he lost a family member. So very sad."

"Yeah, but he's doing better, first few days were really rough. I hate seeing him like that, he is always the strong one ya know?"

"Yeah but even the strong need some down time. I will keep praying for him. I love you guys." She said smiling.

"And we love you girly. I am going to head home, text or call me if you need me, ok?" He said kissing her cheek.

She walked him to the door, and as he was leaving she saw Carter coming up the steps. Tim shook hands with him, then left them to be alone. Carter strode over to her scooping her up and carrying her inside the apartment. He set her down gently then began kissing her. His hands all tangled in her hair, as she wrapped her arms around his waist. Slowly he walked her over to the sofa and laid down pulling her on top of him. They did not speak, their actions were their words tonight. Their bodies melded together and both were engulfed in a longing that defied explanation.

She had definitely missed him, but his desire for her seemed proportionally grander and she wondered what was on his mind. He could not seem to get enough of her and was almost desperate for her touch.

"Carter…?" She whispered.

"Marry me Jesse." He beseeched.

"What?"

"Marry me, please. I love you so much."

"I love you too. Carter are you sure?" She asked a little bewildered by his sudden proposal.

He leaned up on one elbow and looked longingly into her eyes, and asked her again. She looked at him wide eyed, and said 'yes' that she would marry him. This seemed to calm him and he laid back down and held onto her firmly, she laid her head on his shoulder and gently rubbed his chest with her fingers. They laid there for a while when she finally sat up, causing him to rise up too.

"Carter, are you ok? You seem upset or unsettled. I'm worried about you."

"Jesse, the more time I spend with you the more I am convinced you are the one for me. I know it seems sudden, but I love you so much. I long to be with you, I want to know you are mine and I am yours." He said his steely blue eyes searching hers.

"Carter, I love you and want to be with you too. I will marry you. What did you have in mind? I mean there is still so much I don't know about you. I haven't met any of your friends or family. You are a wonderful mystery to me." She said smiling sweetly at him.

"I know there is a lot I want to share with you and I will, very soon. I promise." He started to kiss her but his phone beckoned and he sat up with his head hanging down in disappointment. "I have to go. I am so sorry baby. Please forgive me."

"So soon you just got home?" She stated trying not to whine.

"This project is winding down, and soon we will get to spend some quality time together. I love you Jess." He said lightly kissing her lips.

"OK. I hope so, I miss you Carter." She said touching his face. He picked up her hand and kissed her palm.

She walked him to the door, then watched him walk down the stairs then out into the night.

Dean started reviewing the tapes of Andy's apartment, and saw the attack that took place. He was still trying to find out how this got past Adam who was supposed to be monitoring him. When he was quizzed he stated that Craig had come in with an urgent request that had him distracted. Dean was starting to smell a rat, and was now turning his attention in a different direction. He called Tim and they started devising a plan. He also called Derek then Ninja to give them a heads up and it was all to be kept on the down low. Craig was either a mole, or highly inept and he intended to get to the bottom of this. Sometime after midnight he arrived back home and collapsed in his bed his mind reeling with information he was trying to piece together. Eventually sleep overtook him and his dreams were frantic and fraught with conflict, he was actually relieved when his alarm finally went off.

Jesse woke the next morning, a little unsettled. She was thrilled to finally see Carter, but then that was short lived as once again his work called him away. She was beginning to loathe computers and networks. She dressed and headed over to Reed's. When they had a mid-morning lull, she tried to call the hospital to see how Andy was doing. They would not give her any information since she was not family but she did secure a hospital room number and planned to go see him after work.

She tried to hail Dean on the ear piece, and he immediately answered.

"Jess, I am so happy you called in, listen, I am in meetings all day with the New York team and I will not be available. I know this is not ideal, but just for today, Craig is taking reports. Everyone else on my team is participating in the joint meetings. I'll check on you this afternoon, once I am out of the meetings ok?" He said in a hurried tone.

"Ok, good luck." She replied knowing that protesting at this point would do no good. He was in a bind, and it was important. She would be fine, she would just have to be.

Her day was busy and she only had time once to text Carter and say hello. He did respond, but it was brief and she figured he too must be still focused on his project. The crew got the diner cleaned up, and Jesse was giving the floor one last go over with the mop. Libby had taken the deposit earlier today and Hannah had just come back with the register change for tomorrow's business. Jesse saw them both off and stayed behind to finish some paperwork for Reed. It was close to 5:30 when Jesse thought she had heard a noise in the kitchen.

"Report." She stated tentatively.

"Charge 25 go." Craig answered.

"I'm hearing a noise here at Reed's, can you see anything on the video feed? I'm in the office alone."

"No I cannot." He replied.

"Ok, I'll just check quickly. Will you hold?"

"Go." He replied distractedly.

Jesse stuck her head out the door and did not see or hear anything, so she went back in the office and sat back down.

"Ok, sorry, I guess I'm just hearing things."

"Handler out."

She called in the bread order and then called the Atlas Food line to order menu items for the upcoming week. Once she had that completed she was just about ready to go, and heard a commotion in the kitchen and this time she knew it was not her imagination. Slowly she got up and prepared to see what was happening, perhaps one of the staff had forgotten something and had come back?

"Report?"

"Yes?" Craig replied impatiently ready to leave since it was nearly six o'clock.

"I'm sorry, but I definitely heard a sound this time and I am going to investigate."

"Ok..."

Jesse slowly opened the door from the office and walked out into the main kitchen area, and that is when she saw him.

"What are you doing here? How did you get in..."

It was a little after six when the joint meeting convened and Dean walked back to his war room noticing that all the monitors were turned off and the head set was lying on the desk. He looked around and there was no sign of Craig. *Great, where is he?* He thought perturbed. He turned the monitors back on and put his ear piece back in, perplexed as to what it was he was looking at on the screen.

"Jesse honey, did you lose your camera pin?" He asked.

"Dean?" She whispered.

"Jesse, are you still at Reed's, if so you need to check your camera, I'm looking at...honestly I'm not sure what I'm looking at but it looks like it's lying on the floor or something." He stated still trying to make out the odd picture it was sending back to him.

"Please don't let me die alone." She barely managed to whisper.

"Jesse come back? Say again." The hair on the back of his neck standing on end.

"He... stabbed... me." She said softly then there was nothing.

Dean grabbed his phone and put in the member down alert with Reed's address. Now the picture made sense she was lying on the floor and the pin camera was looking at the bottom of the double freezer at Reeds. He took off running out of the building to get to her. He cleared the lobby then bolted out the front door his legs carrying him as fast as he could and turned in the direction of Reed's, as he cleared the entrance, he looked over and saw Tim running from the private parking garage area over the grassy knoll area and towards the back of Reed's. They arrived near the dumpster at the same time guns drawn to clear the perimeter and their eyes locked communicating a world of information in that one moment. They cleared the outside and then Tim entered Reed's first with Dean coming in hot behind him.

Tim cleared the inside while Dean ran to Jesse's side. She was lying in the floor curled up on her left side, not moving at all now. There was blood everywhere and he could see she had attempted to keep pressure on the wound but to no avail. Ninja was the next to arrive on the scene, she pulled up in the SUV and came in the back door, to assist. She threw Dean a hand towel to help him apply pressure to her wound. Jesse was now not responsive and Dean was devastated to think that this was all his fault. He never should have let Craig monitor her today.

"Hold on Jesse, I'm here honey, we are getting you some help. Please hold on baby." Dean pleaded, whispering in her ear. He was checking her vitals and although she was breathing it was very shallow as he tried to maintain steady pressure on her wound until the EMS team arrived.

Tim came back and knelt by her side and looked at Dean with horror in his eyes. She was so still and the amount of blood loss was frightening. Dean checked her pulse and screamed at Ninja to find out where the ambulance was and why it was taking so long.

After what seemed like an eternity, the EMT's showed up and started prepping her for the ride to the hospital. Dean's hands were covered in her blood and he insisted on riding in the ambulance. He left Ninja in charge of the scene, and Tim left to get Susie. He kept praying over her as they worked to get her stabilized in the ambulance, they had already called in for a surgeon to be on standby. She had been stabbed twice in the abdomen and had lost quite a bit of blood.

They arrived at the hospital and Dean was forced to sit out in the lobby of the E.R while they prepped her for emergency surgery. Dean paced back and forth and his mind reeled as he tried to piece together who could have possibly done this to his Jesse. Finally they took her up to the O.R and he was moved to a family waiting area. He looked down at his hands sticky with her blood, and immediately turned to find the men's washroom. He frantically tried to wash the blood off thinking that her blood and possible death was literally and figuratively on his hands. As he scrubbed his hands and forearms over and over he heard someone come in behind him.

"Dean?" The Director asked. Dean froze for a moment, then resumed washing his hands as the water ran crimson down the sink drain. Glancing up in the mirror he saw his boss standing behind him.

"Sir?"

"Member down? What happened?" He asked levelly.

"Sir, I came in to check on Charge 25 after our meeting and realized that Craig had left her unaided after a struggle and she was injured. I reacted and called in the alert." He answered solemnly.

The Director realized that Dean still did not realize he called in an alert reserved for CIA team members only and that he should have called in a civilian emergency alert. He stood there waiting him out. Dean slowly turned off the water and reached for the paper towels. He briskly wiped off his arms then his hands. Then he turned to look at the Director.

"Son, what were you thinking? *Member* Alert?"

"Sir, I know you think I should have called it in under a civilian alert, but sir she is a *member* of my team. We have worked together on so many valuable tangible leads and we would not be as far on this human trafficking case if it had not been for her. Directly or indirectly. I didn't do it on purpose, but I stand by my call. I will pay for the additional expenses." He stated defensively but respectfully.

"I am not concerned with the cost. I want to know what you are thinking." He replied coolly.

"Sir, respectfully. Why are we here? What is our job exactly?" He asked almost as though they were rhetorical questions. Then he began again to answer his own questions. "Sir I believe my job is to protect our country and the citizens of this country against foreign and domestic enemies. To protect its people. She is one of those people sir. One of the ones that I swore an oath to protect, and if I took extraordinary measures to save her sir, then so be it. She is important to me, to my job, and to my project and she is more than just a civilian to me sir. She represents some of the best of what I pledged to protect." He stated controlling his emotions.

"Very well. Carry on." He stated with a slight smile. "Please keep me abreast of her condition as it develops."

"Yes sir. Thank you sir." He stated running his hands through his hair, not knowing what the outcome of that conversation would yield and then walked back into the waiting area.

Meanwhile Tim was on his way to Susie's house and searched for the right words as he weaved through traffic. He knew she had just returned the day before from vacation, and prayed they were at home. He pulled up into their driveway and parked, then made haste to the front door. He rang the doorbell and waited. Matt answered the door first and stared at the tall handsome man dressed in navy blue mechanic workpants, and a navy blue work shirt with 'Tim' stitched above the pocket, while Sue came running up behind him with Sami in her arms. She took one look at Tim's face and handed the baby off to Matt then ran to get her shoes and purse without a word.

Matt stood there with a bewildered look on his face still staring at the stranger standing before him completely confused as to what was going on and how did his wife know this man.

"I'm sorry to intrude, I am Tim, and I am a friend of Jesse's. There has been an incident and Jesse has been gravely injured. I came to drive Sue to the hospital, since I didn't want to call and have her driving while upset. They will only allow one family member at a time into the ICU. Of course if you can get a sitter for the baby, we will be at Ocean Side General." Tim stated as calmly as he could.

Susie skidded to a stop at the front door, kissed Matt lightly and said she would call with news. She and Tim ran to the agency's black Dodge Challenger and he took off in the direction of the interstate.

"Tell me." She pleaded. Tears filling her eyes.

"We think someone attempted to rob her at Reed's and then stabbed her. She has lost a lot of blood Sue. I have to be honest, I am scared." He said his voice quivering ever so slightly.

"What are her chances Tim? What are they?" She demanded.

"Sweetheart, I honestly don't know. We must pray for healing but prepare for the worst." He said.

He reached for her hand as tears spilled out of her eyes. "I'm so sorry baby, I really am. I love Jesse so much and I have to believe she's going to make it through this. We have to *believe*." He encouraged.

She took a deep breath wiping her tears away and then said, "We've got this. I am not losing her. Not today."

"Right. Not today." He echoed.

He sped along the highway weaving in and out of traffic, running with the flashing lights on but no siren. Dean hailed him on the ear piece and informed him as to what floor she was on and where he was at the moment. It was the worst time of day for traffic and Tim was whipping in between and around vehicles left and right. Susie remained undaunted rolling with the pull of the vehicle as it weaved back and forth. He parked in a spot reserved for police parking and they ran to the E.R. waiting area, looking for the area where Dean had indicated they needed to go. Dean was no longer there when they arrived and Tim walked out to the nurse's station to see if he could get an update on Jesse with Susie on his heels.

Tim stood there incredulous as he tried to block Susie's view of Jerry standing at the counter demanding to see the doctor so he could get a copy of Jesse's death certificate. *Death Certificate???* It was too late, she heard his big mouth then started to hyperventilate thinking they had not arrived in time and Jesse had died. Apparently the police still had him listed as an emergency contact for Reed's. Tim grabbed Jerry by the arm and the scruff of his shirt and proceeded to march him out the hospital door to the parking area then finally released him, sending him skittering onto the side walk.

"Get your hands off me you brute!" Jerry screamed at Tim trying to regain his balance. Susie stood by inconsolable at this point watching the two men face off.

"How dare you show up here asking for *anything* regarding Jesse?" Tim seethed at him.

"I have an insurance policy on her and if she's dead, I am collecting! I have bills to pay and new wife and baby on the way!" He yelled at Tim.

Without thinking Tim reared back and delivered an upper cut that sent Jerry flying upwards and backwards onto the side walk landing on his back. Two hospital security guards came rushing out to break up the one sided fight, and Tim flashed his agency credentials, which backed them off.

"He is interfering with business we have here and he needs to be escorted off the premises." Tim commanded and they quickly obliged.

"What did you show them to make them help you?" Susie asked sniffing, stunned by what had just taken place here and so proud that Tim punched his lights out and she was there to see it.

"Well I deal with a lot of undesirables sometimes, so I have Constable's credentials and I flashed that at them. They work for the hospital not the police, so there is an understanding." He bluffed, taking her hand and escorting her back into the hospital and then to the second floor family waiting area.

The nurse indicated she was still in surgery and more than likely it would be another hour. She had been stabbed twice and the blade nicked the liver and colon causing a myriad of issues other than the loss of blood. He found the coffee machine and made Susie a cup of coffee then found her a place to sit in the waiting area. He stepped right outside the door to make a few phone calls and to find out where Dean had disappeared to.

"Dean? Where are you man, are you ok? And do you still have a job after the agent down alert?" Tim asked.

"Roof. No I am not ok, and I have a job for now. I think." He responded in a somber tone.

"I have Sue with me, and I just had the pleasure of punching Jerry which was wildly satisfying, if I do say so myself. Too bad you missed it." Tim stated with a smirk.

"Jerry? What is he doing here?" Dean asked.

"I'll tell you later. Want me to let you know what I hear from the doctors about Jesse." Tim offered.

"No need, I'm a doctor with floor access to monitor her once she is out of surgery." He confided.

"Excellent." Tim replied smiling, realizing that Dean was going undercover to be near Jess, Adam must have hooked him up with a badge.

"Ninja said they found the weapon used at Reed's, and Derek texted me that the police caught the suspects so they are questioning them now. I'll fill you in once I know more." Dean stated.

"Copy that. I need to go sit with Sue, she looks trashed. Check in later." Tim requested.

"Roger that."

Tim walked back over to where Susie was sitting staring into her coffee, mindlessly rubbing her thumb across the textured cup. She glanced up as he walked towards her and then sat in the chair next to her and put his arm around her. She set the coffee down and then leaned into him resting her head on his shoulder.

"Thank you for being here, and for coming to get me." She stated softly.

"No problem. I'm sorry we had to leave Matt behind, he looked a little lost." Tim stated.

"I called him while you were in the hallway and he said his brother and sister in law were coming over to sit with Sami. He should be here within the hour." She relayed.

"Good, I'm sure that will make you feel better." He sat there grateful for the company she provided, and he was impressed with her strength during this crisis. He tried not to focus on how good she felt in his arms since he knew it was completely inappropriate especially in light of the severity of the circumstances. Still he was relieved she was there with him.

Another hour came and went by without a word from the surgical team, and Tim was getting ready to check on her condition again when Matt entered the family waiting area, and Susie jumped up to greet him throwing her arms around him. They sat huddled on a small sofa near the television which seemed to be on an endless game show loop that Tim found maddening. He excused himself and walked over to the nurse's station to inquire after Jesse and learned that she was being moved into recovery, then would be moved to the Critical Care Unit on the fourth floor.

Tim walked back into the waiting area and saw Susie snuggled up to Matt with his arm around her now, and somewhere deep inside him ached. He knew he shouldn't have any feelings for her, but there was something about these Whitmore girls that caused him to fall hard for them.

285

"They will be coming for you soon Susie, she is in recovery and then they will move her to the C.C.U. on the fourth floor." He stated trying to smile encouragingly.

She looked into Matt's eyes then back to Tim. She kissed Matt's cheek then stood and threw her arms around Tim's waist and held him tightly. He instinctively leaned down and kissed the top of her head and then held her for a minute. She then looked up into his big brown eyes and mouthed 'thank you' then released him.

Matt stood and shook his hand then thanked him for everything he had done, and for punching Jerry. He confessed that he was a little envious as just about everyone in the family wanted a piece of that jerk, but was happy Tim was there to stand in the gap and take care of business on behalf of him and the Whitmore's. Tim smirked and said it was truly his pleasure. Sue said she had his card and would call him or text him to update him on Jesse's condition.

The nurse came to escort them to the recovery area where the doctor would meet with them and discuss her immediate condition and prognosis. Tim watched them walk away hand in hand and immediately felt empathy for Dean who was relegated to this position on a daily basis with Jesse. He found it difficult to breathe and it gave him a brand new level of respect for Dean and the man he was.

"Dean?" Tim stated walking towards the parking lot.

"Here. Where are you?"

"I don't know what to do, Matt is here with Susie and I can't go into recovery. I may head into the office unless you need me to do something. Tell me what to do, this is so exasperating." Tim confessed.

"I know buddy. I just need to see her once more before I head back to the office. Visiting hours are over at 9:00 p.m. so I am sure Susie and Matt will head home then come back in the morning. They might agree to let Susie stay but it's unlikely."

"I'll stay and be your ride since you rode over in the ambulance. I may go to the canteen and grab something to eat. I am not sure if I am hungry or just agitated, I have all these emotions pent up and I don't know what to do. I feel like crying, fighting and lashing out all at the same time. How irrational is that?" Tim said knowing that Dean would understand him and how he was feeling.

"I totally understand. It's partially all the adrenaline crashing, and then all the emotion of the alert, finding her injured, then all the waiting. It's hard. Go eat something and walk around some and try and clear your head. I'll text you in a bit." Dean encouraged.

Tim started for the canteen then turned back towards the fountain in the middle of the courtyard in front of the entrance to the hospital. He sat on the stone wall for several minutes running his hands through his hair and then looking up at the stars. His phone started ringing, he looked down and saw it was Wex. *Perfect timing.*

Susie was overwhelmed with the tubes and wires that were hooked up to her sweet sister, with all the beeping and whirring sounds they were making. Jesse looked like a small child laying there and Sue's face crumbled upon seeing her sister look so fragile and pale. The white blankets on top of her were there to keep her warm, and Sue searched for a place where she could touch Jesse that wouldn't interfere with the I.V. bags and monitor leads. She looked at Matt then burst into tears.

The doctor assured her that Jesse would survive these injuries but was still very sick and infection was a major concern since the weapon had sliced through part of her colon. They were able to stop the bleeding for now, but she would most likely be in the C.C.U. for several days. Time would tell. *Time would tell...* Those words echoed through and haunted Susie's mind.

Matt wandered around the hall while Sue spent time with Jesse, and realized that no one had reached out to her parents. He told the nurse's he was going into the waiting room to make some calls then walked down the corridor for privacy.

Finally Matt and Sue decided based on the nurse's recommendation, to go home for the night, but Sue planned to be back up there bright and early the next morning. The nurse pulled the curtain to when they left and returned to checking vitals on the other patients on the floor.

Dean walked in fully dressed in green scrubs, gloves and a mask and shut the curtain behind him. His faux hospital badge listed him as Dr. Xavier Alexander, a visiting physician from Greenville, South Carolina. Adam had run stats on all the hospital staff and Dr. Alexander was the closest match to Dean's height and coloring. Dr. Alexander had a summer home at the beach and often subbed in at the hospital when in town. Adam fabricated the I.D. badge then sent Derek to deliver it to his boss. Dean looked at Jesse and felt like he had been punched in the gut. He walked over to the head of the bed, unhooked his mask then bent down gently kissing her forehead.

"Hey baby. You sure gave me a scare tonight. I will never leave you with another handler ever again. Please forgive me Jess. Please, please forgive me." He whispered into her ear. "I love you Jesse, I need you to know that. I will make this right, I promise."

It was time for the nursing staff to start doing rounds again, so he needed to leave. He kissed her sweetly one last time then hooked the mask back up and walked out of the room. He strode to the elevator and then once he was on the main floor again, he texted his ride home, Tim.

CHAPTER 33

ANSWERS

D ean started digging into the videos, files and reports from the surveillance of Andy's apartment. Then he continued to pour over the reports from the Alpha team and information finally clicked. The European thug from the Chinese Bistro and Reed's was confirmed as being in the car, the same car that hit Casey. So Andy had gotten roped into working for this syndicate and was in so far over his head that he was lucky to be alive. They never got the code hacked, but he did find a way to reroute the security so they could rob the bank in broad daylight.

Dean made a note to be sure to reach out to a buddy of his at the Federal Bureau of Investigation to alert him to the potential break in there. He discovered the email where they referenced hitting Casey and he realized that when Andy was walking Casey that they must have met outside from time to time and they thought the dog was his. No wonder Casey flipped out when the car they were in got close to Jesse. She died trying to protect her master. *Poor sweet mutt.*

The New York team had been running surveillance on a man up there that was apparently the European's boss. Now things were starting to tie together. Dean's team had been running ops locally and were frustrating the syndicate in the area by continuously busting the low level perps like the bartenders and drug dealers night after night, who were setting the unsuspecting girls for exploitation. They were still building a case against the men in the hierarchy, but their time was coming. Dean knew he would never eradicate this from the east coast, but if he could move it out of his territory, and make this area safer, he will have accomplished a great deal. Unfortunately there was no cutting the head off the snake to make this demon die…cut the head off this snake, and three lesser heads sprouted, but it was a fight he was committed to fight.

Tim walked into Dean's office wanting an update on Jesse, and on what happened at Reed's. Apparently the baby faced man who stabbed Jesse was the skateboarder that Jesse thought was a homeless teenager. He was twenty two, and the female he was running with was twenty years old, the motive was they wanted drug money and were trying to catch Jesse before she made the daily deposit. They even recovered the note she had written them and it made Dean's heart hurt to think her kindness towards them was wasted. Dean also discovered that Craig and Mrs. Lane were having an affair, and he was speaking to the Director at 9:30 a.m. about their futures, which if he had his way would be very dim.

Tim was furious to find out that Craig was not only still alive after what happened to Jesse but still employed and he couldn't decide if Dean was getting weak or showed remarkable restraint. Frankly he was ready to tear his head off. He just prayed at this point he did not pass him in the hallway or he might not be responsible for his actions.

"So tell me about you punching Jerry? What happened?" Dean asked highly interested in what brought all that on.

"Well Sue and I had just arrived at the hospital and he was there demanding a copy of Jess's Death Certificate, apparently when the cops called and described her injuries must have led him to believe she had been killed or he was wishfully thinking. Regardless he was freaking Susie out, so I marched him outside. Then he informed me that if Jesse was dead, he was collecting on an insurance policy because he had a new wife and baby on the way. Dean I swear I didn't even blink. I was so angry I just punched him." Tim stated getting all worked up again just thinking about it.

"Better you than me Tim, I probably would have shot him. He is such a piece of crap, I swear I am so happy she is away from him. Good form man, good form." Dean said.

"Well I know Susie was happy I did it and her husband Matt congratulated me. It was kind of funny." He stated smiling.

Dean remarked that Ninja was doing an excellent job as liaison to the local police department regarding Jesse's attack and she showed great concern for her well-being. He also stated that Reed's was of course closed due to the ongoing investigation and probably would not reopen for at least several days. The staff was reeling from the horrific events and were anxious to see Jesse.

Susie had texted Tim to let him know she was with Jesse this morning, and that her parents were in route. She was about the same as she was last night, and to Susie's knowledge had not regained consciousness yet. Jess was holding steady but there was no real improvement, and that had them all concerned. Dean excused himself to go meet with Director Johnson, and left Tim sitting in his office to review some reports and video. Perhaps a second set of eyes might yield some new leads. Dean walked down the long corridor to the Director's office which overlooked the office park courtyard area.

He tapped on the door but waited since he could see that the Director was on the phone. Director Johnson, waved him in and told him to sit. After finishing his call he folded his hands on his desk then looked hard at Dean.

"How are you this morning?" He stated eyeing him.

"Fine sir, I have tied some things together, and have amended my report to the New York office. I sent you the email regarding Craig, and I wanted to know what your decision was going to be?" He stated clearly.

"Mrs. Lane will be fired, and he will be moved to an outpost in Hawaii." He stated levelly.

"What? He gets rewarded? Sir I don't understand." He asked, shocked at the director's revelation.

"Please. Dean you ought to know me better than that, but I can't send a disgruntled employee off to the outer edges of the world and risk him being bought off or defecting for money or perceived prestige to one of our enemies. I will be keeping close tabs on him, you can rest assured his time there will not be pleasant despite his surroundings."

"Yes sir, of course." Dean conceded, remembering that he did not get to be a director of special operations by being a teddy bear. He started again, "Jesse is somewhat stable but as of early this morning there has been no real improvement." Dean offered.

"I see, but improvement is expected, yes?" He inquired.

"Yes sir."

"Dean I also wanted to notify you that you are number two in the safe house lottery and have forty eight hours to secure financing. You understand how this works, if the person in the number one position can't or doesn't secure financing within the first forty eight, then the property goes to the second in line and so forth. I received word this morning you are number two. Congratulations."

"Thank you sir, I have the cash to pay for the house. I have been saving for quite some time, so it should be a non-issue if the first position defaults and it passes to me." He said keeping his emotions in check.

"I am concerned about you Dean, you just came off an emotional week with your family and now this with Charge 25. Do you require a leave of absence?"

"No sir. I agree the issue with my family was extremely difficult, but we are moving beyond it and we are starting to heal. This development with Charge 25 is very upsetting but I am on my game sir, I am clear and focused. I need to stay busy sir, and I won't let you down." Dean reassured.

"I expect you to know your limits Dean, and I will trust that once you have reached them that you will let me know, and we will devise a plan. Until then, you are still in charge. Please keep me posted on Charge 25 and any upcoming events I need to be privy to. You have been here all night, I want you to go home for the rest of the day and I will see you here at 0700 tomorrow."

"Yes sir, thank you." He stated rising to shake the Director's hand.

He walked outside into the sunlight and put on his Rayban Wayfarers, then walked down to Reed's reliving the events from last night. He crossed the yellow tape and examined the crime scene again. Her blood still lay in a pool on the floor. Adam came on in his ear piece.

"Boss?"

"Go"

"You ok sir? I see you are at Reeds."

"Spying on me?"

"Yes sir." Adam stated with a slight laugh.

"Just checking the scene again…Adam, how's our buddy in the hospital? Do we still have security on him?"

"Affirmative."

"I'm going home, please let Tim know."

"Roger that sir."

Dean exited the crime scene and then walked down to where his car was parked in the garage. He sat in the car for a few minutes then started the engine and turned the car towards home. His apartment felt strange to him, like he was a guest in his own space. He turned the shower on full blast, removed his ear piece, undressed then prepared to enter the steamy shower. He stood leaning against the wall as the hot water washed over his tired aching muscles. Dean rinsed his mouth then allowed the water to wash over his head then run down his tan muscular back. He hastily washed then leisurely rinsed again and then turned the water off and reached for a towel.

He threw on a pair of boxer briefs then a tee shirt and flopped into the bed. He was out in a matter of minutes. Images of Jesse danced through his head and he could hear the roar of the ocean behind her then nothing but darkness.

The Whitmore's arrived at the hospital and they all hunkered down to pray Jesse through this crisis and support Susie who had been dealing with it alone for the last several hours. Tim had texted her and was dying to swing by and check on his sis, but held off since her parents had just arrived. Wex showed up on the 2nd floor demanding to see his boy. Tim walked out from Dean's office into the lobby and they just hugged, then Tim walked him down to his work sanctuary, the garage. Wex knew how much Tim cared for Jesse and was devastated when he got the news of her attack. He knew Tim was extremely upset and confused last night, and when he didn't hear from him this morning he decided to drive up and see him for himself.

Tim started off showing him the latest vehicles he was setting up and some of the new toys he was installing and getting to play with, then they went into Tim's office and shut the door. Once they were alone and eyes were not on them then Tim unloaded. Wex listened patiently and tried to let Tim express all his sadness and fears before he spoke. He sat there for a long time as Tim talked it all out not really needing Wex to comment or speak, a nod of his head was sufficient to keep this one sided conversation going. Tim vacillated between animated motions and sad morose postures and Wex could see the inner turmoil he was in and had been in for several weeks now.

Tim wore his feelings on his sleeve and was truly a gentle soul for the most part. Fighting only when backed into a corner or defending someone he loved. Wex could not be prouder of Tim and the man he had become if he were his own child. Finally Tim stopped speaking and just sat there quietly for several minutes. Wex leaned forward and grabbed his hands and then began praying. Tim inwardly thought that Wex missed his calling and should have been a minister, he seemed keenly in tune with God and was a mighty prayer warrior. He wiped his eyes once Wex finished praying and they decided to grab a bite to eat, then Wex insisted that the tall lanky boy take him to the hospital to see Jesse.

Dean woke up and felt like he had been drugged he just laid in bed and stared blankly at the picture that hung above his dresser. It was a city scape of New York City before the twin towers fell, and he absentmindedly wondered why that particular picture was in his bedroom. Not that it was a bad picture or one he didn't like, he just found it an odd choice for his bedroom. His sister Lily had picked it out and hung it there. He loathed the city life and thanked God and the Director every day for getting him out of the rat race that was D.C. He could still do his job for the agency from South Carolina, and the last few cases he worked yielded some of his best work results yet, proving the Director's theory right. *I am so tired, I'm physically exhausted.* He dozed back off while sitting up still facing the picture.

Late in the afternoon Carter made his way to the fourth floor and found Susie sitting outside the nurse's station looking at her cell phone. He walked over and spoke softly to her causing her to jump up and hug his neck. He thanked her for calling and filling him in on what had happened. She walked him over to where her parents were, then they all allowed him to go in and see Jesse for a few moments alone. It seemed surreal to see her lying there with all the tubes, heart monitor leads and I.V.'s attached to her. His chest felt tight as he imagined the pain she must have felt when the attack took place and then lying there on the floor thinking she was going to die right there in that moment. Tears stung his eyes as he tried to blink them back and focus on the fact that the E.M.S got to her in time and that she was going to be ok.

Slowly he walked over and kissed her forehead then whispered in her ear that he was there and that he loved her. Her eyes fluttered ever so slightly and he held his breath thinking she might open her eyes, but she did not. He wondered if she was dreaming, or if she would dream in that drug induced state. A small framed nurse with light brown hair whipped the curtain back startling him. She started checking the machines and noting Jesse's vitals. Carter was disappointed that his brief time with Jesse was being so rudely interrupted. He slowly backed out and went back to the bench where Susie was sitting.

Mrs. Whitmore hugged Carter then Mr. Whitmore shook his hand they all decided since it was time for the shift change that they would all get something to eat. Carter felt awkward, but Sue insisted he come and spend time with them that Jesse would not want him to be alone. They walked down to the hospital canteen to see what the special was today, it was Salisbury steak and rice and green peas. There was a grape salad or jello for desert. Carter decided he just wanted some of the grape salad as his appetite was waning lately. Susie ordered the chef salad, and her parents just drank coffee.

The grape salad was unusually good and he liked the ratio of sweet to salty with the fresh chopped pecans sprinkled throughout. Sue mostly picked at her salad eating the protein out of it and dipping captain's wafer crackers in her ranch dressing. He overheard Sue's parents discussing the amount of blood Jesse had lost and that the hospital needed more 'O' positive blood for the hospital's blood bank. He was type 'B', and could still give blood, but it would not help Jesse who was type 'O'.

They finished eating then sat and talked for a while before he decided to stretch and then walk outside for a few minutes needing some fresh air. Mr Whitmore walked outside with him and they just leisurely walked around the sidewalk that surrounded the building. When they had come around full circle and near the entrance again, they saw Tim and Wex getting ready to

enter through the main entrance. Carter waved them down and then intro-
ductions were made.

Susie was thrilled to finally meet Wex since Jesse had spoken so highly
of him, and once again she hugged Tim then lightly brushed a quick kiss
across his lips. Carter mentioned to Tim that he was going to check into giving
blood, that they needed more type 'O', to which Tim announced he was type
'O' and if it would help Jesse he would surely donate. They both stopped at
the main nurse's station and inquired as to where they needed to go to give
blood and were directed to the second floor central lab for processing. Tim
wanted to see Jesse first and take Wex up there before he was confined in the
lab giving blood. So Sue and her mother walked up there with Tim and Wex
while Carter and Mr. Whitmore went to the second floor lab to see what the
hours were for giving blood. Carter decided he would come back another day
and give since he wasn't quite feeling himself lately.

After Tim and Wex went up to see Jesse, they went down to the lab and
gave blood which took a little over an hour and a half from beginning to end.
Afterwards they called Dean and asked him to meet them for dinner, he agreed
and they ended up at the Sea Shack Gourmet eats diner. The place was dead
tonight with only two other people in the joint besides them. They took a
booth situated in the back. It had been several months since Dean had seen
Wex, and he was happy to hear that he had come up to see Jesse and console
Tim. Wex extended his condolences regarding Camden and Dean shared that
it was more than the death of his twin, it was the death of the hope they had
all clung to for so long. He was doing better but was still struggling with
certain aspects.

The waitress came back with their waters and the complimentary hush-
puppies then took their order. Once she had walked away they resumed their
conversation. Wex shared what it was like when he lost his son, and Dean
was riveted listening to Wex's ordeal. Tim sat quietly listening to the two
men and silently prayed Wex could reach Dean as only Wex seemed to be
able to do with people.

There was a slight lull in the conversation which was perfect timing for
the food to arrive as she brought Tim his giant burger with fries, Dean his
shrimp po boy, and Wex his fried flounder with coleslaw. The men dug into
their meals and for several minutes there was no chatter among them. Dean
didn't realize just how hungry he was and started stealing a few fries off Tim's
plate, and Tim acted like he didn't notice. As the meal slowly disappeared
before them they started talking again, and Dean was extremely frank about
his feelings in regards to all of the recent events and God's part in it.

That was all Wex needed to lovingly explain the gospel back to Dean in a way he could understand it. He started off by saying that God was not afraid of nor would he shrink away from Dean's anger, but that he understood it. Dean and Tim both sat there hanging on every word that came out of Wex's mouth. That man was on roll preaching right there in that dingy diner, pointing Dean right back to the only person who could heal his heart, hear his prayers and make him whole once again and that was Jesus Christ.

Tim quietly slipped out of the booth and paid the bill while Dean and Wex still talked it out. They finally all walked out of the diner moving over towards Wex's truck and Wex grabbed both boys then started praying for them and specifically Dean. Finally Dean let down his guard, and broke down. He knew that Wex's words were true and now that this attack had happened to Jesse on top of the news about Camden, it was too much, he just desperately wanted peace. He was tired of bargaining with God and just wanted to let go and be filled with the peace that his mother and Tim spoke of. Wex led him through the sinner's prayer and implored him to leave it all at the feet of Jesus and accept the love and peace He was standing there waiting to impart to him.

Dean agreed and hugged Wex so tightly thanking him for everything. Tim knew he would need to drive Dean home and stay close for a bit, and Wex said that he would head back to his side of town, but wanted to hear from both of them in a few days, and they would all go out on the boat soon.

Once again Dean's emotions were raw, but he was starting to settle down and was so grateful that they had encouraged him to come out to dinner tonight.

"I'm mad at you Timmy. You set me up." Dean said sniffing.

"Yeah I know…but I love you man." Tim said focusing on driving.

"I know you both are right. I am soul weary and I do believe everything he said tonight. I want peace Tim. Thank you for being there for me man."

"I'm your wingman Dean. I've got your back, and I want you to have the peace you seek. This is the only way man. It's truth."

"Wex is amazing, no wonder you love that old man so much. Seriously, and he isn't about to let go until you relent." Dean remarked.

"I know, right? Well that…and he's a fabulous cook." Tim said grinning from ear to ear causing Dean to smile.

"Shut up and drive." He said with a smile.

Tim drove them to his place and they went in and talked some more then watched a baseball game on the television. Once he felt like Dean was truly in a good place Tim took him back to his home. Dean came in, locked the door, then knelt down in front of his couch and began pouring his heart out to God, no longer angry but truly seeking the Almighty Holy God and hoping that God would meet him where he was...

Dean remained in that position for quite a while and when he finally had run out of things to say and confess he just sat there quietly and listened for God's still small voice. He was not disappointed. Eventually exhausted he crawled onto the couch and slept there for the night and for the first time in months he slept soundly and if he dreamed they were peaceful.

CHAPTER 34

FOREVER

T he next several days were just like the ones before them, Jesse's condition was stabile but not really improving like everyone had hoped. Infection from the disgusting filthy knife that was used in her attack was raging within her petite body and the doctors were rallying back with massive amounts of antibiotics. Susie and her parents kept a vigil at her bedside while Tim and Dean alternated impersonating hospital personnel after visiting hours so that they could spend some alone time with her.

On a positive note, Andy was now able to speak and was recovering from the injuries of the beat down he received in his apartment. Adam and Derek were tasked with interviewing him and moving him to a safe house while he recovered. This near death experience was enough to make him come clean and confess to his involvement with the syndicate that he was now involved with. He truly did not realize at first that he was participating in something so sinister and just got in way over his head. With the information that Adam was able to glean from him, Dean stated that he would help Andy start over or put him in Witness Protection.

Dean was focused and determined to make significant progress in this human trafficking case. He was informed that he was going to have to go to New York soon and work with the team up there for a short time. The director was trying to buy him some time before he had to go, but the time clock was ticking away. The situation with Jesse grieved him deeply and so he just threw himself into his work once again. Tim was still the one voice of reason in Dean's life that he was still listening to, and Tim knew if Jesse would just turn the corner, Dean would relax.

It was in the wee hours of the morning, when the faux Dr. Xavier Alexander was standing watch over her that she finally opened her eyes. She looked a little frightened and confused, and he immediately began speaking softly to her, noticing the beeping of the heart monitor slowing as he continued to soothe her. She was still intubated and so speaking was out of the question for her right now. He continued to lean in close and whisper to her, he had her close her eyes and then he held her hand and reassured her everything was now going to be ok. After several minutes her breathing slowed again and her eyes fought to stay open, eventually succumbing to sleep once again. For the first time in almost a week, Dean had hope that she was going to be ok.

The nurses were getting ready to start rounds again, and would be checking on her soon so he needed to get back downstairs. Stealthily he moved out of the room and made his way to the elevator. He called Tim once he reached his car, waking his best friend to relay the news that he saw her open her eyes and that he had spoken to her. Tim of course was half awake but elated to hear the good news. Perhaps now she would turn that corner and sprint home.

Carter and Tim both received texts from Susie the next morning confirming what Dean had discovered last night and they were thrilled to hear she was now improving. She still had a long way to go before she was fully healed but this was a blessed step in the right direction. Sue also indicated that they were going to be removing some of the tubes, which hopefully would allow her to speak and do a few more things on her own. She remained in the C.C.U for a couple more days then was moved to the fifth floor to a private room.

Dean received the news that he could no longer delay his New York trip and was required to be in the big apple no later than Monday. Once again he had to tag Tim in to be his wingman and watch over Jess in his absence. He planned to make the most of his time and get in and get out of New York as soon as possible.

Tim as always was happy to oblige and enjoyed seeing Jesse and Susie. The Whitmore's were still in town, and were enjoying their time with Sami and Sue while tending to Jess. Knowing Jesse was on the mend was a huge relief and they were all resting better at night now. Reed and his wife Ann had been in to see her as well as Libby, Hannah and Johnny. Also several of the guys from the table of 8 came by to see her like Doc, Yoshi and Mack. She was so happy to see everyone but was still not up for continuous company as much as she appreciated the show of affection, her strength just was not there yet.

The nurses had her standing up now, and walking small distances which she found cruel. She remained hunched over as she moved slowly since it felt like if she stood up her insides were going to fall out and into the floor. Everyone assured her that was not the case, but she was not keen on believing them at this point. Tim tried to stop by a couple times during the day, often on his lunch hour and then after work. Dean had texted her, and Carter had called stating that he had been called out of town on business but would see her soon. Susie assured her that Carter had been there early on, but his trip could not be helped. This eased her mind a bit, but she was missing him terribly.

Each day that passed seemed to find her getting a little stronger and less dependent on any pain medication. Her parents were still in town for now, but her father was set to return back to Florida very soon, and her mother was going to stay until she was allowed to return home from the hospital. Carter had mentioned that he would trade apartments with her temporarily if necessary so she wouldn't have to climb the steps and she was seriously considering it.

Jesse had been in the hospital for the better part of eight days, and the doctors stated that she could be discharged as early as tomorrow morning which thrilled her mother and sister. She was still nervous but knew that in time she would be fine. Tim got the news and passed it on to Wex, who had been praying non-stop for a full recovery for her. She texted Carter the news and he said since he was home now from his trip he would take off time to get her settled and could help get her home if she needed it.

Finally everyone had left the hospital room for the evening and Jesse was laying there absentmindedly staring at the television and waiting for her evening meal to arrive. She was relieved that everyone had gone home early and she had a few minutes to herself. It had been a couple of days since she had heard from Dean and it stung a bit that he had not checked in with her The last time they spoke he was debriefing her on her attack to get her side of the story which corroborated what the recordings and video showed. He did tell her Craig had been assigned to a remote area in the Pacific Ocean but never mentioned the word Hawaii. She seemed relieved.

Her dinner arrived and she had apple juice, ginger ale, baked spaghetti and a small salad and diced pears. At least her appetite was beginning to return and she ate the majority of her dinner and saved her pears for later as a snack. She had just finished eating when the orderly came by to check on her and remove her tray, then her phone started buzzing. It was Dean.

"Hey Jess."

"Hi."

"I hear you are breaking out of that joint tomorrow. Are you excited to be going home?" He asked.

"I suppose. A little nervous. The stairs to my place seem daunting at this point since at the moment I struggle to get to the end of the hall and back."

"Well just take things slowly. I thought Carter had offered up his place for a few days until you feel stronger. Are you going to take him up on that?"

"How did you know about that?" She asked her curiosity piqued.

"Seriously? I'm a spy Jess. I know things." He said trying to make her laugh.

"Is my bed bugged?" She inquired.

"No, but Tim can't keep a secret. He mentioned it to me." Dean replied laughing.

"Ahh. I see. Good to know for the future. Tim can't keep a secret." She said now smiling.

"Jesse I have a serious question for you." Dean started.

"O.K., ask."

"I think it's time we met, face to face. Once you get out of the hospital and feel stronger, I want to see you. I am tired of having to lurk in the shadows. Will you meet with me?"

"How is that possible? I thought that was expressly forbidden?"

"Aside from your worries about the CIA's policies on this, do you have any other reservations as to why you would not want to meet me in person?" He asked now holding his breath.

"No, I don't guess so, I just want to make sure you don't get into trouble and I don't get fired as a charge."

"It's been approved. So after you get home and feel better, I want to pick a day and meet you then maybe eat dinner or something? Does that sound ok?"

"Yes."

Dean attempted to make additional small talk but could tell she was finished talking for the moment and needed to rest. So he told her goodnight then ended the call. He was happy that she was willing to meet but was dying to know what was going through her mind. She laid back in the bed and her mind swirled with so many random thoughts about Dean, and then about Carter, and her feelings for both of them. Finally exhausted she closed her eyes and drifted off to sleep.

The nurses came in during shift change to check on her and of course woke her back up. Jesse reached for her phone and saw that she had missed a text from Carter. The time stated it was 11:15 p.m. and so she texted him back.

Sorry I missed your text, I had drifted off to sleep. It's been a long day. ~Jess

Hey! No worries, I figured as much, I was going to try and come by tonight but got detained. Are you still set to be discharged tomorrow?-Carter

Yes. As far as I know, but I don't have a time. Were you serious about me staying with you for a few days until I am stronger? ~Jess

With me or at my place if you want privacy, I can stay in your place for a while. Just until you are stronger of course. –Carter

Thank you, I think I may do that, I am really dreading those stairs. Mom had planned to stay a couple of days with me but I think I will be fine. ~Jess

I am good either way, I am just thrilled you are finally coming home. I have missed you more than you will ever know. This has really taken years off my life Jesse. I was so worried about you. –Carter

I can only imagine, I'm so sorry. ~Jess

Carter?

Never mind. ~Jess

What honey, are you ok? –Carter

Yeah sorry, do you want me to call you once I am discharged and leaving? I hear it can take time to actually be released. ~ Jesse

"Yes, that would be great, then I can meet you at the apartment. Look you need to get some rest. I love you Jesse. –Carter

I love you Carter. ~Jess

She slept fitfully, tossing and turning with odd dreams filling her sleeping hours. Susie and her mother arrived around 8:00 a.m. ready to pack her up and move her back home. Sue had gone by Jesse's apartment and had gotten her a sundress that was not binding and her sandals to go home in. Her mother helped Jesse get into the shower so she could wash her hair and prepare to be discharged. The doctor had been by about 6:45 a.m. and signed the release order so that they could start processing her discharge papers. She attempted to dry her hair but was still overly cautious about standing up really straight and holding her arms above her head pulled on the abdomen area making her uncomfortable. For now the semi dried scrunched look would have to do.

The orderly brought the wheel chair in around 9:15 a.m. and Tim walked in right behind him. Jesse was thrilled to see him and all at once felt relaxed for the first time in days. She and Susie and her mom were discussing all the paperwork the hospital required and that is why Jesse was named the way she was. Mrs. Whitmore said they had named Susie, Susannah Leighanne Whitmore; but after having to write that multiple times for school and for various paperwork throughout the years when Jesse came along she was named Jesse Jo Whitmore and that was still too long! They joked and said if they had conceived another child and it was a girl, her name would be Ann with no middle name, and if it was a boy it would be Ed with no middle name. Tim thought this was hilarious and they all laughed with Mrs. Whitmore. Then he spoke up, "Hey, hey baby girl. Let's bust out of this joint." He said grinning from ear to ear.

"Boy am I happy you are here with us!" Jesse exclaimed.

"Yeah? You are?" He said surprised.

"Since you are here, I know it will all be ok. Are you coming by the apartment so we can visit?" She asked wanting to talk to him more about Dean.

"Not right now, I mean I am going to help you get loaded into the car and so forth, I actually brought the company Van, which I think will be easier for you to get in and out of. Susie's car is low and tight and I think will be harder for you to get out of, so I will drive you home, and help you get in but I can't stay, I have a meeting at ten."

"That is so thoughtful of you Timothy." Susie piped up hugging him.

"No problem ma'am. Anything for my Jess." He stated unleashing his dimples.

They had gathered all her belongings, had her follow up doctor's orders and prescriptions and the orderly led the way to the outer doors of the hospital pick up area where Tim had already parked the van. Sue and her mom went onto her vehicle and then followed Tim to the apartment complex. Jesse texted Carter once she was securely fastened up in the seat. He replied he would be there waiting on her.

Tim called Dean on the ear piece and relayed that he had Jesse and was taking her home. She called from the back seat and said to tell him hello to which Tim relayed her message. Tim pulled into the handicapped space at the end near her apartment unit and parked the van. Carter came out to assist Tim, and they gently removed her from the vehicle. Tim patted Carter on the shoulder and told him to carry on. Jesse blew Tim a kiss and said for him to call her later.

Carter's apartment was immaculate, not that it was ever really messy, but she could tell he had gone over it with a fine tooth comb and it smelled lemony fresh. He informed her that there were clean linens on the bed and in the bathroom for her. The second bedroom was his work office and that door remained locked. Her mother and Sue arrived about five minutes later and knocked on the door. Carter let them in and offered them something to drink. Jesse sat on the edge of the sofa looking slightly bewildered. Sue was bustling around and her mom was chatting away, but Carter was keenly aware that she was unsettled.

He left the ladies chatting in the kitchen and went over to Jesse and knelt down.

"Baby, are you ok? You don't look ok." He whispered.

"I just want to be with you alone. Can you get them to leave?" She whispered back. "I mean I love them but they have been with me non-stop for days now. I just want to see you for a few minutes alone without being interrupted."

"I will make it happen." He said smiling reassuringly at her.

He went over to the breakfast bar and had a little pow-wow with them explaining that she was tired and wanted to rest, and he was going to be working from home for today so that he had her covered if they wanted to rest themselves or go run some errands. Sue winked at him and said that would be fine, that she and her mom had plenty to do making meals for Jesse to freeze, so she wouldn't have to cook for a week or two. So they hugged Carter and Jess then made their way back to Sue's car.

He went back over to her then sat down as she reached for his hand. He gently kissed her and then asked her if she wanted to lay down on the couch or on the bed. She chose the bed, so he helped her up then they walked together to his bedroom. He removed her shoes for her then lifted her into the bed and made sure she was comfortable as she rolled to lay on her left side. Then he sat in the bed and ran his fingers lovingly through her hair as she let out a long exhale then drifted off to sleep.

Several more days had passed and she was starting to regain some of her momentum and energy back although her condition kept her from doing a lot of what she wanted to do. Carter ended up staying on the sofa to sleep at night so she could rest but could not bring himself to leave her alone in the apartment. Her mother stayed until the weekend then once she was satisfied that her baby girl was truly on the mend she too headed back home, but made plans to come back in a few weeks to check in on everyone.

Jesse had only heard from Dean a handful of times since that last call he made to her in the hospital and did not bring up meeting again, and she wondered if he had changed his mind. There was a part of her that desperately wanted to meet him, see him and another part of her that was secretly terrified that seeing him would upset her balance with Carter. She just kept praying that God would work it out.

By the end of the month she was ready to move back into her apartment and had been practicing getting up and down the stairs on her own. She was still going at a snail's pace, but eventually she did make it to the top of the stairs. Carter was beginning to get spoiled with having her around so much and protested slightly when she stated she was ready to go home, but eventually he relented knowing this was something she needed to do for herself.

She needed to prove to herself that she could and would be ok. He was still very close if she needed anything and so he helped her move back upstairs.

Dean finally called her and asked if she would be willing to come out to the safe house to meet him on Friday afternoon around 4:00 p.m., he stated that Tim would pick her up and drive her out there since she was still on a driving restriction due to her injuries. She nervously agreed.

Dean sat on the steps of the safe house deck near the walkway that lead out to the ocean. He was dressed in his work boots, agency issued navy blue tactical pants, and he opted for the polo shirt, with his baseball style cap to shield his eyes from the sun. His mind raced as he envisioned every possible scenario and played it back in his head tying to anticipate her reaction when she saw him for the first time. There were so many ways this meeting could go sideways, and only one real way it work out and he kept running what the odds were in his head. Finally he had done it so much he had made himself nauseous, and decided to stop and pray instead.

Tim raised him on the ear piece to let him know that they were pulling in the drive way, and Dean acknowledged. His mouth was now bone dry and he was beginning to sweat. He was not this nervous jumping out of an airplane for the first time, or crossing the border into an enemy territory.

Jesse was extremely quiet on the ride over only offering one word answers to Tim's questions and sometimes not even answering the questions correctly. He assured her he would wait on her and would be there to take her home if necessary and she was grateful for that assurance.

Dean sat with his head down praying earnestly as Tim escorted her to the back of the property mindful to assist and steady her in the soft sand. She stood at the end of the decking and just looked at the man sitting six feet from her. Tim kissed her cheek then walked away back down to where the car was, but had his ear piece dialed in to Dean's frequency.

"She's all yours buddy, good luck man. I'll be in the driveway." Tim stated.

Dean slowly started to lift his head, peaking up at her from underneath the brim of his hat as she slowly walked towards him not making a sound. Her face was expressionless, and once she was directly in front of him she slowly removed his ball cap and set it on the step behind him. He was paralyzed and did not utter a sound as he looked up into her eyes. He was desperately trying to read her expression and body language but was at a total loss. She closed her eyes and slowly ran her fingers through his hair, then gently touched his face tracing the outline near his eyes and cheeks. He reached up for her hand and softly kissed her palm.

He started to say something and she 'shushed' him, and then opened her eyes and said, "Kiss me." It was a gentle command, so he slowly rose up and then cradled her face with his hands and kissed her deeply and slowly.

He couldn't decide if this was going to be the first kiss of the rest of their lives, or a goodbye kiss and the thought of the latter terrified him. So he kept kissing her, not wanting the moment to end for fear of it being the last time he would ever touch or taste her beautiful lips. After several blissful moments of connection she started to pull away from him, his stomach lurched and then dropped like a stone. She looked up into his eyes as a few stray tears ran down his cheeks, then said softly, "Thank God I get to keep you both."

"I know I have so much to explain..." He started, but she interrupted.

"I know I should probably be angry, but I am so relieved to see you, that honestly that is all that matters to me."

After hearing that, Tim smiled to himself, started the vehicle and left the safe house, realizing she was in good hands. Dean took her hand and led her inside to sit on the sofa. The walls had been freshly painted and she looked around at some of the changes that were being made.

"Jesse, once everything happened with Jerry, I knew I had to be near you and the only way I could do it and keep it off the radar was to compartmentalize and split myself off. My name is Carter Dean James. I am thirty three years old, I have a set of twin siblings, Derek you have met before briefly, and his twin sister Leah. My twin that I told you about was recently discovered and his tiny body returned to our family. That was the death in our family several weeks ago." He stated solemnly. She reached for his hand and held it tightly.

"Tim of course knew but was sworn to secrecy. His real name is David Timothy Ford. My brother Derek is Christopher Derek James. Anyway, with everything going on in your life, and in mine it was becoming harder and harder trying to keep the two worlds apart. My feelings became so strong for you I had trouble containing them and as Carter I could somewhat let go and love you, but there was always a part of me that had to be hidden. When we discovered Camden, everything in my life fell apart and for the first time in a long time, I had to do what was right for me and pray that it would not alienate you."

"What do I call you?" She asked sincerely confused. He smiled and then responded, 'When I am at work, or on missions or in this uniform, I am Dean Just Dean. When I am home with you or dressed casually, I am Carter. That is still done for safety reasons and for civilians I am acquainted with."

"Why do you sound differently? I mean, why didn't I recognize your voice?"

"The ear piece technology allows us to manipulate the sounds you hear, like changing my voice by an octave or slowing it down ever so slightly or speeding it up or combinations of all of those things. Not to mention the other times I was actually with you, you were so upset and still had your ear piece in so my voice was still somewhat manipulated."

"You spooks know all the tricks." She said with a slight grin.

"Perhaps, but I could see what it was doing to you, I tried as Dean to back off, but then I finally realized that even if you fell for Carter, there were still things that needed to be addressed that I couldn't do without revealing who I was. I truly never meant for all of this to happen like it did, but it was borne out of an overwhelming amount of emotion and good intentions that ran away like a freight train that I was powerless to stop. Forgive me for deceiving you Jess. I truly love you so much." He stated looking longingly into her eyes.

"Like I said I am just so relieved I get to keep you both, I could cry. Oh, poor Tim! Being tossed in the middle of this, it had to be hard on him too."

"Yeah a couple of times he almost melted down because he was having to lie to you, he is not a good liar. Plus he loves and cares about you so much too, as you saw at Wex's that night a few weeks ago."

"Oh wow, now I understand that night you left me in the stairwell was when Tim had his accident wasn't it?" She said now realizing what had taken place that night.

"Yes. One of the worst nights of my life on many levels. I hated to leave you but we truly thought he was dead. It flipped my world upside down for a few hours. Then to realize I had hurt you so badly on top of it all was just about too much." He stated sitting back and pulling her close to him.

"What are they doing here at the house? Getting ready to sell it?"

"Um no, I have some good news for you. It's mine now, or ours should I say." He said grinning from ear to ear.

"What? I don't understand? So you bought it?" She asked incredulously.

"Well when the agency shuts down a safe house its usually put up for auction via a blind lottery where people at the agency can bid on it. It works like this, there is a minimum bid and a maximum bid set for the property and if you want to bid you have to buy a ticket for ten dollars. On that ticket you place your bid amount, and it goes into a safe. Once the bidding closes the tickets are assessed. The highest bid wins. Now if there are several people who bid the maximum then all of those go into a special bin, and they are randomly drawn out one at a time, first place, then second, third and fourth place. First place is then contacted and has 48 hours to obtain all the financing to pay for the property. If he can't do it then it by default goes to the person in second position and so forth until someone finally secures it."

"So you were in first place?"

"No, I was in second place, but the first place person apparently was getting ready to move back to California to be near family since he was close to retirement, and so he defaulted, so then it came to me. I have been saving money for years and years now. So I had the money to pay for more than half of it out right, so then securing the remaining financing was a snap. This was more than just a house to me after I saw how much you connected to being here, so I knew when it came up that I had to try and get it for you. God just worked out the details." He said kissing her forehead.

"I do love this place, you have no idea how much. I feel so safe and at peace when I am here. So are you the one doing the painting and decorating?"

"Yes, for now, I was taking cues from your apartment in regards to colors you tend to lean towards. There is so much to this place that you have never even seen. From what I can tell when you stayed here you pretty much stuck to this room, the kitchen, and bedroom. There are four bedrooms here, three bathrooms, a dining room and office."

"You are right, I didn't feel like I could go rummaging around in someone else's house since I was a guest. But I will say I love that we are at the end of this cove and it's so private. I shudder to think of what you paid for this home." She said sinking into the side of him and he draped his arm around her.

"It doesn't matter its only money and to know that you would be happy here is all I need to know." He stated then got down in the floor and knelt before her.

"I know Carter asked you to marry him but I want to officially ask you again now that you fully know who I am, with a ring. Jesse will you do me the honor of marrying me?" He said his voice quivering slightly as he knelt down and then he showed her the ring. A lovely one carat solitaire in a halo white gold setting.

"Oh Carter it's lovely. *Yes*, I will marry you."

He placed the ring on her finger, and then kissed her sweetly.

"To your family Jess I'll need to remain as Carter, they still can't know about Dean. I can't wait to introduce you to my family. If you are up to it, we can swing by there on our way home tonight." He stated beaming with pride.

"I would love to meet your family Carter. Tonight is fine, I should be ok, since I took a nap today." She stated smiling.

He took the liberty of calling his mother while Jesse used the restroom then investigated the other rooms in the house. His mother was elated to hear that her son was coming over and bringing a girl with him. She prayed it was the one he spoke of when he was there last and that the complications were now behind them. He explained that she had been injured recently and was in a delicate state, but that they would swing by. She insisted that they stay for dinner as his father was grilling out and he agreed as long as Jess was up for it.

Jesse could not wipe the smile off her face while walking through the house as the realization started sinking in that this would soon be *her* home with Carter. Then she looked down at the dazzler on her left hand and was in a state of awe at the size and beauty of it. It wasn't really that size mattered to her, she wasn't that materialistic, but that he thought enough of her to buy her something that beautiful did matter. Jerry's ring that he had presented her when they got married reflected his lack of interest and caring because he had the means.

They arrived at the James' home and she was excited to finally meet the people that raised this extraordinary man that she had fallen deeply in love with. Carter exited the vehicle and came around to help her out of the car and up to the porch. His mother saw them pull up and met them at the door swinging it open wide and then she nearly tackling him with a hug. Then she came over to Jesse and very gently hugged her and welcomed her into their home.

His father was manning the barbeque on the back porch, under the pergola near the pool. They slowly made their way out there, his father was thrilled to see his son. They first shook hands, then hugged. Then he gently hugged Jesse, and Carter found a chair for her to sit in. His mother brought some fresh squeezed limeade outside, along with some taco inspired nacho chip appetizers.

Carter shared with his parents that he was very much in love with Jesse, and had proposed tonight, and that she had accepted. They didn't have a date yet, but that the sooner the better for him but whatever suited her. He also shared that he had purchased a beach house and that it would be their primary residence for now. His parents were thrilled to see him so relaxed and so happy. They were very sweet and loving towards Jesse and encouraged them to come by more now that their relationship could be out in the open and of course as her health permitted.

Jesse took comfort in how normal they seemed and close they appeared as a family, much like her own family's dynamics. Before they ate Carter showed her where he had buried Casey, it was past the pool at the edge of the yard near a tree, and he had placed a small marker out there for her. She was moved to tears knowing he took such great care to put her in such a special place.

They dined on grilled prawns, and filet mignon, with salad and garlic bread. Mrs. James had made a yellow layer cake with chocolate frosting. Jesse surmised she was going to fit into this family just fine. It was finally time to leave as Jesse's energy was starting to fade. They were so understanding and plans were made to get together again in a few days with the rest of the kids and spouses.

The ride home was blissfully quiet, and the music that played softly on the radio was soothing. Carter looked over at his beautiful Jesse, and his heart was full and his mind was finally settled and clear. He walked her up to her apartment and helped her get ready for bed. He stayed with her until she fell asleep then he walked down to his apartment to call Tim and fill him in. Tim was so excited, he walked up and they sat outside on Carter's patio area and discussed the events of the day and the upcoming nuptials. They sat together talking for the next couple of hours, then retreated to the den and watched then end of an action movie together. Just like old times.

Jesse woke the next morning and called Susie to fill her in on the happy news. Once again Susie nearly deafened her with her screams of joy. She insisted that Jesse wait until her mom was there to tell her the news in person but Jesse was not sure she could wait that long. Jesse also received word that the Director had approved for her to become the new unit secretary for Dean's team and would start her new positon the first of October. He wanted to make sure she was fully healed before she started. She was also going to take some classes at the local college until she decided what she wanted to do long term.

This was a load off her mind, and the fact that she now got to work with Dean, Tim and Ninja on a daily basis, made her heart happy. Dean seemed as focused and determined as ever, the team functioned like a well-oiled machine. The Director was pleased with the outcome of his recent decision and it appeared his apprentice was back on track and his team was fully oper ational and productive.

Tim and Wex held a huge engagement party for them on the beach near Wex's restaurant and both families were there to celebrate Carter and Jesse It was a magical night under the stars with the ocean as a back drop, with the families and friends intermingling and getting to know one another better the beach was indeed their special place of communion and healing. They set a wedding date for December first, and planned to move into the newly renovated safe house immediately after their ten day honeymoon to Colorado where they planned to spend time in a mountain cabin and enjoy the change of scenery.

310

Carter was indeed her happily ever after and she was his; this journey that they both endured had been wildly unpredictable, with hurts, confusion, victories and joys but through it all, Jesse now had her own version of 'The Spy Who Loved Me' and it was heavenly.

THE END

CPSIA information can be obtained
at www.ICGtesting.com
Printed in the USA
LVOW04s0336301015

460278LV00004B/8/P